An Introduction to Barth's Dogmatics for Preachers

Books by Arnold B. Come
Published by The Westminster Press

An Introduction to Barth's *Dogmatics*
for Preachers

Agents of Reconciliation

Human Spirit and Holy Spirit

AN INTRODUCTION TO BARTH'S *DOGMATICS* FOR PREACHERS

by

ARNOLD B. COME

THE WESTMINSTER PRESS

Philadelphia

Library of Congress Catalog Card No. 62–17065

Printed in the United States of America

To Bruce and Mac

my sons,
whose companionship in work and play
will always give our year in Basel
a special radiance of delight
and unrepeatable meaning

Contents

Preface

It is with some fear and trepidation that I write this book. It may be more successful than I hope it to be. It may encourage some American preachers to follow the suggestions for using Barth's *Dogmatics* as a preaching resource, without the critical approach laid out in the chapter "How to Avoid Becoming a Barthian." I am not a doctrinaire Barthian, and the last thing I want to do is to contribute to the production of such.

Nevertheless, Bultmannianism is bound to have an increasing vogue on the American scene, and this development will demand, I believe, a clear and honest hearing of Barth. One of the subsidiary aims of this book is to break the cliché that one must be either a Barthian or a Bultmannian. We must learn from both. Therefore, a careful study of Barth is required because, first, he is not well understood, and secondly, his historical and theological breadth will help to keep Bultmannianism from becoming a narrow sectarian mixture of Biblical insight and contemporary philosophy.

The present study is the outcome of a year spent in Basel (1959–1960). I attended Barth's lectures and seminars, and, like all theological visitors, was graciously received by Professor Barth for personal conferences whenever I requested them. My major efforts, however, went into spending eight to ten hours a day for ten months reading straight through the twelve volumes and some seventy-five hundred pages of the *Dogmatics*. Five as yet untranslated volumes were read in German, the other seven in English, with the German always at hand to check every doubtful or crucial passage. Naturally, while reading I made extensive notations of several different kinds. The values of that year's study were twofold. It gave me a synoptic

view of Barth's theology and development that a hit-and-miss perusal
of the *Dogmatics* across the years could not provide. It also supplied
the indispensable aid in interpretation that comes from hearing the
cadences of Barth's own lecturing style and from hearing him give
answer to questions put directly to him.

This personal acquaintance with Barth has also lent to the present
volume a unique distinction. The biographical chapter (II) has been
read and corrected by the biographee himself. Professor Barth very
generously consented to read the manuscript for this one chapter,
and he scribbled some twenty-five corrections and additions in the
margins. These were simply matters of fact or anecdote. He assidu-
ously avoids trying to predetermine critique or evaluation of his
theological position. Yet it is noteworthy that his secretary, Charlotte
von Kirschbaum, wrote that he read the manuscript "attentively"
and "with approval." I wish to express my gratitude to Professor
Barth for this kind service. This at least assures that the account does
not contain any foolish blunders or total misrepresentations.

For clarity's sake I must make two technical observations. First,
I have simplified reference to passages in the *Dogmatics* in the following manner: A parenthetical reference such as (2–1, 365) means:
Volume II, Part 1, page 365. The symbol ¶1 means Paragraph 1.
All such references are to the pagination in the official English
translation of the T. & T. Clark edition. Secondly, it will be noted,
nevertheless, that every direct quotation from the *Dogmatics* is my
own translation. This should not be taken in any way as a criticism
of the magnificent work of the translators to whom the English-
speaking world will be in permanent debt. But scholarship demands
that interpretation be made from original sources, no matter how
adequate translations may be. Moreover, I believe there are a few
places where the translators have used theologically biased English
terms that misrepresent what I understand to be Barth's meaning.

I must close with a note of deep appreciation to the Board of
Trustees and the Faculty of San Francisco Theological Seminary for
granting me the year of sabbatical leave, and to the Sealantic Fund
and the AATS for the generous fellowship, both of which made
possible that enriching sojourn in Basel.

ARNOLD B. COME

San Anselmo, California

Chapter I

Why Karl Barth?

THIS book is for preachers. And teachers too.

I only wish that preachers today were as open and as vulnerable to questions and remarks from their hearers as Jesus was. Then the line between preaching and teaching disappears. ⌐Proclamation of the good news and its explication become inseparable. And the preacher has to know what he is talking about.⌐

This kind of brutal encounter with the Christian faith is in demand today—both by those who have been drawn within the church and by those who just get within hearing distance of a Christian conversation. The vision of the world's becoming a fiery furnace is now very real to most of us. We have to admire the human toughness that responds by building a bomb shelter in the back yard. But many are wondering half aloud if there is an angel who can go with men into the pit and preserve the human dignity and faith of modern Shadrach, Meshach, and Abednego so that they will not take guns to cut down their neighbors. Even more deeply laid is the inarticulate musing about the story of a Son of God who went down into the last pit of creaturely residence and came back to impart to men a core of life that makes them unafraid of all the fires of human existence. In the face of these ultimate questions the shrill voices of latter-day prophets are beginning to crack and

11

grow gravelly with uncertainty. Even communist youths are daring to ask how Marxist theory establishes the value of the person and answers the questions of individual decision.

Do you preachers and teachers of the church have the answers? As I said, this book is being written for you. I am addressing you in a fairly conversational style because I am one of you, and I want you to know that I understand and am as bewildered by your problems as you are. We are stressing today the idea that the mission of the church must be fulfilled by the whole membership as it lives in the world, but this does not mean that the church can get along without a specialized ministry of preaching and teaching. Just the opposite. You are still called upon to perform a variety of other tasks (pastor, administrator, counselor, youth leader, etc.), but if the whole membership of the Christian community is to be the leaven and light of the world, then you must fulfill most diligently your role as the one especially trained to unfold the depths of the gospel's meaning and the breadth of its implications for the whole of life. And this must be done in a way that provides for some lively give-and-take. I know what you are saying. "Sounds good, but where and how does it really take place so as to make the least dent in the lives of church members?" Here there is room not only for bewilderment but even for discouragement and despair. We must face up to the practical (and theological) problems involved with ruthless realism (as in John R. Fry's *A Hard Look at Adult Christian Education;* The Westminster Press, 1961). Yet, there is more readiness than has yet been met, and creative ways of doing so are being experimented with across the country. The real question mark in the whole situation, as I see it, is this: Are there preachers and teachers who have the answers? Or are there those who, on the one hand, fathom the depths of the gospel and, on the other hand, know the hearts of common humankind, so as to be able to help men in the first place to formulate the right questions? I am proposing in this book that you who have this awesome burden will find an almost infinite aid and resource (seventy-five hundred pages) in the *Church Dogmatics* of Karl Barth.

Why Karl Barth? Let me be very clear in saying that it would be a tragic error if you were to restrict your theological reading to Barth's *Dogmatics* (although the twelve weighty volumes so far produced might take you a lifetime to get through). I will give some specific warnings on this point in a later chapter. But why Barth at all? Why not some Biblical theologian? Surely we all agree, in one way or another, with Barth's own major thesis that man does not even understand who he is, let alone where he is going and how to get there, until he is brought under the transforming power of the Word of God as addressed to him in Jesus Christ. This means that the Christian preacher and teacher are inextricably bound up in the toils of Biblical interpretation. Granted. But that is not all. Along with the original Biblical witnesses to Jesus Christ, we today speak in the language and the concepts of nineteen centuries of Christian witnesses who follow in the train of the apostles. Like the very early Christians, we find things "hard to understand" in the letters of Paul (II Peter 3:16), and we bring to their interpretation the cumulative mind of the church from a long history of formulations that are not as such in the Bible: Trinity, incarnation, sacraments, church order and mission, personal faith and works, heaven and hell. The modes of our hearing the Bible have been stamped upon most of us by the formative thinkers of the church. So the Bible has been read and preached down through the ages by men who thought as Origenists, Cyrillians, Nestorians, Athanasians, Augustinians, Abelardians, Thomists, Lutherans, Calvinists, Arminians, and Wesleyans.

We realize today that we can take full advantage of these

nineteen centuries of insight and interpretation and yet avoid being bound and blinded by them only by being fully conscious of their development and of their formative influence upon us. So we also try our best to get behind those centuries to what the original authors said and meant by using the best historical, literary, cultural, linguistic knowledge we have of the Bible. Yet after all the most scientific and faith-full exegetical and historico-theological studies have been made on any single aspect of the Christian faith, the question remains: What does it mean for us twentieth-century Christians and how are we to bring it to speech? And the questions of meaning and of language are not two problems, but one. And this is the problem of what we Americans call systematic theology and of what Europeans call dogmatics. We cannot be ready to preach and teach the Word of God until we have gone through the last agony of formulating the Christian faith in our own language. And this is an affair not of lone, isolated individuals but of individuals in the communion and conversation of the Christian community.

So I say: Have a conversation with one of the outstanding dogmatic theologians of our time, Karl Barth, as you are on your way of preparation for preaching and teaching. But why not some other theologian, such as Brunner, Tillich, Berdyaev, the Baillies, the Niebuhrs, Ferré, Ebeling, Thielicke, Berkouwer, or why not go back to Aquinas, Luther, Calvin, and the others? Of course, read them all! But without making comparisons, which are always odious, let me recount briefly seven positive reasons for reading in Barth's *Dogmatics* (apart from the basic question concerning the validity of the *content* of his thought, with which this whole book deals).

1. Barth's whole unique theological formulation had its origin and rise from the specific problem of the sermon. He tells us that the theology he had been taught appeared less

and less relevant as he was confronted each week with the
needs of the people on the one hand, and the Bible on the
other, and the task of bringing the two together in the
sermon. Out of this torment came his commentary on Paul's
Epistle to the Romans, and a new theological era was born.[1]
Theology for Barth, however, has not only its origin but
also its goal in the problem of preaching. The formulation
of Christian faith into doctrinal statements is no end in itself. Theology does not replace the Bible or the revelatory
event in which God speaks his own Word to men. You do
not preach dogma. But preaching is a human act, using
human words and ideas, and so very fallible. Theology is
the church's own self-questioning about the authenticity of
the meanings of the sermon's words and ideas. How well
do they accord with the Word of God that speaks through
the Bible? (¶ 3:2).

In Barth's *Dogmatics*, therefore, you have a theologian
writing who always has in mind your specific problem as
you set about to preach and teach in the church. The relation may be obscure to you at times. It may appear to you
that Barth is under the impression that he is distilling the
final deathless essence of Christian faith in all its infinite
detail. Nothing could be farther from the truth. In his latest
ten-year reminiscence he says he is under no illusion about
the limited impact that the *Dogmatics* is having in the
theological world, but "I have no cause for complaint. Im-
perialistic appetites in the field of theology would indeed be
a most ugly business." And he goes on to say that rather
than the highly technical analyses and critiques that are
appearing in increasing number, the report that pleases him
the most is that pastors here and there are finding help from
the *Dogmatics* for preaching, instruction, and counseling.[2]

2. Because theology has its rise and goal in the problem
of preaching, theology must have its center in the Bible.
Preaching for Barth is simply the proclamation of the gos-

pel of Jesus Christ. As theology formulates a criterion for
testing the authenticity of this proclamation, it also must
turn to the only original witness to this gospel, the Bible.
The Biblical witness to Jesus Christ is such a direct, pervasive, and self-conscious criterion for everything that Barth
writes that some accuse him of being nothing but a crypto-
Biblical theologian. We will see in the next point that this
is not technically correct, but it is true that for every major
development in his *Dogmatics* Barth includes a sprinkling
of notes that give its Biblical basis. And sometimes these
notes run on to ten or fifteen pages. Barth's use of the Bible
in these notes must be brought under sharp analysis, as I
will do in a later chapter, but at least when the journeyman
preacher reads this theology he is not left bemused as to
what possible connection it might have with Scripture. You
may disagree with Barth's interpretation, but here the man
who must weekly preach and teach the Word of God from
the Bible will not find a theology completely abstracted
from Biblical language, concepts, and events, nor will he
find a Biblical interpretation that gets lost in the interesting
minutiae of linguistic, historical, and literary problems.
Rather, he will find theological thinking that will directly
stimulate his own Biblical study, giving rise to new creative
insights.

3. Nevertheless, Barth is not simply a Biblical theologian
who blandly ignores nineteen centuries of the church's theological reflection and attempts an autonomous judgment as
to "what the Bible says to me." Nor is Barth a "systematic"
theologian in the sense of creating his own private system
of Christian thought according to some philosophical presuppositions. Barth does try to listen, *tabula rasa*, to what
the Word of God is saying to him personally here and now,
as every Christian should. And he does have his own philosophical presuppositions, which obviously operate in his
theological formulations. But Barth has consciously and

rigorously brought these two subjective factors under the limiting control of a definite context, the Christian church down through the ages. His *Dogmatics* is entitled *Church Dogmatics,* and this marks a deliberate shift from his original volume, which was first published under the title of *Christian Dogmatics.* He tells us that as his thought became more Christological it thereby became more churchly.

So along with the many Biblical excursuses in the *Dogmatics,* you will find also numerous and extensive historical notes. In some volumes they will concentrate on the Reformers, in others on the early fathers, then on the seventeenth-century Protestant scholastics, still another on Roman Catholic thought, and the nineteenth- and twentieth-century greats are all brought into sharp debate. American preachers are notably weak in historical theology. Yet I think you will often find these notes fascinating. Some theologians think they are the most important contribution in the *Dogmatics.* Be that as it may, you should feel more confident and comfortable in using a theological resource for your own thinking that has an amazing mastery of what the church has thought and said on these issues down through the ages. Our new age in human history calls for a reformation of Christian faith, but no break in Christian thinking has ever had significant impact on church or world unless it has also found its place in Christian tradition.

4. What, in your view, are the issues concerning which the church today turns to theology for light and help? My answer would be, Ethics and church mission. "Obey the Ten Commandments" and "Follow the example of Jesus" no longer carry automatic weight. "Why?" and then "How?" are being asked. So the ethical dilemma as to the good life is the form that the existential problem concerning ultimate meaning takes for most American Christians. The more direct and more abstract questioning of the significance of human existence, in current drama and novel,

has an important but more limited appeal. And the question as to whether Christian faith can really resolve man's problem of being and behavior raises automatically the question as to what purpose and goal, if any, the church can serve in relation to mankind and its history. The innumerable conferences and books on this latter question undoubtedly are a sign of the church's own inner confusion on the issue.

Here, whether we agree completely with Barth's answers or not, is a point at which his *Dogmatics* is strong. The questions of ethics and Christian mission are not peripheral for him. They are not even to be treated as separate loci or doctrines at the end of theology. By his ingenious organization of his doctrinal structure, which we will characterize in detail later, Barth has made it possible to incorporate ethics and ecclesiology as continuing themes throughout the whole structure. He maintains that the final import of every aspect of Christian faith and doctrine has not been clarified until its ethical impact has been brought to light. Also, the church for Barth has no distinctive reality except as it is rooted at every point in the living Christ himself. Therefore, whether Barth's formulations on these issues prove finally satisfactory or not, at least his *Dogmatics* wrestles with the basic issues of Christian faith in a way that is directly relevant to our most urgent questioning. And I am of the personal opinion that Barth's positions on ethical and ecclesiological matters will have more appeal and more chance of implementation on the American scene than with the tradition-bound churches of Europe.

5. The matter I have just mentioned concerning the unusual organization of his *Dogmatics* should give their reading a certain freshness and excitement. To the casual observer the *Dogmatics* undoubtedly appears to be just one more ponderous, static, abstract system of doctrine that ossifies everything that is vital and alive in the Christian

faith. This is not the case. As I will show in detail later,
the structure of his *Dogmatics* has allowed for a marked
fluidity and dynamism that will be the despair of anyone
who tries to systemize and pigeonhole Barth's theology—as
much so as with Augustine and Luther. The *Dogmatics*
have been in the process of being written for thirty years
now and will continue until Barth can write no more. They
tell the story of his running battle with all the theological
currents and positions of that period. On central issues he
has restated himself several times. And in the evolvement
of his own thought in this living process he has come up
with remarkably creative reformulations of ancient doctrines. So while shocking the traditionalist with his statements on Trinity, predestination, and the devil, he equally
calls into question the validity of the frank disposal of these
doctrines by certain contemporary theological positions.
Barth gives every contemporary position rigorous and chal-
lenging food for thought.

6. Another obvious characteristic of the *Dogmatics,* which
is usually lamented and derided, may actually be regarded
as a strong selling point for the preacher and teacher. I
speak of its length and complexity, its detailed and repeti-
tious character. Even Henri Bouillard, the French Catholic
who has written three large volumes on Barth and the
Dogmatics, complains of the *longueurs et répétitions* and the
style *plus lourd* of these *volumes énormes.* But very few will
ever read the whole of the *Dogmatics,* in fact, even the
whole of one volume in one continuous reading. Therefore,
as you dip in at one spot in one volume, it will be helpful
to find repetitions of the broader themes of previous volumes
and the specific points worked out earlier in the same
volume. They will give you some sense for the broader context in which Barth is making his point and thus give you
a better appreciation of its richness and breadth.

As for the length and detail of his arguments, this is

exactly what will make the *Dogmatics* an endless resource
for serious and creative presentation of the gospel. Of course,
it does not give you a thumbnail sketch of a Christian doctrine that you can jazz up with a little existentialist jargon
and then throw at people. If you really want to think a
doctrine all the way through for yourself, and if you want
not only to proclaim but will also invite questions and conversation and so become a teacher too, then you had better
have all the detail and length you can get on a specific issue.
And the detail had better be historical as well as exegetical,
and existential as well as historical. This *combination* is what
you do not find in most Biblical and systematic theologies.
They just do not take time and space to be comprehensive.
Barth does. When you get used to him, you will thank
him for it.

As for the heavy and apparently even dull style, the only
advice I have to offer is to learn to read the German. I do
not really expect you to do so, unless you already have a
good grasp of German. But it is a fact that the German style
of Barth has real excitement and drive and even clarity in
spite of the interminable sentences. You might not get this
impression, however, even from the German, unless you
have heard him lecture. As perhaps you know, the *Dogmatics* is the steady accumulation of his major lecture series in
the university classroom. The lectures are carefully written
out beforehand but to be lectured, aloud, to an intent and
responsive student body. He often carries a point by the in-
flection of his voice, and most of his spontaneous, irrepres-
sible humor is expressed this way. The apparent dullness is
wholly a product of the exigencies of translation. All laud
and honor to these men who are giving so silently and generously of their life's time and energy to make this enormous
work available in English. It could not conceivably be done
better in such a short time. But the task of breaking up the

long sentences and of putting the concrete German idiom
into understandable and acceptable English has left little
time or possibility for the creation of a lively English style.
With fifteen different translators to date, a consistent style
would be out of the question anyway.

7. Finally, Barth's *Dogmatics* are worthy of your study
because here is a momentous work of unparalleled theological scholarship written by a man who is anything but a
theoretical, academic recluse. Here is a man who is a concerned churchman, a pastor for twelve years, who has an
active sense of responsibility for the political and social community in which he lives, who has a full and rich family life,
who participates in a wide range of cultural pursuits, who
is one of the most friendly, gregarious, cordial, good-
humored, joyous, vivacious of men. This means that he is
deeply sensitive by nature to all the conditions of the human
heart and mind and society of our day. His whole theology
is written out of this sensitivity and is written with the hope
that all men may share in the glory and joy of God's love
in Jesus Christ. Barth's theology in the *Dogmatics* is fully
intended to be "existential" in the deepest and best sense of
that term. Admittedly, it does not appear so to many. But
not many have given him a very careful reading. Admittedly, his language and conceptuality have remained de-
terminedly Biblical or technically theological. But very few
have explored fully his thesis that this is the most existentially effective language if Christian faith is to occur. The
famous American professor of theology who, a few years
ago, spoke of Barth as that "great and austere theologian"
simply revealed thereby that he was totally ignorant of Karl
Barth, the man. No adjective could be less accurate than
"austere." So it is undoubtedly necessary that these vast
ponderous tomes of theology be placed against the background of the life that produced them if their vital human

quality and concern are to be appreciated. It is for that reason that we will proceed directly to a brief sketch of Barth's life.

These are the seven reasons why you should read in Barth's *Dogmatics*. Later I will give some specific suggestions on how to go about such reading and study in a way that will be contributory to your preaching and teaching. But here at the beginning I would like to say that it would be especially helpful if you could get two or three others to enter the project with you. For one thing, you could exchange volumes, since they are rather expensive. But more important would be the fellowship and discipline of coordinated study. And the sharing of your differing homiletical insights would be very rewarding. You should know that there are already a number of American pastors who are regularly finding deep stimulus from the *Dogmatics* for their preaching and teaching responsibilities. In the last four chapters of this book I will indicate a large number of specific passages that you might find immediately useful. But first we must get a general view of the biographical background and of the structure and contents of Barth's *Dogmatics*.

Chapter II

Barth's Theological Pilgrimage

WHAT kind of theology are you falling in with if you open yourself to Barth's influence? Is it just a recrudescence of the old seventeenth-century orthodoxy (neo-orthodox)? Or is Barth still the liberal wolf in sheep's clothing? Do we have here in the *Dogmatics* a static creedalism, a sterile rationalism, a fundamentalist Biblical literalism, a revelational positivism, a crypto-existentialism, or a simple return to the Reformers? Is the so-called secret philosophy, which is supposed to shape Barth's thought, that of Kierkegaard, Kant, Plato, or Hegel? Strangely enough, every one of these alternatives has been asserted by at least one critic, and then rejected with equal vigor by another.

This is an important even though difficult and perhaps impossible question to answer. You must be aware of it as you read the *Dogmatics* if you are to avoid becoming a doctrinaire Barthian (the methods for which we will discuss in a later chapter). Barth's theology is not the last word or even a wholly adequate word on the many subjects it treats. Nor did he ever conceive of it as such. As I said above, in spite of its apparently systematic form, the *Dogmatics* comprises a running thirty-year debate with the thought and thinkers of that time concerning the live theological issues. The very diversity of the labels pinned on it indicates the vitality with which it entered that debate. Yet this nature

23

of the *Dogmatics* is not apparent if one reads and knows only these volumes. So the following biographical sketch is given with the hope that it will help bring the pages of the *Dogmatics* to life by giving you a brief picture of the man and the life situation that produced them.[1]

STUDENT DAYS

Karl Barth is Swiss. But anyone who knows Swiss provincialism would immediately ask, *Whence* in Switzerland? So Georges Casalis says that in family and being *Barth est un Balois,* a typical representative of the mentality, culture, and character of Basel. One could wish that all Baselers were as desirous of freedom from bureaucratic legalism as is Barth, but still he is one of them. And this means many good things: quick intelligence, assiduous industry, a basic seriousness but lightened by sparkling pleasantry and ironic humor, a passion for knowledge, readiness for lucid polemic, a flair for the arts, especially music. It means life in an ancient but now very modern, middle-sized, industrial, and university city, located on the Rhine where France, Germany, and Switzerland meet, as clean and sedate and beflowered and proud as a city can be.

Theologically, all this means that Barth was born and bred deep in the tradition of the Swiss Reformation. His father, Fritz Barth, was teaching at the Evangelical School of Preachers in Basel when Karl was born on May 10, 1886. Three years later Fritz Barth was called to Berne to become professor of church history and New Testament exegesis. One of Karl's brothers, Peter, later became the coeditor of the famous edition of Calvin's works, while the other brother, Heinrich, became a noted philosopher and just recently retired from the University of Basel. In the line of a family so inclined, Karl Barth grew up in Berne. In the schools there he manifested an aversion to mathematics and the sciences. He preferred history, wrote and produced dramas, and so very early showed signs of that inclination which would lead to his emphasis on the Word of God as action, as event. He never became interested in pure research abstracted from life, even in the fields of exegesis and theology.

At the age of eighteen Barth began his theological studies at Berne under the direction of his father. There he stayed for two years and acquired a thorough grounding in Reformed theology from his father, who was definitely conservative but who stood on the left side of the Evangelical Church. In his fourth semester at Berne, however, Barth read Immanuel Kant and was shaken and shaped to the core of his mind. He decided he must study with the leading neo-Kantian theologian of the day, Wilhelm Herrmann of Marburg. (It should be noted that it is still the custom today for European theological students to move around among the theological faculties of the Continental universities, becoming acquainted with the different schools of thought.) Barth's father tried to guide him to a more conservative theologian, and they finally compromised by his going to Berlin.

So in the autumn of 1906 at the age of twenty, Barth came directly under the influence of the liberal theology that was to dominate his thinking for the next ten years. The seeming deadness and irrelevance of the orthodox patterns of thought in which he had been bred now produced a reflex of eager and enthusiastic response to the practical and warmly personal "new" theology. With only one semester to spend at Berlin, Barth concentrated his whole energies on the task of absorbing the wisdom and insights of that great representative of the new position, Adolf Harnack. Seeking deliberately to become his disciple, and being the youngest of his sixteen seminar students, Barth sacrificed

almost his whole time to his work for Harnack's course on
The Acts of the Apostles—to such an extent that he did not
get to know the city of Berlin at all.

✳ ✳   Harnack's position was one of the major products of the
so-called liberal movement in theology that had had its
origin in Schleiermacher's *Addresses on Religion* (1799)
and its further formulation in the thought of Albrecht
Ritschl (1822–1889). In this "neo-Protestantism" the subject
✳ ✳   matter or center of concern for Christian faith and thought
was shifted from God himself to the impact of God upon
man, and hence to Christian man's feeling (Schleiermacher), to Christian man's history (Ritschl), to Christian
man's conscience (Herrmann), to the problem of Christian
culture (Harnack), to the place of Christianity in the totality
of human religious and cultural history (Troeltsch). Harnack envisioned the ultimate goal of human existence as
the achievement of a moral culture in which the individual
is set free from enslavement to this world. But in order to
attain it, simple universal humanity needs to be lived before
the eyes and by the power of God. Such a living is the
"gospel," and it has been fully realized in the life and teachings of Jesus. Now by responding to the example and inspiration of Jesus, all men may be set free to assume
responsibility for the higher life of moral culture. A
strangely naïve and simple theology for the man who was
the acknowledged expert in all the historical and theological
intricacies of the ante-Nicene period of church history!

This kind of simplified cultural moralism did not capture
Barth's imagination. While at Berlin, he read Herrmann's
Ethic and knew then where he would find his mentor. But
to please his father, for whom he has always had a deep
veneration, Barth returned in the spring of 1907 for another
semester at Berne and even went on in the autumn to
Tübingen for a semester's study with the conservative Biblical scholar, Adolf Schlatter. Finally, in the spring of 1908,

Barth moved to Marburg to sit at the feet (and never was this revolting cliché more appropriate) of Wilhelm Herrmann for three solid semesters.

Herrmann followed Ritschl in insisting that the revelation of God is strictly historical and has its center in the concrete life of Jesus Christ. But he also balanced this view with the thought of Schleiermacher by insisting that the Biblical story is not itself revelation, because revelation is an event in the interior life of man. Furthermore, Herrmann was strongly influenced by the neo-Kantian school of philosophy founded at Marburg by his contemporaries, Hermann Cohen and Paul Natorp (both of whom Barth heard lecture). He was convinced of the truth of Kant's radical disjunction between the grounds of knowledge and the grounds of faith (in the *Critique of Pure Reason*). He also followed Kant's *Critique of Practical Reason* by identifying the unique interior ground of faith with man's moral sense, as opposed to Schleiermacher's identification of it with man's aesthetic (feeling) sense (following the lead of Kant's *Critique of Judgment*). For Herrmann, the sense of "thou shalt" in each man is the potential "still small voice" of God, which is aroused and given content by the impact of Jesus' own life of moral perfection in trust in God. God is not a deduction from the moral sense, as with Kant, but God meets us and reveals his will for us at the point of ethical consciousness (conscience).

It is also important to note that Herrmann's position placed him in severe tension at certain points with the otherwise liberal thinking of Harnack, Troeltsch, and the historicocritical school of Biblical exegetes. Harnack's moralism was too external and cultural. Troeltsch's position finally ended in historical relativism, so he lost any firm ground for the uniqueness of Christ and for his own mystical piety. The critical exegetes sought to develop a method that could handle the Biblical materials according to a strict science of

history, psychology, and sociology. Herrmann could not
accept this kind of reduction of the religious to strictly
objective phenomena and categories. Kant had conclusively
demonstrated that science can neither prove nor disprove the
true elements of religion. And Schleiermacher had convinced him that what is truly human and what is truly
divine have the character of an inwardness and immediacy
that resides beyond the reach of any rational metaphysic or
empirical demonstration. For the young Barth who came
with natural aversion to the natural sciences and with a
flair for the dramatic, for the Barth who had experienced
his first intellectual excitement by reading Kant on his own,
for the Barth who was seeking some kind of dynamic, subjective ground and validation for the principles of Reformed
theology that, as he later said, he "had learned, less consciously than unconsciously, in my native home"[2]—for this
Barth all that Herrmann was and stood for had an overwhelming, irresistible, natural appeal and truth. So Herrmann became his "unforgettable teacher," whose theology
was to permeate his mind as a major force for a dozen years.

It should be noted, in conclusion, that Barth in his university studies gave more or less enthusiastic attention to
the historicocritical approach to the Bible. He listened to
the lectures of Gunkel at Berlin, and to Heitmüller and
Jülicher at Marburg, and he accepted the validity of their
work as far as it went. Nevertheless, it never got to the
heart of faith for him. As he later wrote in a letter to
Thurneysen, "Under the influence of Herrmann I had always accepted (historical) criticism only as a means to
freedom in opposition to the tradition, not, however, as a
constitutive factor of a new liberal tradition."[3]

So Barth ended his studies and entered the pastorate a
convinced and militant liberal. But in his subconscious was
a ground of firm Reformation theology. This built-in
dichotomy has proved to be a formative factor (but not

the determinative factor) in the whole theological pilgrimage of Karl Barth. In spite of his professed attempt to root
out of his *Dogmatics* every anthropological, philosophical,
existential principle, his "system" may still be regarded from
one perspective as an attempt to create a synthesis that keeps,
while transforming, both of the theological attitudes that
he absorbed in his formative years. (So in a meeting of his
English Colloquium in a recent year he remarked that
Schleiermacher *could* be interpreted in a better way than he
understood himself, namely, as a "theologian of the Holy
Spirit," which was perhaps his intention, but he let into his
system destructive elements, such as the principle of identity.) For this reason Barth's *Dogmatics* is of prime interest
for most of us preachers and teachers today, because that
same dichotomy is operative in most of us and still forms
the center of present theological debate.

First Years as a Pastor

With the completion of his studies in 1909, Barth at the
age of twenty-three spent his two years as an apprentice
pastor with the German-speaking Reformed parish in the
old and cosmopolitan city of Geneva (which is in the
French-speaking part of Switzerland). Then he moved to
the town of Safenwil in Canton Aargau in north-central
Switzerland. It was during his ten years as pastor in this
little country village that this intelligent, sensitive, ram-
bunctious, creative young man went through all the agonies
of heart, mind, and soul that finally led to that clear-cut and
shattering theological position that found expression in the
second edition of his commentary on the epistle to the
Romans. It was also in his second year at Safenwil (1913)
that he married Nelly Hoffmann, and so began a rich and
fruitful family life.

During the first five years at Safenwil, Barth made no
serious break with his liberal theology learned from Herr-

mann. But neither did he push forward to any new developments within it. His whole time and energy were consumed in two involvements, the problem of preaching and one major social problem in his parish. Although located in one of the charming valleys of the Swiss countryside, so that a large number of Barth's congregation were farmers, Safenwil was also an important industrial place with three factories. As pastor of all, Barth was faced with the sharp issues between management and labor, between rich and poor. These conflicts, as Bouillard has said, "brought him for the first time into touch with the problems of real life."[4]

Barth was not left to resolve his dilemma by himself. In 1913 his good friend from Marburg days, Eduard Thurneysen, became pastor in the village of Leutwil not far away. Together they were quickly drawn to the side of the laborers and plunged into all the problems of legislation, unions, and management. They were inevitably attracted to the Swiss Christian-social movement whose leaders were two theologians, Hermann Kutter and Leonhard Ragaz. And behind these two men we find the profound influence of the German father and son, Johann and Christoph Blumhardt. We must take a closer look at this group of men because they had a profound and lasting impact upon the direction of Barth's thinking.

Johann Christoph Blumhardt (b. 1805), a pietistic German pastor, had the startling experience of healing a psychopathic girl by prayer. He interpreted this as the victory of Christ over the demonic forces of darkness. The result was a religious revival of such proportions that he established his own retreat center at Bad Boll as a place of healing for body and soul. He took this as a sign of the coming of the Kingdom of God and began to proclaim that a new age of the Spirit had begun, which would end with the return of Christ. He taught that the Kingdom of God is for the healing of the whole man, body as well as soul, and would catch up within it not only believers but the whole of mankind and the universe. At his death, his son Christoph took over the leadership of the movement, gradually purified it of its crass millenarianism, and emphasized the concern of God's Kingdom for the material needs of men. In criticism of the socially conservative church, he finally joined forces with the Socialist Party and entered active politics.

This man was a powerful inspiration to the socialist movement in Switzerland and became the actual mentor and friend of Ragaz, Kutter, and Thurneysen. Through them Barth was also drawn under the spell of the Blumhardts. Kutter through a book in 1903 and Ragaz through a conference at Basel in 1906 got the Swiss movement under way. They bluntly proclaimed that the church was too narrow in its concern for the individual soul and too conservative in its economics. They asserted that God was working in history to establish his Kingdom not only through the church but also through the socialist movement, whether the members of the latter realized it or not. Although they, too, preached the eschatological coming of Christ as the climax of their movement, they were more concerned about the practical steps than the end goal.

With mixed feelings, Barth was drawn into their deliberations and programs of action as he was fascinated by the force and relevance of their ideas for the problems of his own parish. After some hesitation he actually joined their Social-Democratic Party in February of 1915. By September he had come to discern a real distinction in the directions of the thinking of the two leaders and knew immediately where his sympathies lay. In a letter to Thurneysen he made such points as: "Ragaz: experience of social needs and problems; Kutter: experience of God. Ragaz: ethical demands; Kutter: the Kingdom of God as promise. Ragaz: belief in progress; Kutter: insight into the bondage of men without

God. . . . Ragaz: opposition to the church; Kutter: the
religious task *in* the church in the promotion of the pietistic
tradition! . . . Conclusion: the religious-social affair is out;
getting serious with God begins."[5]

Then in the midst of the great war Barth received a
decisive shock to both of his theological norms. The church
in Germany swung its forces behind the kaiser and preached
in church and at the battlefront that this was a war for
God and fatherland. And not one of the voices of his hon-
ored theological masters was raised in protest. Barth rea-
soned: since their ethics were so wrong, their theology must
be wrong, and if their theology were wrong, their exegesis
must also be wrong. But how about the religious-socialists
whose fellowship had been international? On neither side
of the front did any socialist party rise above the chauvinism
of their own nations.

Where to turn?

The First Break: Getting Serious with God

Barth's letters to Thurneysen from the middle of 1915
(like the one just quoted) cry out with a thrashing restlessness and an agonizing, rending self-inquisition. He was
finally consciously facing up to a frustration, even a hypoc-
risy, that he had thus far kept buried below the threshold
of serious attention by his involvement in activistic socialism
and church work. The dilemma and contradiction that had
been mounting in intensity since his first days in Safenwil
was this: What is really going on when I rise on a Sunday
morning to look into the faces of shopkeepers, managers,
factory workers, farmers, knowing as their pastor "the
infinite contradiction of their lives," and then to read from
a Book that is supposed to contain a "no less infinite message," and then to *speak*?[6] Speak what? Supposedly the
Word of God from the Bible. But what he read and heard
there did not seem to make sense in the light of Herrmann's

theology and the social-democratic political program. About the same time as his drawing of the line between Ragaz and Kutter he wrote Thurneysen: "Before the second sermon today I looked out the window and saw the people of Safenwil strolling joyfully in the sunshine instead of coming immediately into the church, and I understood them so well, although I thought theoretically that they should certainly hear all that about sinners and joy in heaven. As yet, however, I simply cannot so tell them that they *must* hear it— and who knows whether I ever will?"[7] Pathos, but at last honesty! He looked with envy at the emphasis of the pietists on individual conversion, at their advancement personally and in good works. Yet he could not join them.

What was the source of this break? Certainly his own enormous sensitivity and intelligence. But here too he was helped. His capacity to be aware of a God whose Word would transcend his best sermons, a God who would stand above the battle lines of warring nations, a God whose Kingdom could not be identified with the program of a Ragaz—this capacity came in part from a source to which the socialists themselves had introduced him, the elder Blumhardt. The depth and permanence of the impact upon Barth of the Blumhardt stories (Bultmann has said, they "are an abomination to me") can only be measured by the fact that in one of the latest volumes of the *Church Dogmatics,* Barth takes Blumhardt's own motto, "Christ is Victor," as the key designation of Christ's prophetic work, and he writes a long footnote telling about the healing of the girl and why this event was so significant theologically (C.D. 4–3, 168–171). He first got a complete picture of the whole story in June of 1915. He writes Thurneysen: "Today I finished reading the Blumhardt book by Zündel, above all with a sense of shame. Next to such a one I appear to myself so small. Last Saturday a local drunkard shouted at me from a second-story window of his house, with clenched

fist and flowing speech: 'Get lost, you rotter, you priest, you
thunder of God! Where you walk, the grass grows no more!'
What could I do! The old Blumhardt would have broken
out into a hymn of praise and cast the devil out."[8]

It is perfectly clear that Barth did not become, then or
ever, a naïve Bad Boll pietist and apocalyptist. But out of
this spiritual crisis in Barth's ministry did come the resolve
to "get serious with God." The immediate effect was that
Barth and Thurneysen formed an agreement to turn their
backs on political and ecclesiastical affairs and to enter a
program of study and of reevaluation of their whole theological position. Barth entered this project with intense anticipation, seeming to sense that something dramatic might
come out of it. They plowed through all their old historical
and theological studies, with Barth even refreshing himself
on the whole of Kant "as if I were going to stand examina-
tion again." By July of 1916 they settled down to reading
the older exegetes (Bengel, J. T. Beck, Oetinger, Tholuck,
and back to Luther and Calvin), and Barth had finally come
to concentrate his studies on one thing: Paul's epistle to the
Romans.

This revival of theological studies first of all resulted in
the opening of the floodgates of Barth's mind and voice, so
that there began in 1916 a flow of speeches and writings that
gradually increased in size across the years, reaching a flood
tide in the forties and fifties. Two addresses given in that
year even show the immediate impact of his Biblical studies.[9]
In "The Righteousness of God" (January) he spoke pre-
dominantly of man's conscience as the voice of God, of
faith as an inner quiet way of letting God speak within
us and so work his righteousness within us. This kind of
thinking remained with him for the next several years but
it began to be challenged by another line of thought coming
out of his searching of the Scriptures. This is expressed in

the very title of the address he gave in the autumn of 1916, "The New World Within the Bible."

The most important product of these studies, however, was the accumulating notes on <u>Romans</u>. They were started only as a means for the clarification of his own thought but gradually took shape as something worth publishing and were finally completed in August of 1918. That this work and its rewriting consumed a major portion of his time and energies is indicated by his apology, in the Preface to the second edition, to the people of Safenwil who "have had to put up with a pastor who lived in his study."

We will not spend much time on the first edition of Barth's commentary on Romans because it was not this book but <u>the second edition</u> which exploded like a bomb and <u>shook the theological</u> world to its foundations. The first edition was the product of his first two years (1916–1918) of note-making on Romans and reveals Barth in all the agony of his transition from a liberal theology of human moral conscience to a theology of the absolute centrality and sovereignty of God. He is already clear that everything human is corrupted with sin, and that justification and salvation are the pure gift of God. He already has launched his slashing attack against all religion, moral idealism, individualistic pietism, historicism, and psychologism. Nevertheless, once God and the new age of his Kingdom has broken into man's world of sin, Barth still conceives of man as having some ground in himself to see, to recognize, to accept, and to cooperate with God and his Kingdom. By faith as the gift of God his will becomes the law of our nature, and "we are able to see in ourselves God's invisible essence." Our world, this world, now becomes God's Kingdom by God's becoming organically united with and at work in it.[10]

This first edition, of only one thousand copies, was mostly

ignored in Switzerland, but caused quite a stir in the explosive conditions of postwar Germany of 1919–1920. It made Barth the center of a lot of theological discussion, but it mostly puzzled its readers rather than startled them. Barth has said that he instantly knew something was wrong with it because the wrong people liked it. Somehow the real and radical "newness" of the "world in the Bible" had not come through to dominate his thinking and writing.

THE SECOND BREAK: THE INFINITE QUALITATIVE DISTINCTION

Barth had completed the writing of the epoch-making second edition (September, 1921) just three years after the first. What so affected him that in the rewriting he could not leave a single stone in its old place?[11] In this short time a flood of new stimuli poured in upon his reflection and gave him the perspective, the insights, the concepts, the very words and phrases that he needed to forge the sledgehammer with which he now attacked the existing structures of theology. In the Preface to the second edition he gave his own list of these stimuli: Overbeck, Plato and Kant, Kierkegaard and Dostoevsky, and—the Bible itself. There should be added, in at least a peripheral way, Otto and Nietzsche. Actually, it is impossible to draw the lines of influence and to weigh their relative force with any finality in the development of a personality as deep and complex as that of Karl Barth. Furthermore, any historical figure as influential as Barth is to be understood in part in terms of the creativity of his own person, but also in part as a manifestation of the larger movements of social, historical, and divine forces. As we shall see in the next section, other minds and spirits were moving simultaneously and independently in the same direction as Barth's. So the listing and characterization of the following influences does not mean that Barth became a disciple or simple extension of any one of them. Barth absorbed them all, responding to some more than others and responding to certain elements in each according to his own instinct and driving determination to take God seriously.

Immediately after the publication of the first *Romans,* Barth was reading and being impressed by Rudolf Otto's *The Idea of the Holy.*[12] Otto's emphasis on the absolute mystery of God as the "totally Other" sounded a responsive chord in Barth in spite of Otto's relativizing of the idea as generally religious. The next year (1920) he was deep into the reading of Overbeck, Nietzsche, Kierkegaard, and Dostoevsky, although he had become acquainted with them even earlier.[13] We have time and space here only to suggest the points at which these men were useful to Barth. He by no means was cognizant of or interested in their total systems of ideas.[14]

Franz Overbeck was professor of New Testament and church history at the University of Basel from 1870 to 1897. Friedrich Nietzsche, the German philosopher, taught classical philology there at the same time, and the two became friends. Overbeck, an avowedly skeptical historian all his life, was a severe critic of the church's identification of Christianity with a historical, cultural movement. For him it was not enough simply to stress the divine origin of a now supposedly Godlike life being lived in history. For him, Christian faith must completely negate history and life in this world. Taken seriously, it could only point to the origin of life in a transcendental pretemporal life of God and can hope only in an eschatological posttemporal realization of that life for man. Barth saw in this a profound dialectic between creation and salvation as the true meaning of the resurrection of Christ. These themes found a tentative expression in his address "The Christian's Place in Society" (September, 1919), and a powerful formation in "Biblical Questions, Insights, and Vistas" (April, 1920).[15] The latter is a striking anticipation of some of the main themes of the second *Romans* and marks a real turning point in Barth's

thinking. It was delivered at a student conference at which
Harnack also spoke. Afterward, Barth had an interview with
Harnack in Basel. Harnack shook his head in bewilderment
at Barth's speech, confessing his inability to understand what
Barth was trying to say, and expressing unbelief that a
student of his would ever talk in these terms. He predicted
that Barth would be the founder of a new sect. In describing this interview (and a subsequent one with Overbeck's
widow) to Thurneysen in a letter, Barth concluded: "Now
we both must spit in our hands to prepare for new work.
It is clear that the idol totters."[16]

His own reading of Nietzsche's *Birth of Tragedy* and
Beyond Good and Evil strengthened him in his growing
conviction that the truly Christian surpasses all that is humanly religious, moral, cultural, and historical. In Paul he
now heard that faith is sheer miracle, a completely new
creation, life out of death by the resurrection of Christ. And
not as something we possess here and now but as promise
and hope in the *eschaton*. It is in this regard that we may
gain a right perspective on the impact of Kant and Plato
that Barth acknowledges in this period. His philosopher
brother, Heinrich Barth, persuaded him to look again at
these philosophers as stating in philosophical form what
Barth was struggling to see and to say theologically, namely,
that reality really dwells in a transcendent world, that it
descends into the world in a completely nonscientific form
of "revelation," and men must follow that reality hence out
of this world into the transcendent "eschatological" sphere.
It is impossible to determine conclusively from the evidence
at hand what role this philosophical study played in Barth's
thinking, but it seems to me that the lavish praise accorded
Plato in the writings of this period appears as the result of
his being persuaded that this philosopher is saying the same
thing as the Bible and so must be recognized as a "pagan
prophecy of the resurrection." But I do not get the feeling

that Barth is actually being influenced by Kantian and Platonic conceptions in the formation of his own theological constructions. It is obvious that Barth had not worked out, even in the second *Romans,* his rejection of all natural theology, which was to receive such vigorous statement later on in his *Nein!* to Brunner (1934).

This radical eschatology, formulated in its negative terms under the strong influence of several philosophical currents, was also heard by Barth in more Biblical Christian accents in the writings of Dostoevsky and Kierkegaard. His attention was drawn to the great Russian novelist by Thurneysen, who at this very time was writing one of the more acute studies on Dostoevsky. In fact, Thurneysen wrote improvements of certain portions of the first *Romans* that so impressed Barth that he included them verbatim in the second edition. It was from the characters of *Crime and Punishment, The Brothers Karamazov,* and *The Idiot* that Barth was recalled to a profound and permanent grasp of Luther's *simul justus et peccator.* Therein Barth saw graphically that God's grace does not come to righteous saints but only to abject sinners, that these sinners are able to believe in God's grace only by God's own act, because God's grace does not become their possession to make them all clean and perfect but leaves them still sinners who live in eschatological hope and trust. Only if you have read not only Barth's *Romans* but also his whole *Dogmatics* can you appreciate what a decisive and lasting contribution Dostoevsky made to his thinking.

One of the most problematic contributors to Barth's development is Søren Kierkegaard, the unique Danish genius (1813–1855). It is obvious that Barth borrowed many of his central terms and phrases from Kierkegaard, thereby enabling him to define more exactly the concrete character of the eschatological inbreak of God's grace and judgment. We hear much in the second *Romans,* and in the works that immediately followed it, about God's revelation as "paradox," about the inexplicable "moment" of "crisis" in which God judges and man is brought to "decision." There is the constant play with the Kierkegaardian dialectic of simultaneous No and Yes, incognito and revealed, doubt and faith, sinner and righteous. Then there is Barth's own well-known statement in the Preface to the second edition of *Romans,* "If I have a system, it is limited to a recognition of what Kierkegaard called the 'infinite qualitative distinction' between time and eternity, and to my regarding this as possessing negative as well as positive significance."[17]

At the same time, I agree with the judgment of Bouillard that it is an error to think that Barth became a Kierkegaardian or even that Kierkegaard is the prime source of Barth's theology of this period.[18] One of the major problems in present Kierkegaardian studies is concerning the way in which he interrelates his vision, on the one hand, of the absolute paradox of God's encounter with man in Jesus Christ with, on the other hand, his plumbing of the existential heights and depths of the individual human subject. To be truly Kierkegaardian one must accept both of these constructions as of equal importance and seek the definitive character of human existence in the interplay between paradox and subjectivity. It is clear that Barth borrowed only from the first theme, paradox, and so his position became known as dialectical or crisis theology. Kierkegaard's subtle and thorough development of this theme was of immense help to Barth but only a help in giving clear formulation to what was already the central drive of Barth's own theological passion: giving all glory to God in a way that leaves not a shred of initiative, of actions, or of possession, with man as regards the event of salvation.

Not that Barth was unconcerned with the individual. Back at the very beginning of his first break (September, 1915) he had written Thurneysen, "It seems to me that the

[Margin notes, handwritten:] Borrowed S.K.'s emphasis on sovereignty of God, Rejected S.K's equally strong emphasis on the subjectivity of man.

deeper and broader we work out our universal orientation, to the same degree more decisive emphasis must fall again upon individual conversion," but, he added, "in a very different sense than that of the pietists."[19] Bouillard has, I believe, captured this "different sense" by noting that "according to Barth, the decision of faith, the believing existence, is not characterized by the passion of inwardness. . . . Decision, existence, simply signify act, event, real movement. They are opposed less to 'objective' than to 'idea.' "[20] This emphasis on the objective presence and act of God as a unilateral transformation of the condition and reality of humanity gradually grew to be the stable ground current of Barth's whole theological development. So before the decade was out, he tried to get rid of the title "dialectical" and to dissociate himself from Kierkegaard. I believe Barth is either unfair or ununderstanding toward Kierkegaard, but his attitude is to be appreciated in the light of the one-sided development of Kierkegaard's principle of subjectivity by some existentialists. At least from this perspective Bouillard is correct in saying that Barth's thought is not an existentialism but an "actualism." At the same time, this overwhelming emphasis on the real sovereign presence and act of God created severe problems for Barth later on as he moved to develop a complete theology, and we will point these out as we come to them.

Another, final "source" of this second break in his theological development is regarded by Barth as the most important and decisive one, the Bible itself and more particularly Paul himself.[21] Even the first edition of *Romans* had given grounds for accusing Barth of "Biblicism," of taking the actual text too seriously. But in the years that followed, Barth tried even more conscientiously simply to listen to the Bible, to listen to this man Paul. He tried deliberately not to dominate the Bible with his own expectations or philosophical and theological categories. He obviously succeeded in hearing only one theme in Paul's witness, as he later admitted. But the second *Romans* is important at least in that its production established for Barth the basic methodology or hermeneutics that he would elaborate and defend throughout his whole career. The content of the second *Romans* was determined by Barth's dogged attempt to be utterly loyal to Paul and his vision of the Christ and so to hear the Word of God himself, no matter how much his other "sources" of this period determined what he could hear.

The actual content and major emphases of the second *Romans* itself can be pretty well surmised from the foregoing account of its sources. The main points can be summarized under three headings. First, Jesus Christ is the vertical inbreak of God from above into the horizontal line of human history. But he does not merge with history, and even the fact of his presence is known only by the resurrection, which is sheer miracle, inexplicable by any human categories of understanding. So the Christ is present in Jesus incognito. We meet him but cannot see or describe or understand him as he really is. So the paradox of human and divine, reason and grace, time and eternity. God's presence therefore encounters us as crisis, as a thundering No, a judgment on all that we are and do and have. Secondly, faith then appears as the negation of all our ideas. It is the sheer gift of God at the point of intersection that comes after all our human desiring, thinking, and striving break down. It is the acceptance of God's judgment that we are deserving only of death. So faith is inexplicable psychologically; it is a hidden thing, and yet a real personal decision not to be equated with any idea or feeling or emotion. God becomes the only reality in a new life because it is a life given out of death. Thirdly, all this means that the real church is also a hidden reality, not identical with the historical church. Yet it is to be reached only through the empirical church, and we must care for the latter even while we seek the former. We are pilgrims always moving out to the frontiers of this world because our real home is beyond it.

In conclusion, we may say two things about this period in Barth's theological pilgrimage. One of them has been said beautifully by Douglas Horton, the translator of the early essays that lead up to and just beyond the second *Romans*. When he first read them in German he knew that something cataclysmic had happened in the theological world. To those bred in the thought of Reinhold Niebuhr and the postwar developments, this may not seem to be the case. As Horton says, "Only those of us who are old enough to remember the particular kind of dessicated humanism, almost empty of otherworldly content, which prevailed in many Protestant areas in the early decades of this century can understand the surprise, the joy, the refreshment which would have been brought by the book to the ordinary and, like myself, somewhat desultory reader of the religious literature of that time."[22] In other words, the need for and justification of such a radical, negative, bludgeoning statement of God's sovereign judgment can be understood only in terms of the context to which it was addressed.

The second thing is this, that Barth has time and again repudiated his commentary on *Romans* as not being representative of his theology as developed in the *Dogmatics*. Even in the prefaces of the immediately following editions he began to say it should be rewritten, until in the sixth edition (1928) he admits that he would have to express these matters quite differently if written anew because he has become aware of new strands in Paul's thought. In the volume of the *Dogmatics* published in 1940 (2-1) he gave a detailed account of how he came to the radical position of the second *Romans* (pp. 632–638). He insists that it was right in what it did say, as against the then prevalent theology. But he states in full how wrong it all was also because of what it did not say. He clearly recognizes that his one-sided emphasis on "a pure and absolute futurity of God and Jesus Christ" was just as mistaken a reduction of God's being and life as was the liberal emphasis on the immediate fulfillment of God's Kingdom here and now in human culture. And he sees the dangerous consequences his position could have in the life of the church if it should go uncorrected. Again, in his address entitled "The Humanity of God" (1956), he repeated the same story and said, "It must now quite frankly be granted that we were at that time only partially in the right, even in reference to the theology which we inherited and from which we had to disengage ourselves."[23] It is strange that this latter statement is taken as heralding a "new theology" of Barth, when he had made the same point fifteen years before. And it is pathetic and inexcusable when supposedly well-informed American theologians keep characterizing Barth's theology in terms of the 1921 commentary on *Romans*.

IN SEARCH OF A THEOLOGY

As Barth was writing the last pages of this revolutionary book, he was packing up to leave Safenwil and the pastorate for a new job (September, 1921). Some churchmen had decided that the Lutheran theological faculty of the University of Göttingen should be balanced by the presence of a Calvinist. American Presbyterians contributed the money to set up an honorary professorship, and Barth was selected to fill it. It was with considerable nostalgia that Barth and Thurneysen faced this break in their long and intimate friendship.[24] They could not even imagine that they would one day be reunited in Basel, Barth as professor and Thurneysen as pastor of the old cathedral church. But immediately upon the publication of a new edition of his *Romans* (1922) Barth was caught up in the battle of European theological debate, and he is not yet free of it.

The professorship in one of the preeminent universities of Germany gave him a good platform from which to sound his new note in theology. Barth insisted from the beginning that it was no more than this. When asked at a ministers' conference in July of 1922 to explain his "new theology," he protested that all he had was a "marginal note" or a "corrective," which anyone could apply to his theology without leaving his own school. So he chose to speak to them about "The Need and Promise of Christian Preaching."[25] Nevertheless, the dialectical or crisis or Barthian school of theology was formed in the minds of men.

It must be noted that Barth was not alone in the trend of his thoughts, though no one put them as drastically as he did. Just prior to the publication of his second edition of *Romans* there had come off the press Friedrich Gogarten's *The Religious Decision* and Emil Brunner's *Experience, Knowledge, and Faith*. They and everyone else immediately noticed the striking similarity in their concerns and the general direction of their positions. Actually, Barth had contacted Gogarten two years before (June, 1920) when the latter had published an article called "Zwischen den Zeiten" ("Between the Times"). Barth had congratulated him and "challenged him to speak out."[26] So in the autumn of 1922 Barth and Gogarten, along with Thurneysen and George Merz, met in Oberrieden near Zurich and launched their little magazine, giving it the title of *Zwischen den Zeiten*. It was dedicated to the development of a truly Biblical theology, in line with the Reformers and opposed to the liberal theology. Brunner, Bultmann (!), and many others immediately agreed to identify themselves with this movement by publishing in the magazine, and still others (Karl Heim, etc.) expressed sympathy while remaining apart. Still others, like Paul Tillich and Paul Althaus, entered into interested debate with Barth and the members of the circle.

Surely, a loose-knit and rather strange "school" from the

beginning! Differences with Bultmann especially began to show up almost immediately. Yet, according to Barth, the group held together pretty well, at least in what they opposed, until 1933.[27] The constant discussion with this circle and its opponents helped Barth to solidify and clarify and to see the weaknesses in the position he had taken in the *Romans.* The letters, which go up to 1925, are replete with references to the excitement and meaning of these exchanges. His public debate with Harnack in the pages of *Christliche Welt* (1923) is a notable example. The developments in these debates are too complex to relate here, but one item should be noted. In this period Barth was tremendously stimulated by his constant contact with Gogarten. The latter was a complex thinker with diverse interests, and under the influence of Ferdinand Ebner and Martin Buber he began to use the concept of I-Thou as a determinative principle. Likewise, Thurneysen met Buber and urged Barth to do the same in a glowing report of the meeting and of the man.[28] As a result the whole language and concept of "I-Thou" and "person" became a central and permanent part of Barth's theological equipment.

In the letters of this period, however, a completely new and different struggle in Barth's theological development manifests itself. He entered into teaching with great anticipation but also great agitation. He began to realize that he needed something more to teach, and his students needed something more to preach, than a "marginal note" to theology. As one called to teach Reformed dogmatics, he could not continue forever lecturing on Paul's letters. He turned with a great sense of inadequacy to the study and teaching of Calvin's *Institutes,* and then to other historical problems. The real crisis came, however, in his third year of teaching (1924) when he finally felt obliged to give some straightforward lectures on dogmatics. "No one," he says, "can ever have been more plagued than I was with the problem, could

I do it? And how?"[29] Then there came to his hands a new edition of Heinrich Heppe's long forgotten *Reformed Dogmatics*. He of course saw that it was a summary of the "old orthodoxy" of the seventeenth century which he had learned and rejected as a youth. But in his desperation, "I read, I studied, I reflected; and found that I was rewarded with the discovery that here at last I was in the atmosphere in which the road, by way of the Reformers to Holy Scriptures, was a more sensible and natural one to tread than the atmosphere, now only too familiar to me, of the theological literature determined by Schleiermacher and Ritschl. I found a dogmatics which had both form and substance, oriented upon the central indications of the Biblical evidences for revelation, which it also managed to follow out in detail with astonishing richness."[30]

Barth was perfectly aware of the severe limitations of orthodox dogmatics, yet in the next years he found a great stimulus in reading them and the more recent conservative theologians such as Kohlbrugge, Böhl, and Lecerf. So in a letter to Thurneysen (June 7, 1925) he wrote: "It is turning out that I, with pondering and astonishment, must finally admit the correctness of orthodoxy in almost every point. And I hear myself expressing things of which I had never even dreamed either as a student or as a pastor in Safenwil."[31] The lasting impression of this study is abundantly present in the long footnotes of the early volumes of *Church Dogmatics*. Although Barth in these volumes is as severe a critic of orthodoxy as he is of liberalism, he had been convinced that orthodoxy at least set the right problems and the right method for theology.

In 1925, Barth moved to the University of Münster to become the regular professor of dogmatics. This meant he took a deeper step in his identification with the German people because as an employee of the state he had to become a German citizen (while retaining his Swiss citizenship).

It was here also that a very important person came into
Barth's life, Charlotte von Kirschbaum, who, since 1929, has
been his secretary and constant aid. Without her capacities
for scholarship, her keen intelligence, her friendly and pa-
tient spirit, the *Church Dogmatics* would never have as-
sumed the breadth of scope and excellence of quality they
now possess. Another significant and lasting impact was
made here on his thinking by his contact with living Roman
Catholic theology. It was also while at Münster that there
appeared the first clear-cut evidence of the fact that he had
made a decisive step beyond his dialectical theology as a
result of the impact of his studies of Calvin and of conservative dogmatics. With the publication (1927) of his *The
Doctrine of the Word of God: Prolegomena to Christian
Dogmatics,* the distance that had been developing inwardly
between Barth and the other members of his "school" now
came out into the open. During the next decade all of them
but Thurneysen were to drop away to follow separate paths.
Eventually the debate between Barth and Bultmann was to
mark the great divide in the theology of mid-century.

Again, we do not have space here to make a detailed
analysis of the shift in Barth's thought that is evident in his
Prolegomena. Bouillard has reached the heart of the matter
by noting its difference from Barth's *Romans.* In *Romans*
the main theme is the creative act of God that first of all
takes the negative form of devastating judgment upon all
that is human, of the old man Adam, and which then has
a positive form purely in the transhistorical event of resurrection in which the new man Christ is created and in whose
life mankind can only hope to share in a totally futuristic
eschatology. In the *Prolegomena* God overcomes the conflict between himself and man by addressing his Word of
faithfulness to faithless man in a way to give that man hope
where he is, in the sinful world, not just beyond the rim of
space and time. Reconciliation is accomplished not simply

in an eschatological resurrection but in the incarnation. The dialectic is no longer between time and eternity but resides in the paradox of the unity and diversity of God and man in the person of Jesus Christ. So between the transcendent events of creation and final redemption, Barth now envisions a middle time and ground, that of reconciliation, which men now know and live in. Bouillard concludes that in Barth's passage from *Romans* to *Prolegomena* "the Platonic and Kantian aspects of his thought are dimmed."[32]

This *Prolegomena* was announced by Barth as the first volume of an *Outline of Christian Dogmatics* that would be quickly completed in another volume or two. This project was never continued. Instead, five years later (1932) there appeared another Volume I (first half) of a wholly new work that was to grow into the massive *Church Dogmatics*. In the interim, Barth had discovered that he had to make one more agonizing shift in his perspective and direction before he could settle comfortably onto that path down which he could walk to the end of his days. In the Foreword to the new volume (1–1, ix) Barth states explicitly the main disturbance that led to the rewriting. He says, "In this second rendition of the book I have eliminated practically everything in the first one that might appear in any way a grounding, a supporting, or simply a justification of theology by existential philosophy." And in a long footnote (pp. 140–149) he explains that what he means by "existential philosophy" is the attempt, that he was still making in the *Prolegomena,* to find a point of departure for theology in anthropology. This attempt he now repudiates completely. He maintains that Christology is the only starting point, that no matter how much theology gets involved in anthropology, not even a theological anthropology must be allowed to determine the initial form and direction of theology. Here begins Barth's explicit war on all natural theology. It must be noted, however, that this development did not mean the elimination of the existential anthropological element from Barth's thinking and concern. His likeness and yet difference from Bultmann on this point I will elaborate in a later chapter (VI).

How did this final decisive shift come about? Probably the most important contributing factor was his own detailed studies in historical theology. His readings in Heppe and the theologians of the "old orthodoxy" had the result that "I found myself in the circle of the church." But the church and its theology obviously had not started or ended in the seventeenth century. While at Münster, Barth held seminars for five consecutive semesters in the history of theology. And when he moved to the University of Bonn in 1930, he continued this process of study and lectures.[33] Once again he found his roots in Calvin. Gradually he became convinced that Christian theology must be church theology, and that church theology is grounded in God's act in Jesus Christ, and that is the starting point for everything, rather than man with his felt needs and his intellectual constructions. Then, one of his first seminars at Bonn was on Anselm's *Cur Deus Homo*. Also aroused by a lecture of Heinrich Scholz on Anselm's *Proof of God's Existence,* Barth worked out (1931) his own position on Anselm in *Fides Quaerens Intellectum (Faith in Search of Understanding).* Barth has said that this is the important document of the 1930's, rather than his *Nein!* addressed to Brunner.[34] Barth concluded that Anselm was not at all concerned with proving God by sheer unaided reason, in the sense of helping the unbeliever who conceives of "God" as not existing to believe that He does exist. Just the opposite. Anselm sought to show that faith is a revelation in which God *gives* his existence to man with such compulsion that man can no longer think *about* God or *beyond* God. He can now only think *to* the God who has revealed himself. This thinking or understanding within faith or revelation is theology. This is the only proof that counts. "It is a question of the proof of faith by faith which was already established in itself without proof. . . . God gave himself to [Anselm] to know and he was able to know God." (P. 170.) This note in a sense becomes ✳ the ground theme of the whole *Dogmatics* as Barth reiterates again and again, "God is known through God and through God alone" (1–1, 255; 2–1, 39, 44, 161, 179, 665). Of course, Anselm scholars are far from agreed that Barth is correct in his interpretation of Anselm. But what is important for our purposes here is only what Barth thought he heard Anselm saying, and how this which he heard became constitutive in his theology.

Thus, with the publication of Volume I, Part 1, of *Church Dogmatics,* Barth had, as he says, "come out into the clear." He had found his basic position. But had he "arrived"? No! In his early forties he felt his life had just begun, with the real age of responsibility, of testing, of development of implications, still ahead.[35]

A DECADE OF OUTWARD STRIFE

During the thirties Barth remained the explosive, pugnacious young theologian on the make. In the recasting of his *Prolegomena* he made a clear and final break with Gogarten (1932). With his *Nein!* (1934) to Emil Brunner, there began an ever-growing distance between the two friends which has often been marked with some bitterness (but which was dissolved by an auspicious and happy, if somewhat nervous, reunion in Basel in October, 1961). With Barth's denial of the normative character of existentialist modes of thought, it became increasingly apparent that his and Bultmann's theological programs were in serious tension. The case can be argued that Bultmann has remained faithful to the basic dialectical viewpoint of Barth's *Romans,* while Barth drew away from it.[36] So already at the time of his break with Gogarten (1932) Barth also regarded as "a piece of liberal-

ism" Bultmann's search for an existentialist understanding
of man that would precede and be the prerequisite of faith
(1–1, 39). It is little wonder that he rejected Bultmann's
program of demythologizing and later branded it as a recrudescence of liberalism.[37] By the end of the decade the
dialectical "school" was completely demolished, and Barth
felt moved to speak of Gogarten as "a sinister-looking German state theologian," and of Brunner as "a new apologist
of his own invention" and a "Buchmanite" (Frank Buch-
man of Oxford Group and Moral Re-Armament fame).

During this period Barth also startled both his friends and
opponents by declaring open war on the Hitler regime.
Barth maintains that this action was just a consistent application of what he had stood for from the beginning—
that there is only one God, that we are guided to all truth
by his Spirit in the Scriptures, that the grace of Jesus Christ
is sufficient for the forgiveness of our sins and the ordering
of our lives.[38] The relation between Barth's political action
and his theological ethics is a hotly debated issue that we
cannot go into here. It is covered in a large and wide-ranging
literature outside the *Dogmatics*. But it should be remembered that Vols. I, Part 2 (1938), and II, Part 1 (1940), were
written during his private war with Hitler, and Vols. II,
Part 2 (1942, containing his general ethical position), and
III, Part 1 (1945), were written during the world's war with
Hitler. The reflection of the external events of these years
in the substance of the *Dogmatics* is mostly indirect and can
hardly be traced. Yet it is clear that Barth's active participation in the political life of both the church and the nation
had two general results. His conviction that theology grows
out of and is directed to the life of the *church* was greatly
strengthened. But also he saw that the Word of God to
which the church listens is the Word *incarnate,* identified
with and concerned for the broken, sinful life of common
humanity in its everyday life. So, whereas in Vol. I, Part 1,

the emphasis was upon the Word as pure sovereign act, six years later in Vol. I, Part 2, it is on the Word "made flesh."[39] In this context he mounts a slashing attack on all theological and political attempts to subvert man's freedom by turning man into a "stone" manipulated by God or a puppet controlled by an authoritarian state.[40] And he insists in the next volume that the open declaration of opposition to the corruption of the church by the Nazis (Barmen, 1934) was theological to the core in that herein Jesus Christ asserted his sovereign right over the church, and the church is called to confess him over against all natural theology (2-1, 172-178).

The external public form of this battle was to have profound results for Barth's future. In January, 1933, Hitler came to power. As his intentions toward the church became clear that spring, Martin Niemöller began to organize his Pastors' Emergency League, gathering in two thousand members.[41] This led to the formation of the Confessing Church as over against the church supported by the state. Karl Barth became the recognized theological resource and spokesman for the group. Already in June, 1933, he issued a pamphlet entitled *Theological Existence Today*. It consisted of a violent attack upon Hitler's establishment of the "German Christians" and against the official church that was not standing against this encroachment. This pamphlet became the title of a magazine edited by Barth and Thurneysen and was followed quickly by twenty-two issues in two years as the organ of the new movement. In May of 1934 the Confessing Church met in Barmen, and out of that meeting came a confession of faith that was to be the heart of the whole movement.[42] It declared Jesus Christ as he is witnessed in Holy Scriptures to be the one Word of God and pledged obedience only to him and opposition to all false gods. This Confession was wholly the work of Barth except for one sentence. Meanwhile, in his classroom

at Bonn it was very clear that Barth did not intend to
pledge loyalty and to do obeisance to Hitler. In December
of 1934 he was suspended from his post. Barth appealed to
the tribunal in Berlin. While he was waiting for an answer,
he gave his first commentary on the Apostles' Creed, entitled *Credo,* at a ministers' conference in Utrecht. Then in
June the word came from Berlin, "Not guilty!" But the
Minister of Education simply dismissed him, and three days
later the Basel City Council elected him to the chair at the
university. So Barth finally returned home, and there he is
probably to stay to the end of his days.

Barth tells us that it was also in the decade of the thirties
that he broke out of his former isolation within the Swiss-
German culture. Now he began to wander physically over
the geography of Europe, becoming reacquainted with the
French life he had known in Geneva, studying ancient
classical culture enthusiastically in Italy, traveling to Hungary in 1936 and 1937 and to Scotland to deliver his Gifford
Lectures of 1937 and 1938. In his travels he came to know
firsthand the churches of other lands and developed a deeper
sense of responsibility to the whole church. In this period
also his mind stretched out beyond the theological sphere
to embrace general intellectual history and literature, from
Goethe to English and American detective novels. But then
came the war. Switzerland became an isolated island, and
a new era in Barth's life began.

It is interesting to note that the three volumes of the
Dogmatics produced in this decade (1–1, 1–2, 2–1) do have
a unity of perspective and mood. The next volume (2–2)
marks the first break and innovation in the development
within the *Dogmatics,* and this we will speak about in the
next section. It is not that I am suggesting that you will find
a "new theology" or a "new Barth" every three or four
volumes. I would agree with Barth's own judgment that
throughout the whole work "there have been no important

breaks or contradictions in the presentation" (4–2, xi). But there have been unforeseen developments as he followed out his basic point of view in its ramifications in the various parts of dogmatics. So there have been breaks, not as contradictions but as innovations. Recently, Barth agreed with this point and remarked, "I hope I have learned something in thirty years!"

We will spend some time in analyzing the structure and summarizing the contents of the *Dogmatics* in the next two chapters. So it will suffice here to say that Barth's treatment of the doctrine of the Word of God (1–1, 1–2) and of the knowledge and the reality of God (2–1) is characterized by a certain formality and dryness of tone, an almost studied scholasticism and reserve, a seemingly deliberate withdrawal of the verve that animated his previous writings. I do not know whether this was consciously performed by Barth, or whether it was the dictate of the topics he was treating and of the seventeenth-century orthodox models he was following. Practically all of his basic themes to be developed later can be found preformed in summary statement in these volumes. But they simply are not marked by the richness, the depth, the imaginativeness, the conceptual and literary lilt and beauty that break out in wild profusion in each succeeding volume. As we draw near to the end of his treatment of the perfections (attributes) of God (2–1), some of these qualities begin to appear. They appear precisely where he begins to apply, tentatively and a posteriori, his principle of determining every theological statement Christologically. In the very next volume (2–2), where he was brought to the necessity of evolving his grand reconstruction of the doctrine of predestination, he became convinced that this Christological principle must be radically applied throughout the whole of Christian theology. He has frankly admitted that if he had seen this and applied it from the beginning, the first three volumes would have been cast in quite a different form and tone. In his first description of "The Dogmatic Method," Barth had clearly asserted that "in point of fact dogmatics must in principle be Christology and only Christology" (1–2, 872). But the real ground and the full implications of this statement became clear to Barth himself only in his elaboration of the doctrine of election.

However, the general character of the first three volumes may have been determined not only by their internal subject matter and method but also by the general character of the life of Barth during this decade. For a man trying to become a dogmatic theologian, his life was too filled with outward strife. A certain amount of peace and quiet and stability are necessary for the full turning of a man's energies inward to the contemplation of the mysteries of life that range through the flux of events and take form in the structures of his own being, there to be fathomed by the human spirit. In the next decade Barth had that peace and quiet.

A DECADE OF INWARD CREATIVITY

When Barth crossed the Rhine into Baselstadt in 1935, he thought it was a temporary refuge. He fully expected to return to the hurly-burly of ecclesiastical and theological life of Germany. It turned out otherwise. As the war closed around Switzerland, Barth was penned up physically but the tremendous drive and vigor of his mind and person were not abated in the least. He continued in the fight against Hitler by a vigorous correspondence urging resistance to the spread of nazism. So there came into being his famous letters to Hromádka in Czechoslovakia, to the Protestants in France, to the British, the Norwegians, the Dutch, and the Americans. And at the age of fifty-four he became a Swiss soldier, helping to patrol the border on the alert for Hitler's hosts. But gradually he came to concentrate his energies more and more on the task of composing the

Dogmatics. He has himself said that in this decade he was
still possessed of a "great intellectual restlessness" and that
it was of "the greatest benefit" in his work as it led him into
startlingly new ways of thinking. Although he traveled
around his native Switzerland, his life was relatively quiet,
and he soon discovered that in this more pacific state he
accomplished more work than "in the belligerency of my
earlier years."

As the war closed, Barth returned to Germany in 1945 to
attend the reconstitution of the Evangelical Church in freedom from the Nazi tyranny. But he was aghast at the German desire (including the church) to return to "normalcy,"
and at the victors' (including the Swiss) inability to extend
understanding in order to help the Germans to purge their
nation of fascism. Barth saw that he had to make a choice:
either to give the rest of his life to help resolve the German
problem or to go home to Basel and complete the *Dogmatics.* He chose the latter. As he neared the age of sixty he
learned to accept the growing limits on his time and energy.
He made a few more forays outside of Switzerland. He
visited Hungary in 1948 and became embroiled in another
political debate by advising the Hungarian Christians that
"protest against . . . the communist system was not exactly
the first and most urgent duty." Rather, he told them to
convert the Hungarian people because "communism can be
warded off only by a 'better justice' on the part of the
Western world." His open letter to the Reformed Church
undoubtedly helped to elect the communist-dominated
Bereczky as bishop. But it was hardly fair that his later
letter to Bereczky, criticizing his conduct as bishop, was not
also made public. He also went to Amsterdam (reluctantly)
for the constituting of the World Council of Churches, and
he came away surprised at his own enthusiasm for the
project. But after each of these trips he gladly returned to
his study in Basel. He says, "In pursuing this path of knowl-

edge, I experienced the most important of the 'changes' " of
these years. He gladly left the fighting of fights and the
making of speeches in order to center his whole life and
thought on the progress of the *Dogmatics* "in the midst of
all the relativity."[43]

What, then, was the major theological thrust of this
period? We have already noted that it took its start from
the identification of the electing work of God, with God's
act in Jesus Christ. But put in another way, Barth says that
in the decade of the forties he learned that it is more important to say yes than to say no, that God's grace encompasses God's judgment.[44] Of course, he had already laid the
ground for this emphasis in his insistence that the love and
mercy of God must always be stated before his freedom and
judgment (2–1). But after his statement of the doctrine of
election as the love of God in turning from himself toward
man in Jesus Christ in eternity, and after his development
of basic Christian ethic as one in which Gospel rules over
and encompasses Law (2–2), the overwhelming and all-
enveloping thunder of God's sovereign loving YES goes
echoing and reechoing down the corridors and caverns of
his *Dogmatics* with even greater majesty and force than did
even God's NO blast forth in his commentary on *Romans*.
The startling originality of Barth's application of his major
Christological perspective comes out in each of the three
other volumes produced in this decade: in his doctrine of
creation (3–1), in his doctrine of man (3–2), and in his
doctrine of providence and the demonic (*Das Nichtige*)
(3–3). And it is further reflected, in his first volume of the
next decade, in his treatment of "Reverence for Life" in
the midst of his ethic of human freedom before God (3–4).

The actual content of these doctrines as treated by Barth
will be summarized and discussed later. But one point concerning Barth's theological pilgrimage must be clarified here.
From the recent publication in the United States of Barth's

"The Humanity of God" it might be concluded that his break with his old "negative" theology and the beginning of his new "positive" theology is to be marked from the time of this little speech (1956). The phrase "the humanity of God" (*Die Menschlichkeit Gottes*) was apparently coined for a portion of the *Dogmatics* probably lectured in 1956 (4–3, 36). But this is just a term invented by Barth to describe the main theme of his thought that had been developing ever since his lectures on predestination (1940–1942). It is clearly stated in his doctrine of creation (especially 3–1, 381), and it is the heart and meaning of his elaborate and complicated doctrine of *analogia relationis* by which he explains the life of man to be related to God, as the eternal Son is related to the Father in the Trinity (especially 3–2, 218 ff.).

As Barth completed the four volumes of his doctrine of God the Creator he reached his sixty-fifth birthday. There is now another noticeable shift in his theology, not in basic content or direction but in form and emphasis. To this last phase in Barth's theology we now turn.

THE DECADE OF MATURITY

During these last ten years (1951–1961) Barth has become more and more "the old man in Basel" (4–2, ix). He has consistently turned down a flood of invitations to lecture all over the world. He has had a growing sense that he has been given further time on this earth for one reason, to make progress in the *Dogmatics*. So, in his most recent ten-year retrospect in *The Christian Century* (1960) he notes with satisfaction that he has got through the bulk of the doctrine of reconciliation (4–1, 4–2, 4–3). When I heard him lecture during the year 1959–1960, he was making a very leisurely start into Part 4 of Vol. IV on the ethics of reconciliation. In the midst of this topic he is constructing his formal treatment of Baptism and the Lord's Supper (he has long since

ceased referring to them as "sacraments," maintaining that
the incarnation is the only sacrament). And between Baptism and the Lord's Supper he is injecting an exposition of
the Lord's Prayer.

With his formal retirement from teaching in the summer
of 1961 at the age of seventy-five, he has been relieved of
the pressure of three weekly lectures that were the external
compulsion that has moved the *Dogmatics* forward across
the years at Basel. Now the progress will be even more
leisurely. This does not disturb Barth. He is content with
what he has done. He does not seem to be anxious or even
particularly interested in getting to his concluding Vol. V
on the doctrine of redemption (his term for eschatology).
When I expressed concern about his completing it in retirement, he replied whimsically, "Oh, maybe I'll do that one
in heaven." He maintains that he has already said everything
he needs to say on the subject. Some critics have suggested
that Barth does not want to get to the problems of eschatology because they will give his system trouble. This is true
in several respects, and we will discuss this problem in a
later chapter. But for whom does eschatology not give
trouble? I believe Barth is sincere and correct in suggesting
that he has already had his say on the subject. Moreover,
although he still has remarkable physical vigor and re-
silience of mind and spirit, he has a right at his age to get
tired and to relax. However, there is perhaps a deeper
motivation in his seeming reluctance to complete his system.
Barth does not believe in a system. He does not regard his
Dogmatics as "a new *Summa Theologiae*" (3–4, xii). He expects and invites the younger theologians now coming up to
be dissatisfied with his *Dogmatics* and to try to improve
upon it. He wants no narrow school of Barthians. If the
Dogmatics is left incomplete, it is possible that this point
will be understood (although doctrinaire Barthians would

also have a field day in vying to complete the *Dogmatics* for the master).

Although Barth has stayed close to home and to work these last ten years, he has been no recluse in his interests and in his social involvements. His now well known passion for Mozart, which began in his youth, has resulted in several speeches and small writings in recent years. Recently he has limited his preaching almost entirely to sermons for the inmates of the Basel jail, and a volume of these has been published. In the autumn of 1959, Barth did travel to Strasbourg to receive an honorary doctorate from the university, the solemnity of the occasion being magnified by the august presence of Charles de Gaulle for the opening of the new school year. Then in the spring of 1962 he typically confounded all the prophecies to the contrary and visited the United States. His appearances at Chicago, Princeton, and San Francisco were a huge personal success as thousands felt and responded to the warmth and genuineness of the man. And he was given the ultimate American accolade of being featured on the cover of *Time* magazine. The theological effects of his visit will not be measurable for some time. But by far his most intense preoccupation apart from the *Dogmatics* was in the political field. Since his early socialist days in Safenwil, Barth has never lost his interest in the relations among social, political, and Christian forces. I have already mentioned his advice to Hungarian Protestants in 1948.[45] In 1953 he became involved in the situation of communist East Germany by protesting the arrest of pastors. And again he spoke what seemed to some very ambiguous words about a Christian's relation to a communist regime in his *Letter to a Pastor in East Germany* (1958). And when he remained silent after the brutal Russian suppression of the Hungarian revolt of October, 1956, he was severely taken to task by Reinhold Niebuhr. Barth's exact position on this

whole problem, and its justification in the light of actual
events and conditions, is far too complex for us to treat
here. There are already full and competent books on the
subject.[46] In his ten-year retrospect of 1960, Barth goes to
some pains to try to explain his viewpoint, but he also says
there that the space he is giving to this problem is way out
of proportion to its importance in his life.[47] His real concern has been his *Dogmatics,* the growing number of
critiques written about it, its use by pastors, and particularly
the special interest it has aroused among the Roman
Catholics.

What, then, was the nature of his theological development in these years? Was there another shift? I have characterized it as a "Decade of Maturity." In the three volumes
(4–1, 4–2, 4–3) in which he developed his doctrine of reconciliation, Barth used the old Reformed schema that di-
vided the saving work of Christ into the three "offices" of
prophet, priest, and king. As usual when he borrows from
the orthodox theology, Barth gives this schema a completely
new and fresh twist in both the order of treatment and their
meaning. Actually, there is hardly an idea in the three
volumes that Barth has not developed or anticipated already
in some prior volume. The uniqueness of this twenty-five-
hundred-page explication of reconciliation lies in the con-
summate achievement of a grand symphony in which all the
diverse themes and melodies and counterpoint that had been
experimented with across the years are now brought under
perfect control of the master composer and unified into a
harmonious whole of infinite complexity and subtlety. It is
beautiful and wondrous to behold, and its impact is enormous. It does have a Thomistic flavor in that it seems to
comprehend within it all possible positions and emphases
and so is hard to pin down and grasp with any sharpness.
Hence, I would have to say that it is not as startling and
exciting and provocative as the first three volumes of the

Doctrine of Creation, with their eruptions and angularities and lack of complete control and synthesis. Of course, each kind of treatment has its own strength and attractiveness, reflecting the differing gifts of the different ages of man.

There is one relatively new and creative development in this last stage of Barth's theological pilgrimage that should be mentioned. In treating the problem of the communication of reconciliation to all the world (4–3), Barth develops a direct and full-blown resolution of a problem with which he had been struggling from the beginning: How is the continuing creaturely existence of man related to his new life in Jesus Christ? In the early volumes of the *Dogmatics* Barth still contended that there was no relation, only the relation of disjuncture and antagonism. In the volumes on creation Barth came to assert that creation (even fallen in sin) and reconciliation (as covenant) are profoundly interdependent in the will and act and goal of God. In his latest volume on reconciliation (4–3) Barth has followed these insights out in a way so as to envision a profound correlation and correspondence between the Creation itself and the historical event and progress of reconciliation. Barth has admitted that this is an insight and emphasis that grows throughout the *Dogmatics*. So when he can now speak of an authentic Word of God to man outside and independent of the Scriptures, something relatively new has come to light at the end of his theological way. And Barth chuckles with glee when he tells how some of his faithful followers now complain that in his latest volume he seems to be more interested in the people outside the church than in those within.

CONCLUSION

Now let us ask our question again: What kind of theology are you falling in with if you open yourself to Barth's influence? I think it should be quite apparent from the foregoing account of his pilgrimage that it is impossible to classify Barth and his theology. One must stand in amazement at the profound sensitivity and radical mobility of his mind and thought. Yet one gets the impression of a ground stream of conviction that keeps flowing relentlessly in the same general direction, no matter what twists and turns, no matter what shifting patterns appear on the surface. What or who is it that gives the *Dogmatics* its fundamental direction? I think that Bouillard has shown conclusively that it is nonsense to point to Kant or Hegel or Kierkegaard.[48] Certainly one can see profound parallels with each of them but also decisive differences. In a similar way, one could make out a case for saying that Barth is a return to the old orthodoxy in that he takes the contents of the Bible with utmost seriousness and seems to regard his theology as a direct deduction from the Biblical revelation. But what he means by the "Word of God" in the Bible, and the results he gets from listening to it, are both so different from the positions of orthodoxy that contemporary American conservatives are mounting a growing attack on Barth. Again, one could argue that Barth still preserves the essential concern of the "liberalism" of Schleiermacher and Herrmann in that he has never forsaken their concern for *humanitas,* for mankind and its practical, ethical, social reality and need. So when many were amazed that the author of the commentary on Romans would get mixed up in a battle with Hitler, Barth replied, "The abstract transcendent God . . . , the abstract eschatological awakening . . . , and the just as abstract church . . . , all that existed *not* in *my* mind, but only in the heads of many of my readers."[49] But in the *Dogmatics* Barth has stood liberalism on its head. Whereas it found God to be the answer to man's needs, Barth found that God is both the determination and the satisfaction of man's needs. Again, one can find a strong strain of *Heilsgeschichte* in the *Dogmatics,* in that Barth takes Israel's history, Jesus' history, and the church's history all as modes of God's own history within human history. Yet Barth by no means is guilty of a "positivism of revelation" (Bonhoeffer's enigmatic charge) but works with a radical distinction between mere empirical history and the revelational event that is not subject to historical analysis. Again, it must be clear that Barth is not antiexistential, that throughout the whole *Dogmatics* there is a deep concern about the subjective event of man's responsible decision. As Barth finished his doctrine of creation and turned to his doctrine of reconciliation (1951), he explicitly said, "Existentialism proves itself without any doubt to be a profitable instrument insofar as theology is concerned with critique, polemics, disputation, demythologizing, etc., and of course theology must always be concerned therewith" (3–4, viii). Yet, in the same place he strongly rejected the possibility of actually grounding theology, exegesis, and preaching on a preformed existentialist philosophy. And since then he has carried on a running debate with Bultmann on this issue.

So Barth seems to encompass all of these theological positions, yet is identical with none. There is one decisive factor that we have omitted thus far: Barth is a theologian of the Reformation. He was born and bred in Calvinism. And Luther dominates Vol. I of the *Dogmatics*. In summarizing the influences that led to the decisive edition of the commentary on Romans, Bouillard concludes, "By instinct, by tradition unconsciously received, the theology of Barth was more Reformed, more Calvinist, than he knew."[50] And concerning the theology of the *Dogmatics* as a whole, Bouillard comes to this judgment: "Let us take Barth's thought for what it is: its originality is irreducible. Its context is truly designated only by reference to the Reformers, from whom it received its basic elements with the desire to make them bear fruit in a consistent way, in the midst of a new mental universe."[51]

It is true that the cutting edge of the driving intellect of Barth's theology is formed from the perspective of the Reformers and particularly of Calvin. But that edge would be too fine and light a thing to cut deep into our life if it were not backed up with the weight of the centuries of the church's Catholic theology behind the Reformers. And that edge would soon grow so dull as not to make an impression at all if it were not tempered with the modernity of the theological, intellectual, and social developments since the Reformation. All this is there in Barth's theology. As far as I can discern, it has no secret hidden core around which are wrapped some flimsy tissues of old and new. Rather, Barth seems to have honestly, sensitively, deeply opened his very life and being to these diverse streams of Christian thought and non-Christian philosophy, and *in himself* they have found their irrefrangible unity. The only names that occur with regularity across the pages of all twelve volumes of the *Dogmatics* are those of Augustine (205 times), Thomas Aquinas (147), Luther (320), Calvin (297), and Schleiermacher (139). Whether approving or disapproving them, these are the thinkers with whom Barth wrestles. Plato and Aristotle, orthodoxy and pietism, Kant and Hegel, socialism and millennialism, Kierkegaard and Bultmann—all these play their restricted roles in the interstices of the structural giants of Barth's theological edifice. It must be no real surprise to Barth that Roman Catholics have found points of great interest and even supposed agreement in the *Dogmatics,* because Thomas has had his part in shaping it. It will come as a surprise to many of Barth's Protestant critics to discover that Schleiermacher's system, far from being brusquely set aside by Barth, has simply been stood on its head in the *Dogmatics.*

Barth has written, "When I should arrive in heaven, I would make inquiries first of all concerning Mozart, and then next for Augustine and Thomas, then for Luther, Calvin, and Schleiermacher."[52] This is the kind of theology, these are the theologians, that you will be opening yourself to in reading the *Dogmatics*—all set to the tune of Mozart, and all filtered through the mind and life of Karl Barth, a man of our own times par excellence.

Chapter III

The Labyrinth

BEFORE you begin wandering around in the vast criss-crossing maze of the *Dogmatics'* corridors, you had better have at least a simplified map of the main paths and their interconnections. Few people have the time to read this work in its entirety, and fewer still have tried to get a synoptic view of the whole. In the next two chapters I will try to help you to grasp the rudiments of such a view. In this one I will give a sketch of the main structures and dominating drives of the work, and in the next chapter I will attempt a brief, chapter-by-chapter summary of the contents. Without some such overall perspective you would be understandably reluctant to dip into the middle of one stray volume you happen to pick up for help on a particular theme. All sorts of doubts might beset you. What if this is just a peripheral treatment of a theme to which he gives major attention elsewhere? Has he changed his position on this subject? If he says *this* here on this topic, what must he say *there* on that topic? If I am persuaded to preach on the basis of this doctrine of atonement, what are the implications for the mission of the church? Many of the major questions along this line I hope to be able to answer for you in these two chapters. At least you then should know where else to look in the *Dogmatics* for the answers to your questions.

As you read this analysis of the structure and this summary of the content of the *Dogmatics,* I invite and urge you
to keep a certain question always in the back of your mind:
What is dogmatic (doctrinal or systematic) theology? What ⚹
is it for? Unless you have asked and answered this question
for yourself in a critical way, you may very easily misuse
Barth's *Dogmatics* in preaching and be tragically corrupted
by them. I will tackle this question directly in Chs. V and
VI, but I want you to be thinking about it seriously as you
read these next two chapters.

THE GENERAL OUTLINE

I have had the Table of Contents of all twelve volumes
reproduced for you on pp. 84 f. From it you can gain some
sense of the scope and complexity of the whole. Yet the
main structure is quite simple and obvious. The five main
divisions consist of the doctrines of: the Word of God, God,
creation, reconciliation, redemption. If you did not have the
full Table of Contents, but only these five topics, you might
immediately begin to ask, Where is his treatment of sin, of   -
the church, of man, of the Person of Christ and the incarnation, of the Christian life? And you would have struck upon   -
one of the distinctive features of Barth's approach to theology, and for the pastor who tries to read on the run, one
of the more frustrating characteristics. There is no place in
the *Dogmatics* where you can go to find his full and definitive exposition of these latter doctrines. In other words, he
does not allow them to be "doctrines," loci, that is, elements
of the Christian faith that can be separated out and dealt
with independently. Barth is arguing that man, his sin, his
Christian living, the church, and even the incarnation are
not events or realities that have their distinctive meaning
and reality in themselves as such. Hence, they cannot be
adequately described by themselves. Of course no system of
doctrines or loci ever intended to imply that they could be

so handled. But Barth contends that their isolation in treatment has always fostered that illusion. So here is a grand
experiment to see if that fragmentation of Christian truth
can be overcome at least in its major aspects.

The way Barth attempts this is to work from the hypothe-
sis that for Christian faith there is only one truth: the living
God. Nothing has any reality except in relation to and in
dependence upon him. This includes the laws of nature, the
human subject and human history, and sin itself. Therefore,
Barth asserts, dogmatics in all its diversity and complexity
"can wish to say nothing else than this: God is" (2–1, 258).
There is only one doctrine, the doctrine of God. So Vol. I
on the Word of God is not "prolegomena" in the strict sense,
because Barth contends that we cannot establish the authority of Scripture and power of preaching by themselves
and certainly not in a preliminary way. The Word of God
is only and always God himself, never identical with the
words of a human book or voice. So in dealing with the
formal and preliminary question of how we know God,
Barth goes to the very heart of the material question of
theology, Who is God? And his answer is, Father, Son, and
Holy Spirit, incarnate in Jesus Christ. So the doctrines of
Trinity and incarnation are the "prolegomena," the ground
of all theology. Likewise, in Vol. II as a general doctrine of
God, Barth does not aim at developing a philosophy of religion to show how the Christian idea of God fits in with
other ideas of God. Rather, he will talk only about the God
whom we know in his act of electing man as his covenant
partner in Jesus Christ. And in this context alone does he
begin to talk about what it means to live as a Christian
(ethics).

The remaining volumes are, then, merely elaborations of
the three basic elements in the general doctrine of God.
Volume III is really a doctrine of God the Creator. Man
has his meaning not in himself but only as *creature* of the

Creator. The cosmos can be ultimately "explained" not in terms of its own laws but as the Creator's *creation* of a locale where his purpose with man may be played out. Volume IV is the doctrine of God the Reconciler. Man   IV comes to the knowledge that that for which he was created is not realizable by means of the given potentialities of creation itself, but the achievement of his destiny comes in the inexplicably gracious gift of God's own self in his humble condescension in Jesus Christ and in God's gift of man's exaltation in Jesus Christ. The whole life of the Christian community has to do only with the knowing and the telling of this act of God. In the projected Vol. V, we are supposed to hear about God the Redeemer, who shall   V bring to perfect fulfillment in man all that he started in creation with man and all that he realized in reconciliation for man.

INNER ARCHITECTONICS

This broad, simple program was set up by Barth thirty years ago when he started the *Dogmatics* (1–1, xiii f.). But the endless refinements in the substructures and their subtle interconnections could never have been dreamed of. They developed at such depth and breadth that it is now impossible to give a definitive exposition of any one part of the *Dogmatics* without making some reference to almost every other part. This fact raises the serious question as to whether the contents of the *Dogmatics* are so subjected to an imposed "system" that the voice of the Bible and the needs of man are not given their proper freedom in this theology. We will try to answer this question at the end of this chapter, but first we must take a frank and honest look at what goes on within the general outline described above.

One of the most interesting results of Barth's general   ✳ ✳ ✳ organization is that it allows, or even requires, him to restate and to develop anew his positions on man, the church,

Christology, etc., throughout the *Dogmatics*. For example, the answer to the question, Who is Jesus Christ? is given in a preliminary way in Vol. I under Trinity and incarnation, receives a radically new twist in Vol. II under election, becomes the regulative criterion for the definition of true humanity in Vol. III, and arrives in Vol. IV at a grandiloquent treatment in the picture of the One who is simultaneously Humbled God and Exalted Man and Victorious Lord. The same program for the development of a doctrine of the church can be seen by simply glancing through the tables of contents. Of course, the most notable example of this phenomenon is Barth's deliberate and announced intention of making ethics an integral part of *Dogmatics*. Thus we find a special chapter (sometimes a whole volume) at the end of the doctrines of God, creation, reconciliation, and (maybe) redemption, in which the broad issues of man's life before God are explored and reexplored.

This character of Barth's schematization gives the whole *Dogmatics* a flowing continuity, an organic and living quality, that is so often absent from chopped up, static systems of theology. It has also allowed Barth to express his own growing insights on the major focuses of our faith. He has admittedly shifted emphasis, filled in omissions, responded to criticism, experimented with different terminologies, and even dropped some earlier formulations (e.g., on the sacraments). It is little wonder that theologians hesitate to assert what "Barth says" on any one problem when what he has to say is stretched out in twelve large tomes covering thirty years of his own intellectual development. Even when one comes to a major exposition of a topic in a later volume, one has to remember that the basic theses have probably already been evolved in another context in an earlier volume. This character of the *Dogmatics* may seem rather threatening to the busy pastor who wants to proclaim on this Sunday one particular aspect of the gospel and to preach

from a particular text. I will deal with this problem in the
later chapters on preaching, but let it be said that Barth's
Dogmatics is simply demanding that you, the preacher,
speak each week out of the Living Center of the Christian
faith. Jesus Christ as this center should give a oneness and
connectedness to everything you preach or teach, and should
prevent you from simply reflecting in an unthinking way
the latest book and author you have read.

Barth's schema has also resulted in some rather (for
modern minds) startling dislocations of emphasis by restricting his treatment of certain themes. We are used to having
a doctrine of God balanced or even preceded by a doctrine
of man. In a way Barth does this because his chapter on
ethics at the end of each major doctrine is his doctrine of
man. Real man exists for Barth only in his relationship with
God, and only in the relationship that is initiated and maintained by God. But what about man as such, in and of and
by himself? It is a cliché of Barth's critics to say that he
denies the reality of such a man and negates therefore any
possibility of considering man as such. This is a mistaken
statement of Barth's position. It is far too complex a question to treat here, and I will touch on it in several of the
later chapters. Barth does restrict his treatment of man as
such within his doctrine of creation, and there, according to
the criterion of Jesus Christ, as true man. But there also in
extended footnotes he does recognize the limited validity
even of nontheological attempts to understand man on his
own terms. Another dislocation in the *Dogmatics* that
amazes almost everyone is the restriction of the doctrine of
sin, since recent theology and philosophy have so emphasized
the sinfulness and tragedy of human existence, partially as
a result of the impact of Barth's own commentary on
Romans. But as a result of his unique formulations of the
doctrines of predestination and of the demonic (*Das Nichtige*), Barth gives only limited reality to the range of sin,

corruption, and death. He makes them basically God's own problem, and their true nature comes to light for man only as he is confronted by God himself in Jesus Christ. This means that sin is dealt with by Barth only in an integral unity with the doctrine of reconciliation in Vol. IV. This also means that the *"Ja!"* of God overwhelms his *"Nein!"*

There is one other result of Barth's general outline that might be said to have a restrictive nature. Although he argues strongly that the Trinitarian God is One God and is active as One God in creation, in reconciliation, and in redemption, yet he also wants to allow the relative "appropriation" of creation to the Father, reconciliation to the Son, and redemption to the Holy Spirit (3–4, 33). This restricted nature of the three main doctrines is intensified by Barth's further interpretation of them within his time schema. The problem of time is of major concern to Barth. In his eternity God has time for us. Time and eternity are not mutually exclusive. So God is related to us in three ways: pretemporally, cotemporally, and posttemporally, which is another way of saying as Creator, Reconciler, and Redeemer (2–2, 549). This restriction of the modes of God's being as Father, Son, and Holy Spirit to the spheres of creation, reconciliation, redemption, and to the spheres of pretemporal, cotemporal, and posttemporal, simply could not be maintained consistently by Barth who makes the oneness of God so basic. But this "appropriation" and the application of the temporal schema do determine some of the things he does and does not say about creation, reconciliation, and redemption. And the preacher should be aware of this restriction as he reads under one of these main headings. I will draw some of the implications of this restriction later on and also make a critique of it.

We have now seen how the main structure of the *Dogmatics* has resulted in the recurrence of some themes throughout all the parts, and likewise in the restriction and subsumption of other themes. Barth's concern to make his whole *Dogmatics* just one inclusive doctrine of God, expressed in a continuous flowing stream, has also resulted in a large number of interconnecting substructures. There are many that I probably have not noticed, and space here allows for only a few examples. One of the most obvious ones is the use of the Trinitarian format. We have already called attention to the broad use of it in the major doctrines of creation, reconciliation, and redemption. Another interesting application is found within the doctrine of reconciliation where Barth speaks of the "judgment of the Father" (¶ 59:3), the "direction of the Son" (¶ 64:4), and the "promise of the Holy Spirit" (¶ 69:4). This would seem to imply an appropriation of the Priestly Office of Christ to the Father, and Kingly Office to the Son, and the Prophetic Office to the Holy Spirit. And within this same context we find reconciliation analyzed into the three elements of justification, sanctification, and calling. And sin is also there analyzed into pride, sloth, and lie, resulting in fall, misery, and damnation. All this makes for a certain beauty in the architectonics of the *Dogmatics,* especially if you like the number three. But this kind of schematization makes one nervous when he thinks that there may be a fourth character of sin that is being totally overlooked. Likewise, as I will discuss later, this schema in Vol. IV blurs the fact that Barth really does not conceive of the prophetic communication of reconciliation as part of Christ's basic act of reconciliation but as a kind of secondary work for which he can give no convincing reason and urgency.

Another example of the subpatterns that Barth's mind has followed at different places in the *Dogmatics* is that which he developed first in Ch. 10 on man the creature. He discusses man in relation (1) to God, (2) to fellowman, (3) to the created order, and (4) to time. In Ch. 12 he analyzes the freedom of man in the same four relationships. And

again he shows how man's sin as sloth (the refusal of freedom) operates in the same four ways (4–2, 409). Still another pattern that Barth is especially fond of is that of:
Jesus Christ, the community (church), the individual. It is
found in its basic form in Ch. 7 where God's election is
described as moving in this order. It is repeated in many
subsidiary ways and notably in the three main chapters of
the doctrine of reconciliation. The justification, the sanctification, and the calling that really occur only in Jesus
Christ have the result then of gathering, upbuilding, and
sending the Christianity community, and then is reflected
in the faith, love, and hope of the Christian individual. This
is a very important schema in Barth's theologizing because
in this way he, first, asserts that all human accomplishments
are no more than reflections and echoes of God's own work
in Jesus Christ. And, secondly, he manages by this pattern
to postpone all questions about man's own, uniquely creaturely *subjectivity* in the event of salvation to the very end
of every doctrine, and there he gives it very short shrift.

We have now taken a quick look at the major skeletal
frame on which Barth has built his *Dogmatics,* and we have
caught at least a glimpse of a few of the different kinds of
substructures. But these are not what make it live. What is
the meat and muscle that covers these bones and makes
them move with power and punch in the theological world?

THE MAIN THEOLOGICAL DRIVES

The *Church Dogmatics* is the work of a single human
person, Karl Barth. It is not the work of a synod or a com-
mittee of the church. Nor is Barth a machinelike researcher,
who drinks in oceans of material in order to distill its essence, or who seeks to produce an all-inclusive syncretism
of all possible positions. He is a highly individualistic,
imaginative, creative person of sensitive and restless energy.

A person of such temperament must have had deep motivation and intense, almost passionate, theological concerns in order to stay with so vast and demanding a project as the thirty-year work on the *Dogmatics*. It is important to understand the theological drives of any theologian you read. They are what give his work a cutting edge and a definite sense of direction. They are the source of its inner unity, weight, and power to shed light. They also are what limit his perspective and the scope of his treatment. Therefore, a man's work should be judged by what he is trying to do, not by what he omitted doing. No human work and so no theology is able to embrace all the truth or to meet all needs. In a later critical chapter (V) I will try to help you to see that Barth's *Dogmatics* must certainly not be taken as all true or the whole truth. But here let us try to capture the strength and passion that informs his theology.

Barth has said that the one thing that he hopes will remain "inexorably unchanged" to his life's end is that the object, source, and criterion of his thinking is "the Word of God which is the mystery of God in his relation to man and not . . . the mystery of man in his relation to God."[1] This statement was made in 1939 when he had completed only Vol. I of the *Dogmatics*. He would now say that the former mystery encompasses the latter mystery also, but never, never, the reverse. If I had to choose the one dominant theme and drive and concern in the whole of Barth's theology it would be this: to proclaim, to plumb, and to protect the *mystery* of God's Word in Jesus Christ. What Barth misses most in the theology and piety of the twentieth century is the element of mystery. What he has in mind, however, is not the generalized *mysterium tremendum* described by Rudolf Otto but the particular and unique mystery of God's love and freedom as present to man in Jesus Christ. And this one dominant drive in Barth's theology must be analyzed into its three distinct but inseparable aspects to be fully understood.

First, the mystery of God takes the *form* of the Trinity. For Barth, the Trinity is not simply the mystery of God's own inner eternal being, nor is it the mystery of the Trinitarian formulation in the mind of man, nor is it the mystery of the analogy between these two (i.e., how do we know that this finite and temporal human concept captures and holds the infinite and eternal being of God?). Rather, the mystery of God that takes the form of the Trinity is this: the way in which the concrete, historical, and existential relationship that God establishes with man is rooted and grounded in the eternal self-contained being of God in himself. In other words, the Trinity for Barth is the reality of God's being simultaneously transcendent and immanent. There are not two trinities, one in God and one in his relationship with us. The Trinity is God himself precisely *in* the relationship he establishes with us. The mystery lies in the fact that in this relationship the absolute qualitative distinction between God the Creator and man the creature is maintained, while at the same time God and man are united in a way that, far from contradicting God's being, actually reflects and reveals him. This drawing of the creature by God into a relation of communion is the mystery of our life just because it is a direct reflection and analogy of the relation of the Father and the Son in the communion of the Holy Spirit in the eternity of God. When the very life of God is reflected in our life, then we can do no other than gaze in wonder and awe before its mystery and cease our human drive to "explain." Barth's sharpest and yet most debatable formulation of this relationship is found in his principle of *analogia relationis:* as the Father is related to the Son, so God is related to man, and so man is related to fellowman. I find this principle to be the most pervasive

and most formative one in all of Barth's theology, even
where it is not made explicit.

Secondly, if the Trinity is the *form* of the mystery of
God's relation to man, its <u>content</u> must be defined in terms
of love and freedom. What kind of God is it that can be
absolutely other, transcendent and omnipotent and yet be
bound and united to human creature on a plane of mutuality? Barth answers: Only the God whose freedom and
sovereignty is love. God in his oneness is Person, and he
he has his own life and history and freedom because he is
in himself three: the lover, the beloved, love (Barth uses
Augustine's terms). Barth never wearies of repeating in a
thousand variations that, <u>first and last, the thing we must</u>
always say is that God is love, he is gospel. <u>God's judgment,</u>
<u>God's wrath, God's NO, are all contained within and serve</u>
<u>his loving being and purpose.</u> But, just as strongly, Barth
wishes to make undeniably clear that it is precisely in his
love that God is absolutely free and sovereign. Before God's
loving, nothing has any other right or claim or power or
possibility. Outside the circle of his loving there is nothingness, impossibility. All that has any being is a creation of
God's love, is sustained by his love, is the goal of his love.
Any movement from "below" to "above" can only be a reflection and an echo of the original movement of God from
"above" to "below." For Barth, all faith must be confessed
and all theology must be written from this perspective. Only
then can <u>men</u> recognize and gladly accept the mystery that
<u>in being determined by God's sovereign love they attain</u>
<u>their only and true freedom.</u>

Finally, the <u>mystery of God's loving</u> in the Trinitarian
relationship <u>is also lodged in its *method* of achievement,</u>
namely, in Jesus Christ. For many readers of Barth, his constant Christological reference becomes oppressive and numb-
ing, with the result of blurring all distinctions to the point

Content
=
love &
freedom

Method
=
Jesus
Christ

of meaninglessness. This is due partly to a misunderstanding
of what he means by "Jesus Christ." For many the name
refers to the Jew who lived a short span of some thirty years
about nineteen hundred years ago and in whose life God
came to us in a unique way. It means that for Barth too.
But it means much more. For Barth, Paul's words in Róm.
11:36 apply to Jesus Christ, "from whom and through
whom and to whom are all things." Jesus Christ is the
eternal God in his temporal creaturely form, spanning the
past, the present, and the future, the origin, the history, and
the goal of human existence. Jesus Christ is the "humanity
of God," God's turning to dwell with man in his decree
before the Creation; God's going with man through man's
whole toilsome way, decisively in the form of the birth, life,
death, and resurrection of Jesus of Nazareth; God's waiting
for man at the end of his road in readiness to receive man
into the glory of his own eternal life. Barth is certain that
we can say nothing meaningful about God or man unless it
is something we say in the direct light of Jesus Christ. God's
willingness in his own eternity to have time for us takes
concrete form in Jesus Christ and is the ultimate mystery
of our life. Barth's Trinitarianism, his emphasis on the
finality of God's love, his absorption with the meaning of
time, his insistence that all life and reality are historical in
nature, all find their ground and explanation in his
Christology.

There are serious reservations and questions that we will
later want to bring to bear upon these main drives of Barth's
theology. His concerns and aims have their strengths and
weaknesses. They allow certain things to be said with force,
but they also seem to prevent other things from being said
at all. At this point, however, I simply want to emphasize
the importance of keeping these basic, formative convictions
of Barth's in mind while you are reading in every part of
the *Dogmatics*. There is not a sentence in any volume after

the exposition of election (2–2) that is not colored by these concerns.

THE QUESTION OF SYSTEM

Barth denies that valid dogmatics can be "systematic." He claims that everyone who has dealt with philosophy or theology that way has understood "system" to mean: "a self-contained and fully established coherence of principles and deductions, constructed on the basis of the presupposition of a certain fundamental perspective and with the rise of certain sources of knowledge and axioms" (1–2, 861). To the contrary, Barth asserts that the theologian must bring to his task no presuppositions, no established knowledge and axioms. The theologian must simply unfold and present the content of the Word of God as a way of checking the authenticity of the preaching of the gospel. And even this act will not be an "objective exhibition and analysis" because the "content" has the character of "a conversation, a process, an active struggle, an act of guidance" (1–2, 858). The only autonomy of the human theologian lies in his decision to do nothing but to listen and to obey the Word of God as he speaks. We will see in a later chapter that Barth of course recognizes that everyone who listens to the Bible has his preformed philosophies, theologies, mythologies, sociologies, and psychologies. But the theologian is not to impose them deliberately upon the content of the Word in order to systematize it. Rather, if the theologian "allows Christ to be the center, the point of beginning and ending of Christian thinking, then adequate provision will have been made to guarantee for it unity and coherence—systematics in the best sense of the concept" (4–1, 528).

Barth, therefore, honestly does not believe that he is imposing a system on the vast range of the materials of his *Dogmatics* when he allows them all to be informed and formed by what he calls the mystery of the Trinity, of God's loving in freedom, of the humanity of God in Jesus Christ. Rather, he sincerely believes that this theme of God's mystery is imposed on his thinking by the Word of God that God spoke in Jesus of Nazareth and that he continues to speak through the apostolic (Scriptural) witness to Jesus. Whatever control man brings and must bring into the development of a dogmatics, he must operate from the free and unpredictable and uncontrollable ground of "that encounter with the work and activity of God given to him" (1–2, 860). The theologian must never seek or expect "a secured platform from which he could survey and control his object" (1–2, 866).

It must be clear, then, that when Barth says, "In actuality, theology must fundamentally be Christology and only Christology" (1–2, 872), he is not thinking of Christology as a well-formulated principle, nor is he restricting it to the event experienced in reconciliation. As I have heard him say, "Jesus Christ is not a clue to be wielded but a Person to be followed." Theology is Christology because Christology is all the truth of God's whole range of activity toward man, from the beginning to the end of time. And this being of God is God in his Word who, speaking decisively and finally in Jesus Christ, is the free and prior source of all faith, all Christian thinking, all dogma and doctrine. From this perspective, Barth insists that even the doctrine of the Trinity must not be allowed to become an all-controlling principle, as if we have caught God in a scheme of thought. The Word confirms the doctrine of the Trinity and is confirmed by it but is not exhausted in it (1–2, 879).

Is Barth faithful to this definition of theological method? Can any man wholly be? Has he never used a Christological formula as a clue and a club? Has he never forced the intractable materials of God's creative and reconciling activity into the restrictive mold of a Trinitarian schematization? Has he never let his sense for the beauty of balance lead to overly nice analysis and arrangement of parts and details? If so, he must accept criticism on his own grounds. We shall have to see for ourselves. In Ch. V we will ask, among other things, whether or not Barth has forced the Biblical witness into the system of monistic idealism to such an extent that he is deaf to the full Biblical message about man. In Ch. VI we will seek to discover whether there is a real difference between the theology of a man who admits that certain philosophical schemata are working unconsciously in his thinking as he tries to listen to the Word of God alone (Barth), and the theology of a man who deliberately chooses one contemporary philosophy as the best available and then submits it to be used and corrected by the Word of God in his self-communication and revelation (Bultmann). These are not easy questions, but they are important ones for everyone who seeks to preach and teach the Word of God and who reads the theologians for help in this task.

CONCLUSION

I would hope that by now you might have a little idea as to "what the *Dogmatics* is all about." We have glanced briefly at the main outline, some of the substructures, the basic drives, and Barth's intended theological method. Now a word of warning. Please do not assume that I have succeeded in systematizing what is purportedly an unsystematic theology. You must not take these four clues and use them to run lightly through the labyrinth of the *Dogmatics*. If you do, you will miss the real helpfulness of this work for preaching and teaching. Much of the richest and most rewarding materials are not to be found in the main galleries but in the incidental side rooms and happenstantial burrowings that Barth carves out along the way. In spite of the amazing coherence and control that he has been able to maintain across seventy-five hundred pages and thirty years of work, the *Dogmatics* is a labyrinth and not one over-

KARL BARTH'S CHURCH DOGMATICS

powering cathedral room hollowed out within the "magic mountain" of Christian faith. Theological experts and doctoral candidates will have a heyday for years to come as they either attempt to harmonize or point with glee at the irreconcilable inconsistencies and the inexplicable lacunae in the *Dogmatics*. It is a fascinating game for those with the penchant for it. But it is not an end in itself. It is not what these volumes are meant to serve. They are meant to serve you who must week by week face groups of people who want to know the truth that will set them free.

Better than half this book, therefore, is strictly introductory. It is simply trying to provide some tools for the clearing of the ground so that the real intent and usefulness of the *Dogmatics* may be explored and suggested. And there are still two more preparatory steps that must first be taken before we are ready for a direct treatment of the relevance of the *Dogmatics* for preaching.

Chapter IV

A Quick Tour of the *Dogmatics*

THE long biographical complexity that lies behind the *Dogmatics,* plus its labyrinthine structure, is enough to discourage most preachers. The sheer bulk of the whole and of each part looms like a stunning mountain massif. If you turn to seek light, for example, on just the one doctrine of reconciliation, you are stopped cold by the shuddering task of chopping through twenty-five hundred pages. Nevertheless, Barth has the audacity to speak about the "page turner" who might miss the fact that this doctrine runs through three big volumes instead of just one, and he insists that we hold our critical breath until we have heard him out clear to the end (4–1, x).

To meet this problem a number of summaries and general introductions are being produced. Standing by themselves, however, they are often more puzzling and bewildering for the average American reader than the original volumes. What we are trying to do in this book is to give just enough familiarity with the general background, structure, and contents that you may find your way around in the *Dogmatics,* not as a master theologian and critic, but as one who seeks to hear the Word more clearly so that you may proclaim it more effectively. As a further help to that end, there now follows a page or two on each of the main chapters. Obviously, these brief statements are in no wise a summary.

The richness and creativity of Barth's thought do not yield to summarization. It will prove helpful, however, to have in mind the dominant and distinctive ideas of each part of the whole while you bore in deeply at any one point. There is no single bit or single theme in the *Dogmatics* that is truly isolated. Every statement and aspect has broad and subtle connections with what is both near and far in the architectonics of this vast edifice. In order to make such a brief account, we will again have to submerge and ignore the contradictions and critical problems that we mentioned in the last chapter and to which we will address ourselves directly in the next chapter. So again a word of warning. Barth is not at all as simple and as undifferentiated as the following digest might seem to indicate.

One other word of caution. To condense seventy-five hundred pages into fifteen thousand words took some doing. It required a careful selection of words, often technical ones that save space, and no repetition or expansion could be allowed. So you may find it rather difficult reading. You might even want to skip it and get on to the "practical" bit. But if you have the patience to plow through it, I believe you will be better prepared to follow and to use what comes later.

Now to the summary. I have given first the general titles of the whole volumes, then the chapter numbers and titles as the major subdivisions (indicating in parentheses after them when we pass from one part volume to another), and finally, I have put in parentheses at the end of my paragraphs the number of Barth's "paragraphs" or subsections within each of his chapters.

INTRODUCTION (1–1)

Truth for the Christian community is simply God himself as self-disclosed in Jesus Christ. The church's authentic speaking about God takes place in and from this existential

determination of man by God in the faith-event. But all of
this speaking is human and therefore fallible. Dogmatics is
the church's speaking about its speaking, testing the latter's
authenticity against the norm of Jesus Christ. So the first
task is to explicate this special way to knowledge in Jesus
Christ—not as a bridge to unbelief but as a correction of
heresy. (¶ 1, 2.)

<h2 style="text-align:center">THE DOCTRINE OF THE WORD OF GOD</h2>

Chapter 1. The Word of God as the Criterion of Dogmatics
   The church's speaking about God includes proclamation,
prayer, singing, confession, social action, Christian education, theology. Proclamation in preaching and sacraments
uniquely expects human words and acts to be used by God
himself as his own word to men. This peculiar kind of
speaking creates the church's own inner life and defines its
task toward the world. Dogmatics has the secondary task of
exposition, investigation, polemic, criticism, and revision in
the service of more authentic proclamation. So dogmatics
cannot prescribe the content of preaching, nor is the theologian necessarily a superior man of faith. (¶ 3.)
   The event of God's free self-revelation by his sovereign
address to men is his Word. The Word of God never occurs
in sheer immediacy. It was objectively and concretely present
in Jesus Christ. Proclamation is a recollection of Jesus Christ.
Scripture is the precipitate of the earliest proclamation. Both
the Written Word, and the Proclaimed Word based upon it,
become the Revealed Word when God freely chooses to be
immediately present to men through them. So God's speech
is his presence in his whole Trinitarian Person. He speaks
with the rational power of truth, directed purposively to
men in their need of renewal and fulfillment. His speech is
concrete contemporary act, with the power to demand an
act of decision from men in response to God's decision about
them. We know it is God's speech because of its mystery:

worldly, human thoughts and words both hiding and mani-
festing God's free Word. The listening of the ear verges
imperceptibly into the hearing of faith, without any ex-
planatory capacity on man's part. So we must speak of the
miracle of the Holy Spirit. (¶ 4, 5.)

It is, of course, *men* who hear and know God. But the
capacity is not to have or to hold God's Word but to acknowledge him. And this capacity is given men in the
event. God's acknowledgment of men empowers them to
acknowledge him. "The possibility of the knowledge of the
Word of God lies in the Word of God and nowhere else.
. . . This miracle is faith." (1–1, 255.) It is a product not
of a prior likeness between God and man but of the free
event in which God chooses and establishes man as an "I"
in relation to his own "Thou." Man's acknowledgment is
always incomplete and imperfect. It is the task of dogmatics
to test man's acknowledgment against God's acknowledgment. This means to listen to the Trinitarian God. To listen
to him means to listen to the Bible against all human
philosophies and sciences, even against all the deliverances
of the church. (¶ 6, 7.)

Chapter 2. *The Revelation of God*

Part 1. The Triune God

The doctrine of the Trinity is not even part of the Scriptural witness to revelation, let alone revelation itself. But
the doctrine, as a work of the church, is a necessary interpretation of Scripture and therefore of revelation and therefore of God himself. The fact that (1) God speaks, (2) in
the historical reality of Jesus Christ, and (3) is heard by men,
and the fact that this irreducible diversity is represented as
the single act of the one God, means that the Biblical witness itself distinguishes among Revealer, Revelation, Re-
vealedness. So church doctrine rightly speaks of one God in
three modes of being. Personality in the modern sense be-

longs to the one God. Yet, since God reveals his *self* to us, the three irreducible, interdependent modes of his operation in making himself known must point by analogy to three eternal modes of his being. So God's oneness does not indicate singularity and solitude. Thus the doctrine of the Trinity is occasioned by the church's faith in and proclamation of Jesus Christ as the Word of God (not by the so-called *vestigium trinitatis*) and rightly stands at the beginning of all dogmatic statement. (¶ 8, 9.)

[margin note: Trinity stands at the beginning of all dogmatic statement.]

In the Trinitarian formula, "Father" points to God as he transcends Jesus himself, God whom Jesus reveals as man's Creator, with whom alone is life and who therefore holds man in being over the abyss of nonbeing. Known as such, he is therefore also known as the One with whom the Son and the Spirit have dwelt eternally. The "Son" who is with us as Jesus is the same Lord God as the "Father," but now is the sovereign Lord as he turns toward us, comes to be one with us and speaks to us. Here is God in his second act as Reconciler, completely new and different from the act of creation. This turning did not begin as a new thing with God at the birth of Jesus, but the latter reflects an eternal turning outward of God from himself, a speaking even while creating, the eternal "Son." However, the turning and speaking of God to us must be received, heard, and believed by us. This subjective acceptance also is the work of God, the third act of God as Holy Spirit, *in* us, setting us free to be children of God in hope. So Holy Spirit is the same Lord God who created and reconciled us, who now goes with us as guide and as empowerer of our words to be God's Word. This communion of God and man, of man and man, in love, is rooted in the eternal bond of love between "Father" and "Son." God has eternally lived in this third mode of being as "Spirit." So his work as Spirit is inherent in the whole of creaturely existence, yet to be worshiped as divine gift, not as human possession. (¶ 10, 11, 12.)

Part 2. The Incarnation of the Word (1–2)

Jesus Christ, as temporal historical event, is the objective reality of revelation. But this reality can be described only in the broken twofold statement: The Son of God is this man; this man is the Son of God. God's freedom for man is marked with mystery and miracle, is "known" only in Jesus because in him we know that incarnation is not based on anything possessed by sinful man but on God's turning in eternity toward his "Son" who is our image and original. This revelation of God also means that God has time for us. So our meaningless and endless time and its history are now transformed by God's presence, giving to men a genuine present, a new fulfilled time in Jesus Christ. It has a pretime of expectation in the Old Covenant's trust in the coming of God's Kingdom in the form of God's concrete acts toward Israel and in the form of hope beyond tragedy and suffering. Fulfilled time is also followed by a time of recollection, because fulfillment was accomplished in Jesus Christ. It is hidden in the suffering of the cross, but revealed in the resurrection that imparts God to us as living presence and future hope. (¶ 13, 14.)

The mystery of revelation as God's having time for us is described as to *content* by the "two nature" doctrine, and as to *form* by a statement about Jesus' birth by a virgin. The two natures of Christ are explained best in terms of "the Word became flesh." "The Word" declares Jesus as subject to be the eternal God in a free act. "Flesh" declares that in this act the Word assumes all the qualifications of real human existence, including individuality and sin. "Became" means a concrete act of mercy in which the Son unites himself with human existence without ceasing to be himself. The virgin birth is the sign, given by God, of the mystery of the reality of incarnation. It is not the reality itself. (¶ 15.)

Part 3. The Outpouring of the Holy Spirit

How is it that man has freedom for God, so that revelation *reaches* man? Objectively, God elects men historically in Israel, Jesus, the church, the sacraments. Subjectively we believe and accept in an act of self-determination but are at a loss to explain how or why. We can only say, it is the miracle of the work of God's own Spirit. He responds to the Word of God for us, first in Jesus and now in us in that we follow (not imitate) Jesus. And our ability to continue in the service of obedience is explainable only by the Spirit's continued presence and control. (¶ 16.)

This presence and acknowledgment of the Spirit's control permits the Christian religion continually to submit its doctrine, worship, art, morals, fellowship, etc., to the judgment of revelation. Thus true religion replaces autonomous religion, which works with only a *concept* of God, which confirms man in his attempt to determine his own life, but which ends in self-doubt, leading to mysticism and atheism. (¶ 17.)

Likewise, living by the Spirit of God enables the individual Christian to live in freedom from the law. He lives by and in the love of God. Love is not a concept or a sentiment but is God in his being, act, and relationship. God's giving of himself to us enables us to find our self-fulfillment in giving ourselves to him as the one to whom we belong. This love of God becomes praise of God in our love of neighbor. My neighbor in need reveals to me my own need (sin), and so I must show him the compassion God shows me in Christ and so be a sign of revelation. (¶ 18.)

Chapter 3. The Holy Scripture

The whole revelation of the Triune God is set before us in the Bible. The revelation takes place in Jesus Christ, and the Bible is a collection of witnesses to the event in the form of expectation and recollection. "Witness" means that the Biblical writings are not revelation themselves, but are ordinary human words that point away from themselves. Yet

revelation occurs with and through them, so the church
cannot free itself from the very written texts. "The Bible is
the Word of God" therefore means not a content we can
control but an event in conjunction with the Bible in which
God encounters and controls us. In this event the Bible becomes God's Word to us, not by our faith but by his power.
Yet the requirement of faith preserves the real presence of
the Word, above and over the fallible human words of the
Scriptures. (¶ 19.)

This continuously present Word of God is the authority
in the church. The Word is not restricted to the past time
of Jesus and his disciples. Their written witness continues
to be the only medium of his immediate presence. So
obedience to God and to Scripture are inseparable. The
written Word prevents a merger of human and divine in
the church. Yet, before I can confess the witness of the
Bible, I must listen to the church's confession before and
beside me, accepting its agreements as concrete authority:
the canon of Scripture, the teaching fathers, the confessional
statements. But even these cannot be a legal external authority. They possess real spiritual authority only as each
generation and individual decides to identify itself with the
decision of former generations. (¶ 20.)

This element of decision is a sign of man's irreducible
freedom, a sign that God's authority is not tyranny. But man's
freedom lies only in obedience to the Word which, in Jesus
Christ, manifests the freedom of power over all evil forces,
power to use and yet to be distinct from the world, the
power to impart this freedom to the church. Individuals in
the church are called to manifest this freedom in the task
of interpreting the Word of the Bible, as involved partici-
pants: first, by *explicating* the sense of Scripture as such;
secondly, by accepting the necessary danger of *reflecting* on
the sense by use of our own prior ideas, images, and philosophy in encounter with those of the Biblical writers; thirdly,

by appropriating and *applying* this interpreted sense to our active life. (¶ 21.)

Chapter 4. *The Proclamation of the Church*

In interpreting Scripture, the church is commissioned to speak about God, and when God himself makes good this proclamation, it is a third form of the Word along with incarnation and Scripture. Dogmatics operates between exegesis and proclamation to see if the content of preaching is "pure," that is, is transparent for the Word. Since the end of interpretation and preaching of the Word is man's living, the existential question of ethics is an integral part of dogmatics. In its critique of preaching and living, dogmatics constantly appeals for a *listening* to the Word as the only way to obedience to Christ. For dogmatics this becomes an explicit rule, manifest in its conscious obedience to the Bible, to the church's teachers and confessions, to the actual contemporary situation of the church. Dogmatics also appeals for a *teaching* of the Word. Herein the church moves on to the material task of unfolding the content of the Word, out of the encounter with the Word. So the coherence of dogmatics derives from its Object (God in Christ), not from a preconceived system of principles. (¶ 22, 23, 24.)

THE DOCTRINE OF GOD (2–1)

Chapter 5. *The Knowledge of God*

Man knows God only by *grace* as God chooses to speak his Word in Jesus Christ by the Holy Spirit, i.e., by faith. Faith therefore is *knowledge, certain* because of God's unique objectivity, *indirect* because clothed in a form suited to the creature. God thus reveals himself as the one we may love and must fear, as certain in his worthiness and mysterious in his otherness. This unity of opposites is the revelation of the Triune nature of eternal God. His presence in

Jesus is sacramental, truly presenting God as sovereign subject to us, yet preserving his mystery and freedom from
human possession. (¶ 25.)

So the fact that man actually knows God is the result
purely of God's readiness to be known. But if revelation
really reaches man, there must be a readiness in man also.
This does not exist in man as such, in fact, man is closed
against God by his sin. This he cannot stand, and so he
seeks his own ways to God. The result is natural theology.
True readiness, then, can be found only in a transcendent
man beyond man as such, viz., Jesus Christ who as Son of
God is ready for God by the Spirit of God, and in whose
humanity our "flesh" is also ready for God. He has stood
"in our place," borne our sin and punishment, accepted
God's grace, and rendered our obedience. So man's readiness
is enclosed in God's readiness, and we are included by being
included in Jesus Christ in faith by the Holy Spirit. The
church is the historical form of this work of the Spirit. So
only out of Jesus Christ can be derived a truly Christian
anthropology and ecclesiology. We can understand and sym-
pathize with the vitality of natural theology, but we must
not allow it within the church. (¶ 26.)

To summarize then: "God is known through God, and
through God alone" (2–1, 179). So faith is first of all a
confession of the hiddenness of God, as judgment on our
need and impotence, and as a sign of the perfection of the
knowledge of God because he is knowable only in that he
chooses to be, and because he has chosen to be in Jesus
Christ. Therefore, faith must also *speak* of the revealed
God, in awe, in humility, admittedly only in analogy (partial correspondence). And faith must even depend upon
grace from Christ for the veracity of our speaking. We have
no human security in our speaking. We live by Christ's
death and resurrection because our knowledge of God is
not ours but Christ's alone. (¶ 27.)

Chapter 6. The Reality of God

God reveals his being in act. As this living God, he unites within himself both spirit and nature, but the dominance of spirit defines his being as self-moved person. This unity is his essential Trinitarian being in which he seeks and creates community, first in himself and then by reflection with another. God is his loving. God is free in his loving in that he is self-sufficient and does not need another, and in that he is not bound in his loving of another. God's being and act as the One who loves in freedom assumes many different kinds of perfection. They truly reveal who God is, yet do not place God under the control of human concepts. We must consider the perfections of the divine *loving* before those of the divine *freedom* in order to avoid an abstract definition of God as impersonal being. (¶ 28, 29.)

The divine loving manifests itself, first, in the forms of God's *grace* and *holiness*. His love is grace because it is free gift, not elicited by the wealth or blocked by the opposition of the other. As holiness, God's loving asserts its claim and breaks down resistance, bringing judgment and calling forth fear. Secondly, God's love is *mercy* in that, in Jesus Christ, he freely identifies himself with man in his sin and guilt and powerfully removes them. But his mercy is also his way of establishing his *righteousness,* fulfilling his law by the perfect penitence and obedience of Jesus Christ and sharing it with other men by faith. Thirdly, God's love shows *patience,* giving man time and freedom to arrive at his destiny, not by saving himself but by believing in Jesus Christ, his savior. But God's loving is not left to chance but is founded on his *wisdom,* which ties together the whole of his creative, providential, reconciling activity in Jesus Christ. (¶ 30.)

The *freedom* of God's loving manifests itself, first, in the forms of God's *unity* and *omnipresence*. God's oneness

[margin note: Manifestations of the Divine loving:]

[margin note: Manifestations of the Divine Freedom]

means he is unique in that he is free from all, dependent on
nothing. It means he is simple, with no division or contradiction. That he is wholly and purely the one God is
known in Jesus Christ. His oneness does not negate remote-
ness, which is necessary for love in himself and with another,
but allows a divine spatiality that is one in his omnipresence,
first with himself, and then to all creation in a variety of
ways. Secondly, God is free in his *constancy* and *omnipotence*. God's constancy means that in his whole eternal
life of loving, he does not change, is not deterred or de-
feated. Even incarnation is rooted in God's eternal willingness, and on this ground creation, reconciliation, and redemption became reality, comprehending the inconstancy
of man's sin within it. God's omnipotence, therefore, is his
definitive capacity to be and to live of and by himself in
Trinity. His power over everything is not sheer undefined
force but is the capacity of his knowledge and will as spirit,
as person. God is his knowing and willing in unbroken
unity. He knows all and wills all that has being and so rules
all. But he does so in loving, purposive differentiation of
concrete active living, and so his omnipotence is not a
tyranny or a blind force. Thirdly, God is free in his *eternity*
and *glory*. His eternity is not timelessness but a duration in
which he is pretemporal, cotemporal and posttemporal. In
his Triune being itself, God moves and lives, and therein
man's time has its potentiality in God's eternal "being for
us." All of God's perfections are summed up in his glory,
in his right, power, and act of making himself *known* as
God. By the beauty of his glory he calls forth man's desire
and rewards him with joy as man finds his goal in being
the mirror in which God reflects his love. (¶ 31.)

Chapter 7. *God's Gracious Election* (2–2)

As the one who loves in freedom, God acts to relate himself to man and the world in covenant in Jesus Christ. So

predestination is all grace and gospel, for the whole world, chosen in Jesus Christ. Even its shadow in God's opposition to man's opposition is God's love for the fallen. God's election is a judgment that creates and enforces the order of his intention for his creature, the order of communion in love. It has nothing to do with naked sovereignty or irresistible power. It is concerned, in the first place, with God's act toward the whole of mankind, only relatively with individuals. Election is that primal decision of God that comes to light in Jesus Christ alone, because in him the elect man and the electing God are united. Any attempt to separate election from Jesus Christ allows it to slip into the irrational darkness of an unknown God. So our only source of knowledge of election is the Scriptures that witness to Christ. The Bible always ties election with God's people, but behind the elect people stands the electing God. So the doctrine should be at the front of dogmatics because creation and redemption from sin are only outworkings of God's primal determination to have for himself a people in Jesus Christ, even as the Father eternally has himself a Son in the Spirit's bond of love. (¶ 32.)

Election, therefore, has its beginning, its end, and its content in Jesus Christ. He is the electing God in that he is the eternal Word through whom in the beginning all things were made (John 1:1-3). In him God turns toward his creature, and so there is no hidden decree behind the birth, death, and resurrection of Jesus Christ. So also is he *the* elect man because only as others share in his humanity by faith do they share in this man's exaltation to fellowship with God. Herein we see election is pure grace, accomplished by God's assumption of our suffering to work man's perfect obedience. Election, therefore, means only salvation and life for man, just because it means for God the bearing of the responsibility, judgment, damnation, and death of man's sin. God elects to do so because the threat to man and his actual fall were provided for in God's original decree, but only as a shadow of his will for communion in love, a provision for man's misuse of his freedom. God's election becomes concrete in the history of encounter between God and man, finding its realization in the awakening of the response of faith in the one man, Jesus Christ. (¶ 33.)

Election will find its fulfillment, however, when all men share in Jesus' faith. The elect people is the intermediate and mediating realization. In it Jesus as the Christ is visible among men. As part of the people, Israel manifests the stark judgment of God on man's refusal of God's love. As the other part, the church reflects the mercy of God in his fulfillment of his purpose for all men in Jesus Christ. The failure of Israel (man), however, does not exclude it from the goal of the chosen people. The two parts of the people form the environment of Jesus Christ and are united in him. The church as the believing community is founded on Israel as the hearing community. The church's mission is to let all men hear God's promise, and to confess its belief that this promise has been fulfilled already in the life, death, and resurrection of Jesus Christ. So Israel signifies the passing old man of sin and death whose lot God elects for himself. The church exemplifies the coming new man, realized in Jesus Christ and proclaimed as the destiny of all men, both Jew and Gentile. The Jews' stumbling does not mean their fall, just as the Christians' believing is not their earning of salvation. God's mercy precedes and will conclude all things in Jesus Christ. Salvation is by grace alone. (¶ 34.)

The individual man is the final goal of God's electing activity, but not man in his natural particularity and capacity, but as the new man who personally hears God's call, is empowered by grace to accept it, and achieves his authentic individuality within Jesus Christ and his community. Man's attempt to be an individual on his own is his essential godlessness, the impossibility that is negated in Christ. The elect is the man who recollects that our judgment has been borne and our humanity sanctified in Jesus Christ alone. The reprobate is the man who still lives in expectation of this reconciliation. So in themselves as such, both are equally ungodly, while in Christ they are equally elect. They are thus brought together because each can be designated only in relation to Jesus Christ, since Jesus Christ is *the* rejected (in his bearing of our sins) precisely because he is *the* elected (the Son of God who became man). The actually elect are distinguished from the potentially elect in that they accept the love of God in Christ and respond in joyful, thankful service. Their service is to break open the circle of election to all other men by witnessing to Jesus Christ. So one's private salvation is not the main point to one's election but is subordinate to sharing in Christ's ongoing work of reconciliation. The rejected man is he who as yet has not heard or who resists Christ's calling. But they are not annihilated because God preserves them in his love and patience. The called see their present rejection only as a shadowy unreality because Christ has already destroyed it in principle. Yet the rejected man makes clear to the called what man, even the called, is without the gospel and what God really wills for man, life eternal, the opposite to the no-future of the rejected.

Chapter 8. God's Commandment

God's election of man is the gracious gift of life but also the rigorous demand for obedience. So the doctrine of God includes the problem of ethics, the question of the human act and therefore of human existence. Christian ethics invalidates general ethics, which are grounded on the assumption that man establishes his own criterion of the good. The good is only what God commands, which is known only as he speaks his Word in Jesus. So theological ethics does not ask about man as such but about God's act of commanding man. (¶ 36.)

God has claim and power to command our obedience only in that we can believe in him as the one who has already graciously fulfilled for us in Jesus Christ what he requires. Man can accept this act as right because therein he sees that man's beatitude lies in being possessed by God. By this acceptance our action is made to reflect and correspond with God's act in Jesus Christ. So law, as a norm requiring man's decision between right and wrong, is at an end. Now the law or obligation of the gospel is God's permission by which man need not sin and may perform the only possible alternative, may live unto God in true freedom. The lack in our lives of any perfect correspondence with God's command does not defeat us because we no longer depend upon heroic deeds to make us good but upon the working of the Spirit of Christ. (¶ 37.)

God's command is not only a claim upon but also a decision about man. It marks the life of every man whether he likes it or knows it. It places man in *responsibility* as the essence of the human situation: man's actions are "a perpetual answer to the Word of God spoken to us as command" (2-2, 641). This word comes to us not in general laws but as specific commands about particular details in the individual's life. In the Bible we see God's command coming to particular people in specific historical conditions. The general laws are summaries of these concrete commands. We are to listen to both, not as general wisdom for our own application but as the medium of the command of the living God to us, today, in our specific situation. When heard in Jesus Christ, we know that all of God's commands are out of his love, directed toward our good. The decision that informs the command is God's will to bring harmony:

reconciliation of man with God, man with man, and each man with himself. (¶ 38.)

God's determination to reconcile this sinner inevitably brings with it judgment on his sin. But in Jesus Christ we see that God loved and accepted us prior to judgment, so we do not fear it. Judgment is necessary to make clear to us that we are transgressors of God's command. Yet its real purpose is to make us his sons by our sharing in the righteousness and new life achieved by his Son in his cross and resurrection. We do not possess it in ourselves but only in the relationship of faith in Jesus Christ who is our sanctification. (¶ 39.)

The Doctrine of Creation

Chapter 9. The Work of Creation (3-1)

The doctrine of creation is an article of faith. It is not self-evident that this world had its origin from God, nor conversely that this world has any reality outside God. We "know" this only in Jesus Christ in whom we see by faith the union of God with the "flesh" of man and the world, as his own creation and possession. Creation is grace by the Word of God. (¶ 40.)

More specifically, creation provides a locale for the history of the covenant of grace. This means that creation itself is historical, in the sense of being a temporal event. But creation time is God's time in his primal turning in eternity toward the creature. We can comprehend this time and event of creation when viewed in the light of the time of grace in Jesus Christ. But we cannot describe it in the terms of creaturely, fallen history. So we must resort to the poetry of saga (not myth). (¶ 41:1.)

The first description (Gen., ch. 1) suggests that creation is "the external basis of the covenant," of the Sabbath rest of God and man. His creation is to be one of light, the light

of his presence, so the "darkness" stands for the unreality
and impossibility of any other alternative, ruled out by God
himself. The creation of man in "our image" means that
man lives in a way that is analogous to the eternal Trinitarian life of God. As the Father is an "I" to the "Thou" of
the Son, so is God related to man, and so is man related to
man (the latter being established and enforced by the
creation of humans as male and female). This is an "analogy
of relationship" not of "being." It means that man has his
being as man only in that relationship where he is addressed by God as a "thou." In this sense man can never
"lose" the "image." And it finds its fulfillment in a reciprocal community of love between God and man in Jesus
Christ, who alone is the actual "image and glory of God"
(I Cor. 11:7). (¶ 41:2.)

The second description of creation (Gen., ch. 2) suggests
that the covenant is "the internal basis of creation"; creation
already prefigures the covenant. What man *is*, in his creatureliness, his work, his very earthiness, his "garden," is
God's will and not a disgrace. There the tree of life is God's
assurance of a future in spite of all finiteness and natural
mortality. The tree of the knowledge of good and evil, on
the other hand, is a sign of the "possibility of an unheard-
of exaltation of the creature," not to judge and to choose for
himself between good and evil (which is death) but to
accept and to obey freely God's judgment of the good and
thereby to share in his life. The impossibility of man's living
by and unto himself is further established by the creation
of woman as the necessary copartner of man. But this created
relation was not an "original state" of fulfillment but only
a promise of what would be realized in Jesus Christ.
(¶ 41:3.)

Creation, therefore, is God's great affirmation, the positive
expression of his sovereign will. And his will is to have
fellowship with his creature. So the "world" is not the

creation unless seen as God's "good work" in service of his purpose of fellowship. And we know this only by revelation, by faith. And only so do men know that they and their world are not an illusion but really exist, and not in mere existence but in the fullness of God's own eternal Trinitarian being. Creaturely existence is therefore "justified," not in a fulfillment of man's natural optimism, nor by an alternative to his pessimism, but only by God's act in which he assumes man's darkness, and himself becomes man's light, in Jesus Christ. Thus God fulfills man's Something and banishes the threat of his Nothing. Thus he gives man a place in the universe, the place of God's love, in which man may live in joy and freedom beyond the contradictions of human existence. (¶ 42.)

Chapter 10. The Creature (3–1)

The Christian doctrine of creation really treats of only one creature, man, because revelation is concerned wholly with the relation between God and man. This "man" is sinful man as encountered by the grace of God, but his essential humanity is not changed by the perversion of sin. So by looking at the humanity of Jesus, wholly under the grace of God, we can know what is the essential humanity of all men as created by God. This does not deny the qualitative difference between Jesus and us, but it does properly ground our anthropology on Christology. (¶ 43.)

The man we see in Jesus possesses his identity precisely in his existence for God, in his service for the honor and the coming Kingdom of God. This analysis gives us a preliminary concept of humanity which serves as a criterion to judge other concepts: the naturalistic emphasis on mind, culture, and history; the idealistic emphasis on personality and ethics; the existentialist emphasis on "self-transcendence." All of these speak only of the phenomena of the human, not of real humanity. They end in relativity, anthroparentism, and obscurity. Real man is man together with God through togetherness with the man Jesus. With Jesus, man knows he is elected to life instead of to the doom of nothingness. With Jesus man knows what it means to live by being addressed by the Word of God. With Jesus, man is able to have a true history, moving from creatureliness to its fulfillment in God's Kingdom. So, living under grace man realizes his true responsibility, spontaneity, freedom. From this perspective the above "phenomena of the human" are seen as symptoms of true humanity and form a valid science of man, from which theology can derive stimulus and knowledge, though not knowledge of real man. (¶ 44.)

In Jesus we see the one who not only exists for God but also the one who exists for his fellowman. This "cohumanity" is his essential manhood because it reflects and manifests in creaturely relations what is the eternal divine relation between the Father and the Son. This means that humanity as such consists of the capacity to be in covenant with God, and also, as a direct reflection, the actuality of existing in I-thou encounter with other men. And the sexual relation is the basic form of the latter, given determination. This mystery of being man only vis-à-vis other men is inherent in all men, prior to Christian revelation and love. In fact, the non-Christian may be even more knowing about this basic form of human nature than the Christian. But man's cohumanity as his given nature is not a self-sufficient end but is a "parable" of his destiny as God's partner. Man is not the latter by nature, but attains it only by grace. Yet there is a correspondence, so that our created nature is an "image" of what we are to be by grace, because in both cases man is not alone but in fellowship, even as Father and Son are, eternally. (¶ 45.)

In Jesus we furthermore see that our created nature is a whole man, the union of soul and body related like Jesus' Sonship and humanity, i.e., as Lord and servant. As body, man is integrally a material organism, but as soul he is a subject, and as both he is to be God's covenant partner. As the Holy Spirit achieves the unity of Father and Son, and the unity of divinity and humanity in Jesus, so his presence makes man able to be that subject who is God's partner. The solidarity of man's soul and body is his by nature. In it man has the capacity of turning back to and discovering himself, and so as soul to be self-conscious. So he has and is true subjectivity, but the "I" is of both body and soul. Within this unity the body-soul distinction still has point. In the single event of apprehending God, man must both perceive (body) and conceive (soul). In *doing* what he apprehends, he both desires (body) and wills (soul). Obviously, in his definitive being as God's partner, there is an order of relationship that gives the primacy to the soul. As addressed by God he is a rational person. Yet he is an ordered unity of both body and soul. (¶ 46.)

The basis of man's life is that God's Spirit gives man to be the soul of his body. But this would be for naught if God did not also give man *time*. To have time is to live, even for God. But man's creaturely time must be caught up into God's own time. This has been done in the incarnation. That is why Jesus is true man: man caught up in all his creatureliness into God's eternal life. So Jesus is God's time sent to and for us, and we know this by his resurrection. Here man's limited time is broken open, and Jesus is seen to be the door to all time—past, present, and future. But God's time is not only sent but actually given to man, first in Jesus, then to his disciples, but ultimately for mankind, the creature as such. This gives man's present time urgency as lived before God. This means man may now remember and accept his past as truly his, and may forget without guilt what is to be forgotten. This means also that man may now leave his future in God's hands with confidence. (¶ 47:1, 2.)

Admittedly, man's creaturely time is limited and fixed.
But this is for man's own good, so he knows he is not God
and so he will receive gladly the gift of fulfilled time by
the grace and power of God in Christ. The Christian can
accept the fact that his life had a beginning because he does
not look back to an empty void but to God, because he
now locates the beginning of his true time and life at the
point of his union with Christ by faith (so away with infant
baptism!). Likewise, the Christian can accept the fact that
his life has an end because he knows Christ has died for
sin in our stead, and his end no longer mean's God's judgment of death. His end is only a sleeping, no longer the
dread sign of nothingness, but the sign of our creaturely
finiteness, placed there by our loving Creator. Only in him
is there life and so only in him is there hope. (¶ 47:3, 4, 5.)

Chapter 11. The Creator and His Creature (3-3)

Providence is God's faithfulness and coexistence with his
creation *in action,* ruling it, preserving it, and bringing to
pass its goal in Jesus Christ. Providence is not a world view
or a philosophy of history but a simple faith-knowledge that
we have to do with God our Father in the spontaneous
events of life. We know this only through hearing his Word
in Jesus Christ. This faith requires the theological statement
that world history is coordinated by God with covenant
history, because both are under his providence for the
realization of his goal. (¶ 48.)

The divine preservation is a qualitative affirmation of
man's existence, working indirectly through creaturely interrelatedness beyond our ken. Man requires preservation because of his subjection or meaninglessness but ultimately
because of his destiny in Jesus Christ. God also accompanies
man not as a tyrant but in love, and so affirms and sustains
man as a free agent. In doing so, God works before, with,
and after the creature's work. God's predetermination under-

lies and overrules the "laws of nature," relativizing but not destroying the creature. God's codetermination is by his speaking his Word with the power of his Spirit. Thus he establishes creaturely freedom and worth. Man's obedience to God's presence produces a history of acts, and God follows them out in their impact, determining their content, meaning, and power. (¶ 49:1, 2.)

God's government of both natural and human history is not to be identified with either miracle or causal determination but transcends both by his power and freedom as Creator. This government comes to be known through God's acting and speaking as "I am" in the midst of the covenant people (Old and New). As such he is known as the ruler of all creaturely history, directing all toward their goal. So covenant history gains its meaning precisely in its interrelationships with world events, and world events have intrinsic meaning in their divine coordination with those events which center in Jesus Christ. This coordination is visible only to faith. Faith is not blind submission but a living as awakened by God's word in Christ, and so a participation in God's providence and rule. Faith also includes obedience, the *doing* of the word under the leading and ordering of the Holy Spirit. And this doing is in the whole world of which Christ is also Lord, so it is social, scientific, and aesthetic. Prayer is the Christian's ultimate form of obedience, consummated in the petition that is intercession for the world, thus sharing in God's rule of the world in Jesus Christ. (¶ 49:3, 4.)

In giving creation a kind of being alongside of himself, God thereby negated its opposite as evil. The occurrence of this accursed factor, while under God's rule, cannot be attributed to either God or the creature. So it is not to be confused with the natural suffering, decay, and death of finite creation. This evil is known in its true uniqueness only in Jesus Christ, because the incarnation is aimed not simply at affirming God's good creation but especially at the unmasking and vanquishing of God's real enemy. Only at the cross is revealed the real character of sin as subservience to the evil emptiness that God negated in creation. Only in the resurrection is revealed the adequacy of God's power alone for the deliverance of man. (So Leibniz, Schleiermacher, Heidegger, and Sartre are incomplete.) This evil factor does not have being like God and his creatures, but it does have a kind of reality under God in that it is that which God does not will and choose. The creature in his sin gives it occasion to become an operating factor in creation. But it can have no permanence, and God assumes the responsibility of destroying it through incarnation. (¶ 50.)

The Word of God in Christ, as witnessed to in the Scriptures, leads us also to a consideration of the nature of the Kingdom of Heaven and the angels in the total relation of God and his creatures. Here we are at the limits of theology because here we move outside the orbit of God, man, and the Word. But if we limit ourselves strictly to the Biblical materials, we will avoid the usual absurdities attached to this subject. God's revelatory activity has made clear that his great movement out of himself in his act of creation is unitary: there is God, there is creation, there is no other between or beside them. Yet within creation there remains the distinction between heaven and earth. "Heaven" designates God's way of being present himself in creation, yet so there remains true distance between him and his creature, thus providing for real dialogue and drama. When God speaks directly to his creatures, it is as his Word, as himself, as Jesus Christ. But at times it serves his purposes to be present indirectly in the witness of a creature. So between his self-witness as Jesus Christ and the witness to him by men there is a third class of creaturely witnesses to God's presence. We can indicate their uniqueness only by the unique Biblical word: angels. They do not replace God, so are not objects of attention or veneration. But they are signs of the real mystery of the divine presence. Demons are not angels because they are not creatures. But demons are the dynamic of the negated evil and so share in its improper reality and sure defeat. (¶ 51.)

Chapter 12. The Command of God the Creator (3–4)

Christian ethics must produce an ordered formulation of the character of and standard for ethical behavior. The ethical event occurs within certain continuities: the one commanding God, human action, and the history of their encounter. Yet it cannot be reduced to rules, "orders of creation," or "mandates" because of its interpersonal nature. In Jesus Christ alone we see the structure of true man as God's creature in perfect obedience and so in him we can see, as in a mirror, what we are meant to be. (¶ 52.)

Man is meant to be free for God. But this freedom, like the Sabbath, is a living in complete, joyous, communal capitulation to and trust in God instead of in men. The coming of such a "day" is the sign of the *eschaton,* the arrival of God's Kingdom. This freedom also takes the form of confession, not just of man's sin but first of all of his positive faith in God, a confession in both word and act. Thus man is also enabled to pray, not as a cry of despair out of darkness, but as the confident asking of a child who knows his Father and who has been granted the freedom to ask. (¶ 53.)

The nature of man as God's partner also determines man's life as set in the I-thou relation with other men, particularly in the sexual relation. So God's command is particularly concerned with sex and transforms it from a merely physical reality to a matter of the whole man in his community of love and work. God's command always treats men as male or female, in their absolute difference and interdependence, so that only in their encounter can man be truly human, whether marriage is involved or not. Yet marriage is the goal and norm of sexual relations. Under the gospel, marriage is an ethical problem, becoming the task of developing a life-companionship, a relation of love reflecting God's love for man. So it is complete, exclusive, and lasting. Before such a command and demand of God, every Christian knows he is an adulterer. But God's judgment is grace. The Christian cannot, will not, rest in his sin, but is enabled by God's forgiveness to "keep the commandment" by joining God in his battle against sin. (¶ 54:1.)

Just as (because) man is man in sexual differentiation, so man is man in being the child of parents. Here, too, is a reflection of the relation between God and man. God is man's true father on whom we depend and from whom we must learn. And our direct knowledge of God in Jesus Christ does not destroy but exactly establishes and defines parental authority. For Christians, having a child, being a parent, is no longer an unconditional commandment but a decision subject to God's Word. Beyond the family relations, man finds also that he is a member, first, of his people or nation, and, secondly, of mankind as a whole. In these spheres man is also met by God's command, so Christian obedience (ethics) extends to all social action and problems. But here there are no distinct forms of God's commands because these spheres are not permanent orders of creation and so of humanity but are fluid and impermanent orderings of God's providence. (¶ 54:2, 3.)

Man's freedom before God and in community with fellowman is based on another freedom: the freedom of each man to reverence his own life (and that of every other man) as a gift, as a loan from God. God's command also relates man to himself. So man must maintain a certain awe and humility before the fact of his own being as an individual person—of course within the limits of God's command, because life is not a natural premoral fact. "Thou shalt not kill," in its positive meaning to love life, is the Biblical formulation of reverence for life and covers such items as: the will to live, the use of nonhuman life, concern for health, the will to joy, concrete self-affirmation, and the will to power. The more obvious negative meaning of "Thou shalt not kill" applies unconditionally, and so rules out every instance of euthanasia and most every case of all other forms of killing, because life is reverenced as a gift and loan of God. Nevertheless, man's life is conditional and finite, and so allowance for the necessity of killing must be made in certain extreme cases of the following: suicide, abortion, self-defense, capital punishment, and war. (¶ 55:1, 2.)

For *what* has God given man the sacred loan of life? To act and to work in correspondence to God's activity. This calling distinguishes men from all other animals. The first actualization of this freedom and honor occurs in the fulfillment of the mission of the church. This mission is to proclaim what the church alone knows, that God has already come in Jesus Christ and transformed the situation of all mankind. This the church does as it simply lives as the church, as it wins new members, and as each member brings prophetic witness to the world where he works and lives. There is no dualism in Christian activity. It is just this work in which man becomes whole, body and soul together affirming human creaturely existence and meeting its needs under the impulse of God's Spirit and the obedience of the human soul. As such, man's work must be purposeful, have dignity, be conducted with humanity, allow reflectivity, have limits to allow rest. The ultimate limit must be rest to listen to God, to his Word, because only then can man truly stand off and see himself and so know and value himself as God's child. (¶ 55:3.)

With such self-knowledge man realizes that the finite delimitations of his life are God's way of affirming man's genuine reality as subject, as "I." So he uses his time well, and does not fear the boundary of death. Within the particular creaturely conditions of his life, a man responds to God's calling and so finds his individual vocation. The criteria for determining a man's proper response (vocation) are as follows: the particular moment in his life process, the particular historical situation, his inner personal ability and fitness, a choice of definite field of activity. The intersection of these forces may be regarded as "the creaturely carrier and medium of the voice of God himself" (3–4, 636), as a sphere where man hears God's Word and command. Only in such a relation with God is there true freedom for man, and so also is there the resolution of the ethical problem, the determination of the "goodness" of human behavior. Herein the honor imparted to man by God in his creation is freed from sin and matched with the wholly new yet corresponding and proper honor of being called to be God's child and covenant-partner. This honor is reflected in those actions of men which are deeds of service, performed with humility and humor, and in which man leaves their goodness to God's judgment and protection. (¶ 56.)

THE DOCTRINE OF RECONCILIATION

Chapter 13. The Subject and the Problems of the Doctrine of Reconciliation (4–1)

The creature receives its true and proper glory, not as a development of its created nature, but by the priorly planned and subsequently performed act of reconciliation. This act is "God with us" in Jesus Christ. God's covenant with Israel is only a means to the fulfillment of his covenant purpose with all mankind in Jesus Christ. In him we see that this good intention of God is not something merely relative to man's sin but is grounded on God's turning toward man in the Son's identification with Jesus in eternity. This means that God is not indifferent to man, so man cannot be indifferent to God and his act of reconciliation. Because of man's sin, reconciliation in Jesus Christ takes the form of an "exchange," God becoming what we are so that we may become his righteousness. This unilateral crossing of the abyss of separation by God results in an absolutely new human being, the reconciled man Jesus Christ. This reconciliation is reflected in the existence of Christians in three ways: in faith, as the acceptance of God's judgment on us; in love, as the acceptance of God's direction of our life; in hope, as the firm expectation of eternal life as God's covenant-partner. These three comprise our justification, sanctification, and calling. But all this does not take place in us but in Jesus Christ. As the God-man he *is* the event of reconciliation. So the doctrine of reconciliation consists of a description of Jesus: (1) as God who has humbled himself to man's estate, (2) as man who has been exalted to God's estate, and (3) as the effective witness of this reality that he is. Only in this context can we rightly speak of man's sin, man's salvation, and the church. (¶ 57, 58.)

Chapter 14. Jesus Christ, the Lord as Servant

The central theme of the New Testament and of all theology is that Jesus is God, humbled and suffering as sinful man without ceasing to be God. This is understood not as a contradiction but as an affirmation of God's true nature as free sovereign love. The only way of understanding the mystery of incarnation lies in the revelation that there is a form of self-humbling *within* the eternal life of God himself, the "Son" to the "Father" in the unity of "Holy Spirit" (love). Thus incarnation is not a contradiction but an actualization of God's unchanging nature as love in freedom. This condescension of God is love because its goal is man's salvation, but because of sin it is first an act of judgment in which the Judge allows himself to be judged in our place. This does not mean we are freed by a mere legal transaction but that by God's becoming one with us in our sin, he accepts responsibility for it, transforms our condition from within it, performs as a man in our place what we are supposed to do but cannot. So he suffers the punishment and death of our sin, not as penal satisfaction but as the way to deal with sin and death *in man* and to conquer it. Thus *as man* God conquers what separates and subverts us, and so opens the way to reconciliation. The victory in Jesus is for all men, whether they know it or not, because he is our representative. The actual transition, however, is accomplished through the resurrection of man in Christ. Although an event in history that cannot be idealized or allegorized, yet the resurrection is an autonomous new act of God without the factor of human cooperation. In this event, he who was "for us" and "in our place" in his death is now the living and active Christ who is with all men on his own initiative. Yet his presence now is indirect, by faith and the Holy Spirit. So the church looks back to Christ's cross and forward to his coming again but now lives by him and under him as the Lord of time. (¶ 59.)

Only in the face of this absolute judgment and mercy of God in Jesus Christ can we really speak of a knowledge of sin. Sin perverts its own self-understanding. Before Jesus alone can one confess, "I am condemned and forgiven, by pure mercy." Before the very person of God and the original model of true man all other men fall, without even a distinction between better and worse. There comes to view the utter irrationality of sin as the impossibility negated by God. So it cannot be redeemed but only forgiven and removed by God. Before God in Jesus Christ, sin is revealed first of all as the pride of unbelief. In contrast to the loving self-humiliation of the Word become flesh, man wants to exalt himself to be a god. In contrast to the Lord become servant, man struggles for power to become a lord. In contrast to the Righteous One who accepted our judgment and punishment, man refuses to be judged but seeks to be his own judge. In contrast to Jesus who trusted God for help in everything, even on the cross, man rebels against every limitation of his freedom as harmful and seeks to save himself. Before Christ, we see how mistaken we are and how nothing but chaos, alienation, corruption, and enslavement result. This does not mean that human nature has been destroyed, but before Christ's gracious forgiveness we know we live in a state of debt we cannot pay. Before Christ's death, we know our life is totally subverted to evil. As Jesus is the new Adam, his judgment and his mercy equally apply to all mankind. (¶ 60.)

However, we must ask specifically how and on what grounds the transition of man from judgment to mercy occurs, how he is justified and reconciled. First, it assumes the right of the Creator to bring to judgment his rebellious creature in a way that fulfills his loving purpose with him. Secondly, this judgment must actually break into man's own life, shattering man into a simultaneous awareness of being both the doer of wrong and the child of God. Thirdly, this creative acceptance of God's judgment by man is impossible for man as such but has been performed for man by God, as the man Jesus. By faith in him, we share in his faith and righteousness. This justification comes to us in the form of pardon, of God's ignoring and shutting out the past and his setting us free to a new future. This takes the form of a history, a movement out of the past into the future. It gives the present real meaning by establishing man as the child of God in real kinship, and by enabling man to hope beyond the contradictions of the present. Yet man has no sure possession of this new life. He sees it in Jesus Christ and humbly believes it is for him. So his own faith is empty of content but clings to Christ. But faith then becomes the way of the entering of the fullness of Christ into the life of the believer. (¶ 61.)

The result of this "justification by faith" is the community of the faithful, created by the Holy Spirit, "the power in which Jesus Christ declares himself" (4–1, 648). So the church is visible only to faith, yet it also always exists in a purely empirical form because it is, by definition, "Jesus Christ's own earthly-historical form" by which his reconciliation is proclaimed to the world. This church is *one*, only because the churches are ruled by one Lord. It is *holy*, only insofar as its members share in God's holiness by obedience to Christ. It is *catholic*, because Christ's rule overcomes all differences that seem to separate. The concrete criterion for these three spiritual marks is the church's *apostolicity*: its being under the normative determination of the apostles' witness as recorded in the New Testament. This church has been given time, between the resurrection and Parousia of Christ, to proclaim the gospel because God's victory is not a unilateral overpowering of humanity but desires man's response of thanks and praise. (¶ 62.) This response, by the individual and the community, is faith, that free *acknowledgment* of Christ as Lord that is enabled by Christ's enclosing a man into his own reality. This acknowledgment involves a *recognition* that makes faith essentially a cognitive event, a knowing with my whole being of the truth of what God says and does in Jesus Christ. Finally, this acknowledgment before God demands a *confession* before men of the fact that Christ died and rose for all men. (¶ 63.)

Chapter 15. Jesus Christ, the Servant as Lord (4–2)

Reconciliation is not complete as the movement of God in humiliation to become man but includes the exaltation of man to fellowship with God. It is an "exchange." The two events occurred in the unity of Jesus Christ. So in him our human nature is transformed into the new man. Although this is not repeated in us, mankind is started thereby on its return to its home with God. This exaltation is no accident or whim, nor is it a natural human development. It has its power as absolute norm of all truth because it is God's eternal purpose. So when it is realized historically, it is the mystery, the only real sacrament of the Christian faith. Herein, God in his mode as Son willed to become a creature. He assumes in union with himself not *a* man but our form of humanity. So the human thou of this man *is* the Thou of the eternal God. This one subject, who is Son of God, therefore shares completely in both the divine and the human. In this union humanity is fulfilled in its true intention, even though we will never know the same union with God. In this unique union, our humanity is not destroyed or altered but raised to its true freedom and destiny of perfect obedience to God. And this is not a static but a dynamic historical event, moving out of the past, to the present and into the future. And this movement encompasses the revelation of this exaltation of humanity. In this self-revelation of Jesus Christ as Son of God *and* Son of Man his resurrection and the work of his Holy Spirit are inseparable. (¶ 64:1, 2.)

In considering Christ as exalted man, the Second Adam, the doctrine of reconciliation is driven back on its factual historical basis in the New Testament witness to Jesus of Nazareth. As a man among men, he was a tangible, unforgettable, irrevocable, disturbing, earthly presence. Yet his life was a parable of God's: he was despised, he sided with the lowly, he threatened every vested interest, he was compassionate. So his whole being, his life and history, was one mighty *act*. It can be distinguished into person and work, into words and deeds, but it was their reciprocal relation that made Jesus as such a single *act* which broke through all barriers of communication and evoked astonishment and opposition. Here was the "miraculous," not as the suspension of natural law, but as the presence of the unconditional power of God to deliver man from the abyss of sin and to give new life. This act of Jesus for man's salvation finds its center and completion in his cross because it was

his perfect human obedience to the will of his Father that
led him there. (¶ 64:3.)

His victory as reconciliation, however, is to be lived out
in us. This is possible because there is an ontological connection between our humanity and that exalted in Christ.
But we must see this victory, there outside ourselves. This
turning outward to Christ is our liberation. Yet, Christ's
victory and our participation in it is hidden, even contra-
dicted, by its very form: the cross. So our turning and seeing, although being *our* decision and including a disclosure
of our true selves to ourselves, actually is worked from the
other side by the power of Him who seizes us and frees us
by his Word in the event. This is the power of Christ's resurrection, as the continuing reality that miraculously makes
us to be, and to believe that we are, new men in Christ Jesus.
This power may also be described as the presence and work
of the Holy Spirit. So the mystery of the event of mediation
and communication between Jesus and other men is rooted
in the mystery of the eternal communion of the Father and
Son in the Holy Spirit. The work of the Holy Spirit, however, does not mean pure magic worked in immediate consciousness but takes the form of concrete guidance from the
person of Jesus Christ. (¶ 64:4.)

It is under the impact of Jesus Christ by the Holy Spirit
that man comes to know fully his true condition as sinner.
In the betrayal of Jesus he sees his own sin and shame in
the betrayal of God. He knows that the new man of faith
cannot build at all on the old man of sin. In the light of
Jesus' true exalted manhood man sees his sin in its form of
sloth, the refusal of God's gift of freedom out of evil, in-
dolent self-contentment. In relation to God it is an irrational, self-destructive folly, because we refuse the only
source of light and truth for our life. In refusing the freedom to live with fellowman, sloth is the stifling of our true
humanity, which was created in the form of coexistence. In

relation to one's self, it is the refusal to live at the level of
Spirit, sacrificing its freedom for the desires of the body and
soul. In relation to the limitation of our creaturely time, we
refuse the freedom of the promise of resurrection, so our
sloth here takes the form of destructive anxiety about the
securities of creaturely existence. There can be only one result of this form of sin: misery. Misery means to be enslaved to evil, yet to remain a man with a drive for freedom.
(¶ 65.)

The Christian is the man justified by faith, who still remains the sinner, and so needs the continuing work of God's
grace in the battle with the old man (sanctification). So
saints are sinners who live in and by Jesus Christ. By his
guidance they are kept aware of their condition in sin, but
even more they are set free from sin to the freedom of
obedience by the power of his Spirit. This obedience means
that sanctification is discipleship: the acceptance of Christ's
summons to service, being bound to him and not to an idea
or program, being led to ever-new kinds of goodness, freed
from old orders and absolutes. Our ability to follow Jesus,
however, is dependent on conversion, which is not just an
awareness of and a looking at Jesus. It is a movement, in
the opposite direction as before, now toward God instead
of away from him. So the old man and the new man are
related as a history, the *terminus a quo* and the *terminus ad
quem*. As we follow after the work of God in incarnation
and in calling us to discipleship, we too are bound to do
good works, works that he praises and that praise him.
Finally our obedience must expect sometime to take the
form of ultimate sanctification: the cross. Not as a repetition
of Christ's experience, absolute rejection in innocence, but
as a participation in his manifestation of love for all men.
(¶ 66.)

God's work of sanctification of men in Christ is directed
to the individual only as he is part of the church and its

mission. So sanctification is aimed at the establishment of
the church, by uniting men in the love of God through the
gathering of the community in corporate worship. As this
community is created by its fellowship in confession, joy,
prayer, service, proclamation, it experiences growth both
extensively and intensively, the latter being normative, the
former being relative. But the church is also constantly
threatened because the world is impelled to oppose this
"stranger" in its midst, and because the church constantly
tends to secularization or sacralization within itself. Listening to Jesus Christ is the only safeguard. This listening to
its one Head also results in order and law in the church. It
is not understood by the world because of its unique and
hidden source. Likewise, it cannot be codified because
Christ's specific commands vary according to time and place.
Yet, it can be said that all church law (1) is shaped under
the church's calling to service, (2) is derived from worship
because here the living Christ is present, (3) is living law
because Christ is alive and men's formulations are fallible,
and (4) has the task of setting an example for the law and
order Christ desires in the world at large. (¶ 67.)

The sanctification of the individual takes the form of a
reflection of God's self-giving love (*agapē*). This is the
transcendent fulfillment of man's created nature, and it engages in the battle to extirpate that self-assertive love (*erōs*)
that is a corruption of man's nature. Man is able so to love
only on the grounds of God's summons to live in a relation
with him whereby God's being as love becomes determinative of man's being. Therein we know God's love to be free
and unmotivated, purifying and victorious, creative of new
life. But man is thereby enabled to commit his own new,
free, joyous act of self-giving. First, toward God in praise
and in obedience and so in participation in his life. Then,
toward all fellowmen as brothers in Christ, either arrived
or on their way. Love for neighbor is the constant reminder

that God loves and is to be loved, that none of God's children are to be alone. Yet, man's love of fellowman cannot impart the real event of God's love, but can only witness, tell, about it. But this witness is necessary in the totality of God's work of reconciliation. The powers given to Christians for this witness are perverted unless used in the service of love. Love alone is victorious and eternal. (¶ 68.)

Chapter 16. Jesus Christ, the True Witness (4–3)

The humiliation of God and the exaltation of man in the single event of Jesus' life accomplishes but does not complete reconciliation. What has been accomplished between God and man in Jesus Christ must be communicated to all men. This is the revelatory prophetic work of Jesus Christ and his church, by the Holy Spirit. (¶ 69:1.)

Unlike the Old Testament prophets, Jesus' own life is the light for men, his work is God's Word to men. The truth is in the doing, so the proof that Jesus is the Light of the World lies simply in our being embraced by, and in our obedience to, his life. He is God for us because he is God with and to us. He asserts himself as such by relativizing all other truth including Christian doctrine. Even the Scriptures point beyond themselves to him. Jesus is the only word of God because he is the eternal Word of God. So he is free to unite himself with the Bible, the church's proclamation, and with human words beyond the church's walls. The risen Christ is now Lord of the *world* as reconciled by his cross. So the sphere of his Word is wider than the church and creates "parables of the Kingdom" beyond the church. So the church must listen for his Word from both the purely profane and the relatively Christian worlds around the church, because the function of this Word in the world is only to guide the church in its work as it listens to the Scripture. The created world, after all, is the theater in which the drama of reconciliation takes place. It has its own

God-given stability, which in turn speaks its own "light."
The light of Christ and this Light of the World are never
the same, but they are coordinated under the one God as
he works his one purpose for his creation. (¶ 69:2.)

The coordination, however, takes the form of a dramatic
historical struggle in which Jesus' accomplished victory
battles to become subjectively true in men. This battle is a
dynamic one that moves to involve all mankind. Christ
himself is not complete until he is victor in this battle for
men's minds. Only so is the subjective-objective antithesis
bridged, the epistemological problem resolved. This battle
has its beginning in Jesus' own concrete existence as the inexplicable confrontation of men with the mystery of the
meaning of human life. It continues as Christ establishes
among men here and now the reality of joyous fellowship
with God and arouses the resistance of that dark negative
possibility of life apart from God, that demonic impossibility
that has enslaved man. The goal of Christ's battle in the
world is not yet, and there can be no certainty of that goal
except that we see that it has already been attained by him.
And we know this only when his Word breaks through the
barriers of the creature's corruption and resistance. (¶ 69:3.)

This breakthrough is achieved only by the resurrected
Christ who gives us certainty by his own inconceivable, free,
repeated self-witness. The resurrection was the first form of
Christ's eschatological Parousia (to be followed by the Holy
Spirit and the Final Coming). By it he was set free from finite
limitations in order to transform the human situation totally,
universally, finally. Here in his soul-body unity mortal humanity was known to share in God's eternal life. This event
did not immediately become true for all mankind because
God's good will allows a "time between" in which men may
respond freely and joyously, not by force and necessity. But
the knowledge of Christ's resurrection by itself does not
materially differentiate Christians from non-Christians. This

difference occurs only as that event is made the living, operating hope of our lives by the presence of Christ in his second form of Parousia as Holy Spirit. This intermediate form of his presence is just as real and full as the other two, and has its special glory in showing that God really does care about man. So the Christian can live with joy in the midst of agony. (¶ 69:4.)

The self-revelation of Christ as the Truth also reveals that man's sin has the character of the lie: man's attempt to assert an alternative to God's Word to him. Christ is the true witness in this respect because in his inner pure form he is the unity of God and man, yet he also assumes the passion form of our existence. By this combination Christ is able to speak the truth of God's will for man in a way that actually creates men who are able to hear him. But when men hear this truth, the wrongness of their condition becomes the sin of deceit in their attempt to oppose or to flee from the truth. In this way man refuses God's pardon and invites its opposite: damnation. But this is still only a threat, not Final Judgment. Man's evil deceit is only an experiment that has been invaded and vanquished by God in Christ. So we must hope and pray for the salvation of all. (¶ 70.)

Indeed, the Christians' special calling takes place against the background of Christ's universal reconciliation and goal. So we must maintain a "borderless openness" to all men as those for whom Christ died, for whom he now rules, and for whom he will come again. Our calling is a concrete historical event, but its definitive nature lies in the setting of our whole life in the light of the truth of God's personal presence in Jesus Christ. To be a "Christian" is to be so called, to have Christ as Lord, to live by his word, to be the confirmation and revelation of God's will and action in Christ. In this relationship (Christ in me, I in Christ) there is an intimacy and immediacy but without any loss of identity and distinction. Christ is here Lord of a man's thinking, speaking, working. The relationship is initiated and held in being by Christ, not by man. The resultant transformation of called men is important but is not an end in itself. A Christian is called to a task, and his personal piety is peripheral to it. That task is to be a witness by declaring to the world what God has done for it and to it in Jesus Christ. The Christian is the one who shares in the life and therefore in the work of Jesus Christ. But this also means that the Christian must bear affliction. The world that crucified Christ will also rebel against the Christian who charges it with sin and guilt. Yet, while being hurt and frightened, the Christian cannot be mournful but must rejoice in his sufferings as the sign of a good witness and the promise of the resurrection to come. In fact, the Christian does know, in the present alteration of his own being, an anticipation of that goal. He *now* knows fellowship in place of solitude, the free land of the human being in place of the despotism of things, the confidence of prayer in place of the anxiety of human seeking amid endless possibilities. Still, this personal deliverance does not replace his call to witness as the chief thing of his life. (¶ 71.)

Therefore, the church's chief object of concern is not itself but the world in which it exists. It sees this world as ruled and corrupted by that absurd impossibility negated by God, as a result of man's act of denying God's good will in his creation. But even more the church sees by faith in Christ the victory of God over this corrupted world and must always act toward the world as so transformed, even though the world does not so regard itself. Being in this world, the church must regard itself, on the one hand, as an empirical sociological structure and in this respect weak and vulnerable, but, on the other hand, as living by the mystery of the Holy Spirit and in this respect strong in the invincible power of God as it speaks his Word. The church, like the Son of God, does not live and act for itself but is sent into the world for the world. It knows the world as that for which

Christ died, it maintains solidarity with the world as God's good creation, it accepts responsibility for the world because all men are brothers in God's election. All this is true only as the church is in the image of Jesus Christ, the man claimed by God to accomplish his mission. (¶ 72:1, 2.)

The church, therefore, lives by its commission, whose content is nothing other than Jesus Christ as Savior, whose addressee is man as sinner in need of help but also as the creature chosen in eternity to be God's friend. The church must guard against adulteration of its commission in its tendency to turn both gospel and sinners into objects of manipulation. The service committed to the church is very definite and limited: letting God's Word be heard in the world. It cannot guarantee reconciliation and revelation, but it does live by Christ's promise that where the gospel is declared and explicated, there will be some concrete anticipations of its fulfillment. The many forms of the church's service (preaching, teaching, theology, prayer, charity) fall into Jesus' own twofold classification: speaking and doing. (¶ 72:3, 4.)

Finally, the prophetic work of Jesus Christ is the work of the individual Christian. He is able to witness to the victory and presence of Christ here and now because his is a life of hope. He goes to meet his end, not as extinction, but as the full revelation of life in Jesus Christ. His present life radiates that hope and joy. And this is possible and actual for him because he does not live by himself now nor have a purely private goal as his hope. He now lives by the power of God's Spirit which has given him freedom, and so by the same Spirit he is free to hope. (¶ 73.)

Chapter 17. The Command of God the Reconciler (4–4)

Barth began to lecture this chapter in the autumn of 1959, and he is still at work on it. By the summer of 1961 he had gotten through the following paragraphs:

¶ 74 Ethics as the Task of the Doctrine of Reconciliation.

¶ 75 The Establishment of the Christian Life and Baptism.

¶ 76 The Children and Their Father ("Our Father").

¶ 77 The Zeal for the Glory of God ("Hallowed be thy name").

¶ 78 The Battle for Human Righteousness ("Thy kingdom come").

Presumably, Paragraph 79 will be on "Give us this day," 80 on "Forgive us our debts," 81 on "Lead us not into temptation," and 82 on the Lord's Supper. And there may be more.

His opening summary statement on ethics is as follows: "In the context of the doctrine of reconciliation, special ethic serves to indicate that, and in how far, the one command of the one God is at heart the command of the Lord of the covenant, in which the behavior of sinful man is settled, regulated, and circumscribed by the free grace of the faithful God, come to light and effectiveness in Jesus Christ."

In the ethics of reconciled man, Barth takes as his key word not "faith" (*Glaube*) but "fidelity" (*Treue*). His main point is that the fidelity or faithfulness that characterizes the covenant relationship is wholly the work of God. The faithfulness of God to man and of man to God are both realized only in Jesus Christ by the Holy Spirit. This leaves two questions: (1) How does God's faithfulness reach out to all men and also to the unique individual? and (2) How can the Christian life, once begun, continue on so as to keep the newness of the original encounter? The first question concerning the foundation of the Christian life is answered in Baptism. The second question concerning the renewal of the Christian life is answered in the Lord's Supper. The Christian life in itself, wholly dependent on God's original and continuing initiative and act in Jesus Christ, can only have the character of thankfulness and praise. So the Christian life is a life of prayer, in which we have been also taught by our Lord Jesus Christ.

No more detail had better be given here, but the general way in which Barth rounds out his doctrine of reconciliation is clear. And it should be obvious from what has already been said that Barth here restates his view of baptism so as clearly to exclude the legitimacy of infant baptism. Water baptism is the conscious, joyous, simple response of man's Yes to the prevenient act of God's sovereign baptism of him by the Holy Spirit in which the individual is engrafted into the death of Jesus Christ and put into a position of hope in his resurrection.

Thus ends our summary, in the last three chapters, of the background, the structure, and the contents of Barth's *Dogmatics*. But before we turn directly to the question as to how they may be helpful in preaching and teaching, we must finally turn a very critical eye on the whole, so that we remain responsible theologians ourselves and not just parrots of another man's words.

Chapter V

How to Avoid Becoming a Barthian

IT IS a sad thing that Barth's *Dogmatics* is not being widely read, either here or in Europe. But an even worse fate could overtake it, that its readers might become doctrinaire Barthians. What do I mean by this? Various things. For example, the story is going the rounds that recently a small group of Barthian-minded graduate students had an evening with Paul Tillich. One was expounding on the universal application of Christology, and finally illustrated it by saying: "You see this ash tray? To really know the truth about it, you must understand it Christologically." To this Professor Tillich replied, "I just don't know what you're talking about." And neither would Karl Barth!

By a "Barthian" I mean one who does not read the *Dogmatics* critically, who assumes that it is a Protestant *summa theologica* like Aquinas', with all questions answered and in perfect balance, and who takes certain leading ideas and turns them into principles whose automatic application is supposed to solve all theological problems. For example, Barth's attempt to make his theology Christological is misused, as it was by the student referred to above. His assertion that Christ's saving work is "ontological" is taken to mean a dogmatic universalism that relativizes both sin and the mission of the church. His rejection of all natural theology may lead to a complete indifference to all scientific, phil-

osophical, and cultural developments. His "Biblical positivism" is supposed to rule out every shred of existential
concern, turning faith into rationalistic dogmatics. The foregoing chapters should have made clear that nothing could
be farther from Barth's intention or desire than the development of such a "Barthianism." Nevertheless, it is easy to
understand how some readers of the *Dogmatics* might come
to such a position without too much difficulty. Barth is
partly, if not largely, to blame himself. Because of the very
length, the wordiness, and repetitiousness of these volumes,
the average reader, who cannot make a thorough study of
the whole, might easily cover parts here and there and come
away with the impressions of our hypothetical "Barthian."

Barth, however, is responsible at even a deeper level. He
is so concerned to drive home certain emphases against
liberal theologians that he deliberately minimizes or even
omits discussion of the legitimate scope of their interests.
Barth does cover himself against most of the ludicrous
exaggerations of his overzealous followers, and so also
against the more extreme of his critics. Nevertheless, it must
be clearly recognized that the *Dogmatics* does give the overpowering impression of having said the whole word and
the last word on every subject. So Bouillard, in his very
sympathetic account of Barth's theology, concludes: "A
Christian is able only to approve his project to reestablish
the sovereignty of the Word of God. But he seems to be
wholly above. He is placed somehow in the point of view of
God (of the God who speaks in the Bible) for the contemplation of his work below." This gives his theology "the
appearance of a *gnōsis* (mystery, wisdom) fallen from
heaven."[1] But even if we are able to establish that Barth
does not mean to be taken this way, another problem remains. Even when Barth does provide ample treatment of
the extra-Christological dimensions of creation, strong emphasis on the historical struggle involved in Christ's victory,

a real curiosity about God's ways with men outside of Christ, and a clear recognition of the existential character of faith, it is precisely then that Barth often seems to leave an irreconcilable contradiction in his own thought. And we are left wondering which Barth to take seriously or how to interpret the one in the light of the other.

In other words, you must not let the *Dogmatics* become your master. You must be able to keep it in its place as a tool, a help, an aid. I know of no other way to help you do this than by discussing briefly and nontechnically a few of the major critical issues concerning Barth's theology as contained in the *Dogmatics*. Simply by being aware of them, you should be forearmed against swallowing some of his positions whole. You are called to preach and to teach the gospel, to interpret the words of the Bible so that they become the Word of Life to men. This task is never achieved by preaching and teaching somebody else's theological formulas, per se. But somebody else's theology, especially that of such an imaginative, dedicated, dynamic, human, intellectual giant as Barth, can serve as a profound stimulus to your reading of and listening to Scripture.

Please remember that Barth would take the following critique with great good cheer. The biographical chapter should have made clear that he sees theology as a pilgrimage that is never done, either for himself or for the whole church. Barth has said on a number of occasions—and if you had spent a year with him, you would know he meant it—that theology without humor can only be bad theology. Only God himself can be taken with utmost seriousness because he is pure joy. Everything human is finite and fallible and so to be taken with a sense of humor. So Barth has often taken German theology and theologians to task for taking themselves too seriously. He traces some of his troubles with Bultmann and even with Bonhoeffer to the fact that they also were purveyors of what he calls "the melancholy theology of the north-German lowlands."[2] If you learn to hear Barth's own self-humor in the pages of the *Dogmatics,* you will be in no danger of becoming a "Barthian."

CHRISTOMONISM

All of the critiques that have been leveled against the *Dogmatics* lead in one way or another to the general charge that he has reduced all theology to Christology. This can be said of both the method and content of his theology. This Christomonism can be seen operating in his method of analogy, his principle of presupposition, and his exegesis of Scriptures. It can be accused of bringing about, in the *Dogmatics,* the relativizing of history, the absorption of humanity, the emptying of faith, and the limitation of the church's mission. We will take these charges up one by one (leaving the question of Barth's use of Scripture for a separate chapter because of the crucial bearing of this question on your use of Barth). You must realize that each of these problems about Barth's *Dogmatics* has already given rise to highly technical discussions of very complicated historical, philosophical, theological, and exegetical questions. Our purpose here is not to review these discussions or to propose fully argued solutions (that is another and quite different book on Barth). But in a very sketchy and non-technical manner I wish simply to suggest what these questions are and how they bear on your reading of the *Dogmatics* for your preaching.

On the general charge of Christomonism it should be pointed out that Barth has been aware of this possible difficulty from the beginning and has sought to guard against it. In the very passage where he first identified dogmatics and Christology, he warned that the Trinitarian revelation of God is not to be reduced to the act of reconciliation in the incarnation, although it is centered in it. Christology for

Barth includes everything from the original creative decision
and action of the Father to the ultimate eschatological redemption of mankind by the Holy Spirit (1–2, 872). Barth
does not like his theology to be called "Christocentric," because the resolution of man's dilemma does not come
through his having a "Christological principle" that he "can
use as a key to open the last lock." It comes through "Jesus
Christ himself as the sovereign Judge and Savior of his
action" (2–1, 251). From a different perspective, in his exposition of God's providential participation in our life, Barth
strongly rejects all "theories of emanation and infusion," all
"pantheism and monism" that would compromise the "autonomy and particularity" of the creature (3–3, 149, also
117). And he makes the same point under the doctrine of
reconciliation, insisting that the reality of the new world
and the new man achieved already in Jesus Christ does not
mean that the distinction between Christ and world history
has been erased. "That would now indeed be 'Christomonism'!" (4–3, 713.)

All of this means that as you read the *Dogmatics* and every-
where find every problem resolved by reference to the work
or act of God in Jesus Christ, you must remember that Barth
is not referring simply to what happened in the words and
deeds of Jesus of Nazareth as witnessed to in the Gospels.
How and on what grounds, then, does he tie everything
together in his Christology, and how can it escape the charge
of "Christomonism"?

The Principle of Presupposition

In seeking the "presupposition" of an event or a condition,
we are looking not for its *cause* but for its *reason*. We are
not trying to explain the "How?" in a mechanical or effective sense, but to understand "How is this possible?" Hans
Urs von Balthazar, the Swiss Jesuit scholar, has asserted,
"We will see the central problem of the theology of Karl

Barth concentrated in its final form in the *concept of pre-supposition,* in the sense that the proper and original positing by God *itself presupposes something in the act of positing.*"[3] Here Balthazar has special reference to the relation of God's act in Jesus Christ to the structure of human life in general, but whether we agree with his concluding clause or not, his main assertion shows deep insight into Barth's theology as a whole. For Barth, God's self-revelation to men in Jesus Christ is the given event and condition of the Christian's faith and life. There can be no human preparation for it or explanation of how it takes place, and so no guaranteed production of it. It occurs by the sheer free grace of God. But granting that it is a reality, man can do two things: proclaim it and seek to understand it. The latter is the task of theology. Within the event and reality of man's being united with God in faith, man's intelligence comes awake to explore this new realm and context of human existence. Within the limits of this faith-relation with God, man presses the question as to how this is possible, as to what are the grounds for such a common life between God and man in this world.

In one way of looking at it, Barth's whole theology is constructed out of the pressing of this question. A few examples are these. In his *Prolegomena* on the nature of revelation, he has one section in which he first talks about "Jesus Christ as the *objective reality* of revelation," and then about "Jesus Christ as the *objective possibility* of revelation" (¶ 13). A little later he has a section on "the Holy Spirit as the *subjective reality* of revelation" and "the Holy Spirit as the *subjective possibility* of revelation" (¶ 16). In his first discussion of ethics he centers on the fact of the command of God as claim, decision, and judgment, and then has subsections on "the ground of the divine claim," and "the presupposition of the divine judgment" (¶ 37:1; 39:1). One of the most problematic and far-reaching examples is his ex-

ploration of "creation as the *external ground* of the covenant," and of "the covenant as the *internal ground* of
creation" (¶ 41). And then he picks this up again to talk
about "the covenant as the presupposition of reconciliation"
(¶ 57:2). All these examples of the interdependence of all
the various aspects of God's dealing with men have, for
Barth, one single ultimate presupposition or ground of possibility, namely, the original decree or determination or election by God in eternity to turn outward from himself and
to identify himself with a creature and creation. And this
determination took the original form of the Son of God's
assuming the form of the Son of Man, Jesus Christ. And in
the next section of this chapter we will see that Barth feels
that theology is compelled to push the question one step
farther to seek wherein lies the possibility of God's act of
turning outward from himself and to find the answer in
the ultimate inexplicable mystery of the Christian knowledge of God, the eternal Trinitarian life of the one God.

Barth's critics among both the Catholics and the Protestant
existentialists find fault with this theological method on at
least two scores. First of all, they would ask, *how does Barth
move* from the existential reality of revelation in Jesus Christ
to what he calls its "possibility"? How does one draw the
lines from creation to covenant and back again? How can
we look behind the claim and judgment of God to something called their "ground"? How can the human nature of
Jesus be the only presupposition, the original image and
ground of a valid anthropology, and yet the very being of
Jesus as the Son of God for mankind in general rest upon
the presupposition of a creaturely mode of human existence
distinct from that of Jesus (3–2, 43 f., 223, 265)?[4] Barth is
charged with a theological rationalism that uses a process of
circular deductions to construct an abstract and obscure system
of concepts that have little or no contact with concrete human
existence. His critics maintain that this dilemma of Barth's

theology would be at least lessened if he would heed their second complaint. They cannot agree with Barth that theology must derive *all* of its presuppositions for the understanding of the Word of God and the reconciliation of man from within the sphere of faith itself. They charge Barth with a wanton neglect and doctrinaire denial of the reality of valid and helpful insights that derive from the vast range of human experience and reflection quite apart from the revelation of God in Jesus Christ.

Barth would answer these charges somewhat as follows. Jesus Christ is Lord of all creation by the power of his resurrection. So all men are now subject to his Word. Men in the profane world outside the church are addressed by him and do receive his Word, even though they do not recognize it as such. Christians must therefore listen for God's Word in the world, quite apart from the Word in the incarnation and the Bible (4–3, 113–135). Moreover, there is an entirely different source of light for man apart from the Word of God in Jesus Christ. The nonhistorical, nonhuman dimension of creation has its own uniqueness under God. It has a duration and stability that, in a sense, "speaks," and men are equipped with reason in order to "hear." This is not the Word or revelation of God, but man can form creation's ordered constitution and relationships into a schema that gives him some light even in the darkness of his sin (4–3, 135–143). Then man has even a third source of some truth, himself. Quite apart from any direct knowledge of Jesus Christ or the special communion of the Holy Spirit, there is the constant of created human nature. Knowledge of this common, creaturely humanity is not what distinguishes Christians from others. In fact, it is often understood and lived more profoundly by non-Christians (3–2, 276). Therefore, the insights concerning man that are achieved by natural science, idealistic ethics, existential philosophy, and theistic anthropology are to be recognized as genuine, justified, and necessary and are to be welcomed by theology as true and valuable within their limits (3–2, 200–202).

Barth is obviously not the obscurantist concerning general human knowledge that he has often been made out to be. Nevertheless, he does ask what all this knowledge has to do with the task and content of theology. The God who created and maintains the constant structures of the world and of human nature, the eternal Word of God whose voice "goes out through all the earth" (Ps. 19:4) and whose "light shines in the darkness" (John 1:5), this God has sent his Word in the form of the human flesh of Jesus, in the midst of and as a participant in the history of the called people of Israel and the church. In actuality, the ultimate meaning and finally satisfactory presupposition of the world order, of human nature, and of all the dazzling truths of human insight are made known to man only in God's free sovereign action and speaking in Jesus Christ and in the history that belongs to him. God is and declares himself to be Lord of the universe and of man in general just and only as he is Lord of Israel and the church in Jesus Christ. Barth insists that all the various activities and relations of God toward creation are really nothing more than diversifications of the one single act of divine decision, the act of the election of man as his covenant-partner in Jesus Christ. So even man in his sin and creation in its corruption are not another sphere of reality outside God's electing grace (2–2, 90 f.). There is no absolute dualism. God's revelation "speaks of a dually determined reality but not of a dual reality" (3–1, 383).

Theology, then, has the task of exploring and explicating all the wisdom concerning God, man, and the world that has come to light in Jesus Christ. This wisdom does not invalidate or take the place of that which is gained by the natural sciences or by purely human experience and reflection. But Barth asks, Why would we consult the restricted, partial, and sinfully corrupted wisdom of creatures about merely creaturely reality when the question concerns the ultimate and eternal meaning and destiny of man before God, on which question we have received the light of the Creator himself? "The presupposition given us in and with the human nature of Jesus is exhaustive and superior to all other presuppositions, and all other presuppositions can become possible and useful only in dependence upon it." (3–2, 43.)

It must also be remembered that by "Jesus Christ" Barth does not mean some Absolute Idea that contains all concrete particular truths that are to be deduced by a rational dialectic (Hegel). "Jesus Christ" is a history in which the living personal God moves *from* his freely made decision to share his eternal life with a creature, *through* the whole process of time that he gives that creature, *to* the fulfillment of his purpose. And the medium in which this history of God becomes visible is Jesus of Nazareth and his special history as witnessed to in the Bible by the Holy Spirit. Theology, therefore, never has a material to work with that is static and objective in the sense of being controllable. It is dependent from day to day and from word to word upon a dynamic history in which the determinative factor is the free, sovereign, personal God. Within the vast sphere of this new relationship and new life of the creature with his Creator "the inquiring and contemplative reason of the creature" (3–2, 44) is free to roam. This is "faith in search of understanding." This is the task of theology. But, Barth would want to make clear, theology is not faith, nor are theologians automatically a class with superior piety. Theology is important and necessary, but it is neither the source, nor the substance, nor the goal of Christian revelation and faith.

In spite of Barth's answers, some questions and problems remain. In spite of his generous remarks about natural science and philosophy, he has not really answered the question as to the value and usability of their insights for theology. He has suggested that the true words of God in the profane world have their significance for Christians only insofar as they lead the Christian community deeper into the Biblical Word (4–3, 134). But in the *Dogmatics* he nowhere allows this to happen in a conscious and explicit way. Since it certainly happens in every theologian's thinking, would it not be better to bring the process out into the open and control it? In his only direct and extended discussion of the relationship between theology and philosophy, Barth struggles to allow proper autonomy to each, but he seems to end up bewildered that anyone would want to continue to make a philosophical approach to reality when the theological one is available.[5] On the grounds of even his own position, such a stance is inadequate. Because of his deliberate relegation of his own broad knowledge of secular learning to an occasional footnote, his *Dogmatics* do give the impression of being a "*gnōsis* fallen from heaven." Their very real relevance to the everyday life of man easily escapes our notice.

This impression that the *Dogmatics* is a kind of revelation in itself, and that revelation consists of theological propositions, is intensified by Barth's obvious confidence in the powers of "the inquiring and contemplative reason of the creature" to derive all the presuppositions, grounds, and possibilities of divine and human existence from the materials of Christological history in which faith participates. For one who insists that our knowledge of God must resist all speculation and be limited to what is spoken to us by God, Barth will seem, to many, to be able to give extremely extensive and detailed accounts of the inner eternal life of the Trinity, of the nature of God's election before creation, of the origin and reality of the demonic and of angels, and of the relation of the whole realm of nature to the purpose of God with man. Furthermore, he makes his statements on all these subjects with a seeming finality that is hardly suitable for one who must know that the principle of *simul justus et peccator* applies to the Christian's power of reason as much as to the rest of his being. Finally, it must be asked, As one who knows that all human language about God can be nothing more than an analogy, is it proper for Barth to build his *Dogmatics* into such a tight system of rationally coherent propositions by means of the logic of "presupposition"? Does not analogical language suggest a looser relation among reality, ideas, and words? Is, perhaps, the "later Heidegger" correct in moving in the direction of more poetic and less propositional language?

For you, the preacher, all this means that as you read the *Dogmatics* you must strongly and consciously resist the impression that here faith has finally been caught in sentences and needs only to be learned and repeated. You must banish the fancy that herein man has at last been able to shed all his confining clothes of fallibility and uncertainty and now is able to dance around in the pure freedom of absolute truth. In order to make legitimate use of the endless stimulation in these pages, you must fight and wrestle within them constantly, asking, "How do I know this?" and "What does this mean for Christian living?" If you ever catch yourself slipping into the habit of unconsciously acceding to whatever is being said as if it were the unquestionable truth and simply repeating it by rote, then I advise you to stop reading the *Dogmatics*.

Let me remind you again that I have here hardly begun to analyze the problem, let alone propose a solution. All that is being done is to draw your attention to it. But as already suggested, the problem of Barth's construction of his theology by means of reason's search for the "presuppositions" of faith cannot be considered apart from the equally complex problem of his acceptance of analogy as the only possible way of describing the God of Christian faith and his dealings with men.

THE METHOD OF ANALOGY

The problem of the nature and use of analogy may be moving toward the center of attention in the whole question of theological method. Diverse forces are encouraging this movement. Contemporary philosophy has long been interested in the problem of language and meaning. Philosophy and theology have in common an intensified concern for symbolism in its broadest connotations. Biblical scholars are passing beyond the consideration of mere exegesis to the wider questions of hermeneutics. Within the latter field Bultmann has made the blunt proposal that the alternative to mythological language in theology is that of analogy.[6] And Barth's own attack on the supposed Roman Catholic usage has called forth a new interest in the medieval Scholastic developments in the concept of analogy.[7]

In common parlance we often use the term "analogy" to refer to any form of comparison. Of course it is recognized that in an analogy we are dealing with a correspondence that is only partial. While there are points of likeness or similarity, there are also points of difference or unlikeness. Barth sticks to this simple definition throughout the *Dogmatics* (1–1, 277 ff.; 2–1, 225 ff.; 3–1, 195 f.; 4–3, 533). But his two major uses of it (*analogia fidei* and *analogia relationis*) are so different, and his own understanding of the general subject has so developed, that it would be fatal to read the *Dogmatics* without some rudimentary understanding of some of the technical problems involved in the subject. Furthermore, the role of analogy is so crucial in all our talking about God and in the communication of the gospel, that preachers in general ought to be better informed on the subject. Only so will they really understand the limits and the possibilities of preaching.

As a form of simple external comparison, an analogy is a metaphor, and so may be nothing more than a natural unsophisticated form of speech. For example, "the ship *plows* the sea" or "a *volley* of oaths." As such, it falls under the larger category of the human activity of symbolization. A. N. Whitehead has defined this activity by saying, "The human mind is functioning symbolically when some components of its experience elicit consciousness, beliefs, emotions, and usages respecting other components of its experience."[8] Analogy, as one form of symbolism, is therefore a factor in broad areas of human existence including the religious. And so the analogical activity of the human mind has been seen to be something more than a form of language or a means of communication. The fundamental human capacity to bring experience into the form of language or speech has been taken as a clue to the problem of epistemology, that is to the problem of *how* we know what we know, to the problem of the limits and possibilities of knowledge. The Scholastic classification of analogy into three types obviously has gone beyond the question of linguistic structures and is trying to analyze the different ways in which the vision of truth takes form in the language of the human mind. (The three types according to Scholastic theology are: inequality, proportion or attribution, and proportionality.)

Whether Barth's uses of analogy fall neatly within one or another of these classifications is a question we will not enter into here. It does appear that in his original formulation on the subject (2-1, 224-243) he sought to classify his usage under one type but in actual practice he broke through the bounds of all three. The important point, however, is that he is dealing with analogy not simply as a form of linguistic communication but as a problem at the heart of Christian epistemology under the general heading of "The Limits of the Knowledge of God," and under the more specific topic of "The Veracity of Man's Knowledge of

God." Barth is concerned with how Christians come to an understanding of the God who is now in fellowship with them in the event of his self-revelation to them. Barth maintains that the only relationship that can exist between the truth of the God whom we know, and the words and concepts in which we know, is the relationship of analogy. "We cannot open our mouths," he says, "to speak about God without recourse to the promise that we shall speak the truth in the analogy of his truth itself." (2–1, 231.)

It must be stressed, however, at this stage of his theology (1940) Barth is not primarily concerned with the classification of the *type* of this analogy. He wants to establish *how* this analogy comes into being at all. When Christians assert an analogy between the truth of God's being and our human words and ideas, they are not dealing with a general principle and tool that is used by all men in their differing quests for the truth. They are referring to a theological principle concerning the very specific relation that is established between God and our knowing in the particular context of his self-revelation in Jesus Christ and of the forgiveness of sin by grace alone (2–1, 238 f.). This is why Barth's meaning of analogy transcends the limits of all three of the medieval types and includes elements of each (in spite of his identification with the analogy of extrinsic attribution).

The situation is not that man has the idea of God but has to find a way to know God and so, among others, uses the way of analogy on the assumption that the Creator must be something like that which he has created. Nor is it even the case of man's having received a nonverbal revelation of God and then is left on his own to cast around for the best way of putting it into words. Rather, Barth insists that the propriety of our thought and language for the expression of God's self-revelation has two grounds. First, the world to which our words and concepts are appropriate is the creation of God; it is his own and so not something alien to him. So in claiming our thought and language as an expression of the truth of his being he is returning to that which is his. But, secondly, our sin has also corrupted this creation of God, so the purification and determination of our language as a proper analogue of his obvious truth is accomplished by the initiative of God himself in his gracious presence in a man, Jesus Christ (2-1, 228-231).

In other words, Barth will accept the inevitability of analogical language in theology only if it can be done in a way that refutes all natural theology, only if the analogies are formed within and are actually dictated by the grace of God and the faith of man in Jesus Christ. This is why he placed the *analogia fidei* (1-1, 279) or the *analogia gratiae* (2-1, 243) in opposition to the *analogia entis* of Thomistic theology. He wanted to maintain that the correspondence between God and our language is established only by the grace of God through faith, not all by man's natural reason comparing the being of God with the being of man. Ten years later (by 1950) Barth had been persuaded by Balthazar that Aquinas never meant what Barth accused him of in the concept of the "analogy of being" but that Aquinas meant something like Barth's own later formulation of an *analogia relationis* (an analogy of relations). So Barth ceases to make this contrast in his later volumes. Nevertheless, though the language changes, Barth still maintains his original point, that our way of speaking of God can never really contain the truth of God himself, the creature never captures and controls the Creator. Yet, our language may reflect the truth of God's own being if we speak of him whom we know by faith in Jesus Christ, and if we use the language that he himself has sanctified in becoming one of us in Jesus Christ.

Finally, we must note that analogy can be used in a third way besides as a type of symbolic language and as an analysis of the epistemological problem. Analogy can pass from being the form or structure of the act of knowing into being the very content or substance of what is known. This is the kind of analogy that Barth began to develop when he took over Bonhoeffer's term, *analogia relationis,* as a concept for explaining in what sense man is created "in the image of God" (about 1943, in 3–1, 194 ff.). Barth argues that the "image of God" consists in mankind's being created male and female, or in more general terms, in their being created to live *with* one another. This essential relationship of man to man is a reflection of the relationship of God to man in Jesus Christ, and this in turn is a reflection of the relationship of Father and Son in the eternal Trinitarian life of God. When Barth says these three relationships are "analogous" to each other, he is not just using a figure of speech, nor is he trying to solve the problem of Christian knowing. In the using of a linguistic form (analogy), on the basis of God's affirmation of our language in his revelation (faith), Barth is making an *ontological* assertion, an affirmation of *what* God has revealed about himself and about mankind. Barth is saying that Christian faith comes to understand that these three relationships are alike (or similar, or corresponding) not because man is comparing them to each other but because the relation of man to man is grounded in the relation of God and man, and the latter is grounded in the relation of Father and Son. They are analogous because God has determined them to be so. And Barth uses the concept and term of "analogy" as the sanctified one for the expression of this divine truth because it indicates simultaneously a real correspondence and a qualitative difference a "real likeness along with complete unlikeness" (4–3, 533).

Our concern at this point is not with the theology of this position (we will evaluate that later). But you, as the reader of the *Dogmatics,* must be very clear that when Barth talks about the *analogia relationis* in Vols. III, Part 1; III, Part 2; and III, Part 3, he is concerned with something beyond the *analogia fidei,* although he places it also in opposition to the *analogia entis.* When Barth became convinced that what he meant by *analogia relationis* is the same concern that the Thomists express in *analogia entis,* he quit using this technical terminology altogether (after 3–3) and retained only the basic simplified concept of analogy. He seems to have concluded that his getting mixed up in the threefold Scholastic distinctions on analogy was a mistake, that they inevitably bring irrelevant and so false categories into theology. So the reader ought not to be confused over the seeming conflict in Barth's own language on analogy, originally rejecting the distinction of likeness and unlikeness in preference for "similarity" and "partial correspondence" (2–1, 225), but finally moving through various formulations to that of "real likeness along with complete unlikeness" (4–3, 533).

It should also be noted that what Barth came to call *analogia relationis* in Vol. III, Part 1, was not a new theme but an old one that Bonhoeffer helped him to see applied also to the definition of the image of God in man. In fact, as I have noted before, I would hazard the thesis that the analogy among the relations of Father and Son, God and man, man and man, is the ground motif of the entire *Dogmatics.* This does not contradict Barth's own thesis that "in actuality dogmatics must fundamentally be Christology and only Christology" (1–2, 872) but rather is identical with it. For Barth, we can say nothing about God (Father and Son) or about man (male and female) except on the basis of that which we see in Jesus Christ (God and man). The analogy of these interconnected relations does form the ground motif of the *Dogmatics* because it answers what is for Barth the basic theological problem; it resolves the central dilemma that confronts faith in its search for understanding. How is it possible for God to be in absolute freedom and sovereignty, to be infinitely and eternally self-sufficient, and

yet at the same time to bother to create a form of finite and
temporal existence and even to enter into this alien sphere
when it has become corrupted by its opposition to him?
This is not for Barth an existential question for which
natural man is seeking an answer. It is the ultimate question
that the man of faith asks within the wholly new and unique
relation he has with God in the life of reconciliation in Jesus
Christ.

The answer that Barth finds is the eternal life and history
that God himself lives in the three modes of his being as
Father, Son, and Holy Spirit. This is why the doctrine of
the Trinity is no mere human fiction for Barth but goes to
the very heart of revelation. In Jesus Christ, God reveals that
what makes revelation possible, what makes his entrance
into communion with man and his world possible, is his
own Trinitarian life and being. Because eternally in himself
the Son is distinguished from the Father yet united with
the Father by the Holy Spirit, so it is possible for God in
his unity to posit man and his world as distinct from himself and yet enter into union with them. Barth stated this
basic theme in his first discussion of "God's Freedom for
Man" (1–2, 34), he developed it more sharply in his treatment of "The Being of God in Freedom" (2–1, 317), and
then it is repeated like a litany again and again in every
possible connection (e.g., 2–1, 616; 2–2, 99; 3–1, 185, 196;
3–2, 220, 324; 3–3, 430; 4–1, 202 ff.). And as Barth explored
more and more the ramifications of this analogical correspondence between the Trinity and God's relation with the
world, he was forced to state ever more positively the
correspondence between God's act of creation in the election
of Jesus Christ and God's act of reconciliation in the life,
death, and resurrection of Jesus Christ (reaching its climax
in 4–3).

In conclusion, then, what do we make of Barth's whole
use of epistemological and ontological analogy? Again, our

purpose and space here do not allow a full critical appraisal
of this complex problem. But readers of the *Dogmatics*
should at least be aware of what Barth is doing when he
talks about *analogia fidei* and *analogia relationis*. Furthermore, we must always be on the alert to question Barth's
own faith-rationalism in this regard. If we grant that the
love for fellowman that Christian faith inspires is a reflection and an analogy of the love that God has shown toward
us in Jesus Christ, does it follow "unavoidably" and "inevitably" that both these loves are modeled on the same
kind of love that exists between the Father and Son in the
eternal Trinity (3–2, 323 f.)? Quite apart from some troublesome implications of such a view, does the logic of faith
really force us to such a position? Indeed, is there such a
thing as the logic of faith at all? Again, even though you
may end up agreeing with him, you must ask if Barth is
correct in saying that by contemplating Jesus "we cannot
avoid . . . the astounding conclusion" of Barth's own particular doctrine of the Trinity (4–1, 202). Do we really know
even by faith that God's activity as Creator is the "marvel-
ously consistent final continuation of the history in which
he is God" (4–1, 203)? Barth's method of analogy is a profound and intriguing possibility, but it must not be accepted
and followed uncritically. And we now turn to state very
briefly some of its problematic results in the actual theological positions of the *Dogmatics*.

THE RELATIVIZING OF HISTORY

By now we have become aware of a number of themes
in Barth's theology that, if taken by themselves, could easily
suggest a kind of Gnosticism or monistic idealism that robs
human history and even the whole of creation of their reality and significance. I have defended Barth against this
charge, although we have bluntly to recognize that his principle of presupposition and his method of analogy could

easily be misused so as to blur if not erase the lines of distinction between God and the world. In this section I want to show specifically how an unwary reader of the *Dogmatics* could easily land in such a position, and to indicate some emphases there that should be kept in mind to guard against such a conclusion.

When by *analogia relationis* Barth says that all of God's relations with the creation are a copy and a kind of projection of the relation of the Father to the Son within God, then the creation appears to be a mode of God's own being. This impression is furthered when one recalls that Barth's doctrine of the Trinity places the first emphasis on the oneness of God, rejects the traditional "three Persons" as too tritheistic, and defines the Trinity as three modes of God's being God. When Barth adds to this that God's identification with creation was already accomplished in all its possibilities in the union of the Son with the humanity of Jesus Christ in eternity before creation, and that everything that happens outside God is already present to God in that his eternity overarches the past, present, and future of our time, one begins to wonder why God bothered creating something outside himself, or whether the distinction of "inside" and "outside" retains any meaning (e.g., 2–1, 462, 559; 3–3, 430). Again, Barth's continual emphasis that everything is created through, in, and unto Christ, combined with his description of reconciliation as a movement of humiliation from "above" to "below" and of exaltation from "below" to "above," tends to erase the distinctions among God's original decision to create, his actual act of creation, and the event of reconciliation.

In counterbalance to this apparently irrefutable monism of God's power and reality, you must remember that Barth insists that an analogy is not an identity, but a likeness with a difference. The difficulty is that until very recently Barth has talked about how the creation is different from the

Creator very little and only in negative terms (God is free, creation is dependent, etc.). To guard against this imbalance it would be helpful if you could read his really constructive view of the universe as having a positive constancy of its own (4–3, 135–165). It must also be constantly recalled that Barth is an adamant foe of the concept of a static, motionless, timeless Deity. He rejects "being" as the ultimate category and insists that God reveals himself as the *living* God who acts in freedom and love, and so has a history and duration in himself. So the giving of life and history (time) to a creature outside himself is indeed for his own glory, but that glory is realized in his loving gift of a share in his own joy to another. However much this other is an analogy to God and an extension of his own life and history, Barth always reminds us that Creator and creature are two absolutely different orders of being who never have been and never will be identical. Their likeness makes their communion possible, their unlikeness guarantees the retention of the identity of each. Barth wrote most of the *Dogmatics* as a slashing attack against a theology that he accused of leaving man's destiny in his own hands and of suggesting even a deification of man. If Barth has reestablished the sovereignty of the Creator over his creation, the reader of the *Dogmatics* must preserve the dominant Biblical emphasis on the dynamic, processive, struggling, almost experimental character of God's involvement in the life and history of his creation.

THE ABSORPTION OF HUMANITY

The relativizing of history in the *Dogmatics* assumes its most problematic form in the placing of a question mark over the very reality of man as a responsible subject distinct from God. In fact, the adequacy of Barth's anthropology will probably be the main point around which uncertainty and debate will revolve for some time into the future. He has frankly admitted that he approached the doctrine of creation in general with great reluctance, that he came out with an exposition that he himself had not expected, and that he was so dissatisfied with his original formulation of his doctrine of man that he had to hold it back from publication in order to recast it completely. (3–1, ix f.) The problems here are therefore so complex, difficult, and far-reaching that we can barely mention the major ones, let alone give any kind of exposition or proposed solution to them. But again the reader of the *Dogmatics* should know that these problems are there and that Barth himself does not pretend to have worked out a complete and harmonious position concerning them. And of all the issues about the substance of Barth's theology, I personally feel that this is the one in regard to which the student of the *Dogmatics* should be most on his guard in order not to accept uncritically positions that might make all preaching pointless and powerless.

The first question I would raise about Barth's anthropology concerns his distinction between created man and reconciled man, between man "as such" and the man of faith (3–2, 276). Most of the time Barth seems to make a radical disjuncture between nature and grace, which sounds very much like the medieval two-level view of man. He wants to deny rigorously the view that in natural man there is any point of contact for grace, any inherent readiness of man for revelation, any natural capacity for his destiny as God's partner, any merely creaturely power to work the glory of God. (1–1, 272; 2–1, 147 f.; 4–1, 576; 4–2, 341, 560, 570.) Taken by itself, this strain of passages would seem to reduce man as created by God to an empty and impotent vessel into which God later pours his grace, a purely animal substructure to which God later adds a totally new and unrelated spiritual superstructure. One wonders if God could not have just as well used a friendly hound dog or a mimicking parrot.

This is not what Barth means to say. This strain of passages is Barth's exaggerated way of saying that when release from sin, and fulfillment of human destiny, comes in Jesus Christ, it comes as a sheer gift for which man cannot prepare himself, which man cannot attain on his own, which presents itself not as one but as the only alternative for man if he is to attain complete manhood. So the emphases made in these passages must always be balanced by another strain in Barth's thought. He clearly asserts that in all mankind as created by God, quite apart from man's fulfillment in Christ, there is an "immanent mystery." Man as such, in his simple creaturely nature, is constructed by his Creator so that his being as a creature corresponds to his destiny as God's covenant-partner. Man is created with a "covenant-capacity," which takes the concrete form of each man's being moved by his very nature to live with, to, and for his fellowmen, in I-thou encounter, in love. (3–2, 249, 265, 267, 274, 277.) It is in this mode of his existence that man is created in God's image (3–2, 323 f.; 3–1, 19–206), and the image in this sense cannot even be touched, let alone destroyed by man's sinful faithlessness to God (3–2, 40, 324; 4–1, 480–484). So here the reader must take caution not to judge Barth on the basis of his earlier view of the image where he talked of its being "totally lost" and "restored." (1–1, 273; 2–2, 517, 532, 560, 566.) On the basis of his revised view he argues strongly that the view and proper glory that come to man in God's command "reverts and reaches back to that first glory" that God gave man in his creation, and which cannot be lost but remains as the "ontological bond that binds every man to God." (3–4, 651 f.) Likewise, the *agapē*-love that comes to man in reconciliation does not alter basic human nature but actually corresponds with it in that man is structured in creation so that he is truly man only as he is with God. (4–2, 742 f.)

In spite of all these glowing words about natural man, a

second serious question arises about Barth's meaning because he repeatedly asserts that the humanity he is talking about, when he says it is destined to be God's partner, or that it is ready for God, or that it is ontologically bound to God, is not humanity in general but the specific humanity of Jesus Christ. (2–1, 148, 284 ff.) Barth's constant theme is that all God's ways and works with man have their beginning in the election of Jesus Christ in eternity and have their goal in the incarnation in Jesus Christ in time. (2–1, 667; ¶ 35:1, 2.) The only "real man" is Jesus Christ. (¶ 44:3.) Men in general only become true men as they participate in the humanity of Jesus Christ by faith-union with him. In this sense all men were crucified, converted, and sanctified in Jesus Christ, and in him mankind was altered at its root. (4–1, 317, 348, 353, 391.) And this is true for every man whether he knows and believes it or not. It is hard to read such statements without seeing in them the complete absorption of man into the humanity of Jesus Christ and therefore into the "humanity of God." And this would mean that mankind becomes nothing more than a mode of God's own being because, for Barth, Jesus is no human person distinct from God but is the second "Person" of the Trinity in human form, and so is God in his Person (1–2, 163 f.; 4–2, 49). Over against such a destructive nihilistic conclusion, we can only point out that Barth also maintains that our humanity is qualitatively different from that of Jesus Christ (2–1, 286; 3–2, 86, 265; 4–1, 54, 131, 210; 4–2, 47 ff.). The difficulty is that he never explores this difference in a positive way. Yet this would seem to me to be absolutely necessary. Barth himself cannot help recognizing that God's identification with man in the election and incarnation of Jesus Christ is not really the end and goal of God's creation. Occasionally, he clearly states that God has turned outward and become incarnate in Jesus "for our sakes," that is, for men in general (3–1, 382). Then surely the unique way in which we ordinary mortals, as different from Jesus the Son of God, believe in, love, and live with God should be explored by theology.

The exposition of this difference would perhaps also deliver Barth's anthropology from a third objectionable contradiction. Because he sees God accomplishing his own glory only in Jesus Christ, Barth quite naturally describes the ultimate service of the creature as its being a wall that echoes back God's own voice, or as a mirror that reflects God's own image to himself for his own self-glorification (2–1, 668–673). Such language is wholly indefensible when our attention turns from the relation of God to his own incarnate Word to the relation of God to men in general. Barth himself constantly contradicts such language by insisting that created man as such is continuously addressed by God as a "thou" and as such is created with a capacity for freedom that God will not smash by the brute force of a tyrant. (2–2, 553 f.; 3–1, 263 ff.) God's Spirit does not operate mechanically or by infusion toward man, but God deliberately preserves a distance from man so that there can be dialogue, intercourse, and drama between them. (3–3, 139, 432.) If Barth really means all this language in any understandable sense of the words, then he cannot mean for man to be absorbed into such a union with God that his true subjectivity and nature as a person are obliterated.

However, we must mention a fourth and final puzzlement concerning Barth's anthropology. He is so anxious not to assign any independent autonomy to man that he even casts a threatening shadow on all his fine words about man's freedom as a responsible person in encounter with the person of God. Here I have reference to his use of *analogia relationis* as the basic way to explain the essential character of human existence. As we have already seen, Barth locates the "basic form of humanity" in man's living in I-thou fellowship with fellowman. This man-to-man relationship, however, is not self-contained nor an end in itself. It cannot maintain itself or achieve its true meaning on its own strength and resources. This relationship was established in God's act of creation to serve as the external ground and preparation for another relationship that is the real mystery and meaning of human existence, mankind's destined relationship with God as his children and friends. Therefore, the fellowship between man and man is an analogy of the fellowship between God and man. And in the realized Kingdom of God these two relationships become but inseparable aspects of the one reality of the communion of love. So far, so good.

Barth, however, insists that Christian faith cannot leave it there. What is the ground of our assurance that human love will find its way to fulfillment in God's love? What guarantee is there that God will succeed in this seemingly risky venture of trying to establish such an unstable relationship as love with so fallible a being as man? How can we hope that it is even possible for the infinite omnipotent King to be wedded happily with a weak and humble creature? For Barth, God himself gives the answer in the revelation of his Trinitarian being. In faith we come to see the ultimate mystery that the relationship of God to his creature, man, is grounded upon and is a reflection and so an analogy of the eternal relationship between the Father and the Son within God himself. Of course, Barth always adds that the two relationships are not identical but only analogous because God and man are two different orders of being. Now if we agree that the Christian confession of Jesus Christ as the eternal Son of God incarnate requires the formulation of the doctrine of the Trinitarian being of God, and if we add to this the Pauline doctrine of Jesus as the Second Adam, the true man who is the image of God and in whose image we are to be renewed, then we may recognize that there is *some kind* of analogy between the relation of Father and Son and the relation between God and man. But there are

a lot of difficult and questionable ifs in this statement, and
even then what is meant by the "analogy" is not at all clear.

Nevertheless, the most objectionable and confusing character of Barth's development of this analogy is yet to be stated.
He goes on to specify that the three analogous relations are
alike in that they are all I-thou relations. Men are able to be
I and thou to each other just because God creates and addresses man as a thou to his I. Again, so far, so good. But
then he adds that both of these relations are possible only
because they are reflections of an original and eternal I-thou
relation in God between the Father and the Son. At this
point it must be recalled that Barth firmly rejects the idea
that God is three "Persons" in the modern sense of person.
Rather, God is person in his oneness, and is three in his
modes of being the one personal God. (1–1, 403, 410; 4–1,
204 f.; 2–1, 284 f.) Then what kind of an "I," or subject, or
person, is man if he is a thou to God as the Son is to the
Father? Is man no more than the projected self-consciousness
of God? We do not have time here to follow out the com-
plexities of this problem, especially as to the nature and
function of the Holy Spirit.[9] But if this is what Barth really
means, then here is the complete absorption or destruction
of man as a free, responsible being capable of the mutuality
of love.

Against such a charge Barth would say that the relations
are only analogous with an absolute difference as well as
real likeness. But he goes too far in the equation of the I-
thou likeness to redeem it for its usual meaning by some
supposed difference that he will not discuss. He asserts that
the I-thou are two individuals on the human plane, whereas
"the one individual, God as such, encloses this relationship
within himself" (3–1, 196). But Barth cannot have it both
ways and still speak meaningfully. Either the relation enclosed within God is not like the interpersonal relation I
have with another man, and then the I-thou terminology is

improperly applied to God, or Father and Son are in an interpersonal relation as men are and then the Trinity consists of three real persons. But the real problem for Barth's schema arises as to the relation between God and man. Is man just a self-projection of God and as the Son is to the Father, or is man a real subject and thou to God's person as a man is to another man? Barth remains equivocal on this issue. His intent and concern is understandable, because he feels that if we grant to man spirituality and subjectivity as a capacity given in creation, then we will not be able to avoid the pitfalls of Pelagianism and humanism. But I for one believe that Barth's two-level view of created man and reconciled man, his ontological identification of mankind with the humanity of Jesus Christ, and his *analogia relationis* comprise more ammunition than is needed to fight this important battle. In making sure that God alone gets the credit for salvation, he is in danger of reducing its object, man, to a nonentity.

The extremes that he will go to and the difficulties he gets into in this battle can be shown in two additional ways.

THE EMPTYING OF FAITH

The reader of the *Dogmatics* might think that all the uncertainty about man as a creature, about his natural capacities, and about his being a spiritual person or not, would be completely cleared up and bypassed once man is brought into a reconciled relation with God in faith in Christ. Such is not the case. While man is justified by faith, he remains that man who was a sinner that is now justified. Bouillard maintains that *simul justus et peccator* is the most persistent theme in Barth's theology, and that everything else is built around it. Barth certainly does not conceive of reconciliation as the fulfillment of man's destiny. He reserves the term "redemption" for this consummation. This something more that lies beyond the peace and coexistence of reconciliation

consists of man's becoming the child of God. In this "kinship of being" not only is man tied to God but God is tied
to man. Their life becomes one. But this is all a matter of
promise and hope as yet. In our present faith-relationship
we know this hope and we live by this hope, so the hope is
truly present and operative, but it is still hope. (4–1, 599 ff.)

What, then, is the substance of reconciliation, of the life
of faith here and now? Barth wants to make this something
very positive, concrete, and of real moment. You will recall
that one of the clearest signs that he had left behind the
dialectical theology of his commentary on Romans appeared
in his insertion of the event and the time of reconciliation
between the hidden, transcendent realities of past creation
and future redemption. God in his saving presence and work
is not only pretemporal and posttemporal but also cotemporal with man. (2–1, 636 ff.) Through God's speaking his
Word to the men the man of faith comes into being as a
definite, particular, temporal, historical reality. By this self-
revelation of God, man's readiness for God is brought to
light, and man attains unto certain knowledge of God. By
God's word of election, man is confronted with the demand
to believe by his own free decision, and a line is drawn between the elected and the rejected. God's command comes
to man as gospel, not law, and so sets man free to do the
law. God makes our time to be his time and thus we see
our nature become what it was created to be. In reconciliation, God declares the forgiveness of our sin and man is
justified. This justified man now lives a life of faith in which
he truly repents and turns to God, a life of love in which
he truly loves God because God has first loved him, a life
of hope in which he looks forward in confidence to becoming the son of God in fullness.

What more could be asked? Has Barth, then, become a
proponent of realized eschatology? Has the Kingdom really
dawned already in the "new life" of the Christian people?

Nothing could be farther from Barth's intention. In every single instance mentioned above, Barth ends his glowing description of the results for man of God's inbreak into his life by asking the question, Where have we actually seen such results? Is there a single Christian who can honestly reply, in *me*? Absolutely not! Then where have we seen such results so that we can proclaim with such confidence that such is the work of God's reconciliation here and now as a concrete event in history? In every single instance described above, Barth gives the same answer: We have seen these results only in the one man, Jesus Christ.[10] The destruction of the old man of sin and the restoration of man to his right and life with God has come *to* me, in Jesus Christ, but has not taken place *in* me. (4–1, 771, 773.) The life of the Christian, therefore, consists substantively in witness to and trust in Jesus Christ. His own personal piety is a peripheral concern. The Christian shares with the non-Christian in the uncertainty, weakness, evil, and suffering of this world. He is distinguished only in that he knows that this world has been overcome in Jesus Christ. (4–3, 342 f.) This knowledge gives to the Christian himself one concrete trait and possession—hope.

This analysis would certainly seem to make the Christian life of faith an empty shell, waiting to be filled at the Parousia of Christ. It would be easy for a doctrinaire Barthian to fill his sermons with a radical eschatology that would seem to leave little for the Christian to do but to beat his breast in penitence and look to the horizon in hope. Again, this would be totally contrary to Barth's intention. He insists that this hope becomes an operative force here and now, and that the Christian man is altered and marked in his very being by being personally involved in the Christ-event. (4–3, 647 ff.) By our being drawn to Christ and by our dependence and confidence in him, we become his analogue, his parallel, his likeness. (4–1, 770.) What has

happened in Jesus is *pro me,* for me, not in theory but concretely, enclosing me in its reality. This is the truth of pietism and theological existentialism. (4–1, 755.) Barth takes
rigorously to task those who puritanically refuse to allow
any possibility of man's returning love to God out of a
legitimate fear of mysticism and sentimentalism. (4–2, 795 ff.)
And in his long section on "the direction of the Son" (4–2),
Barth argues strongly that God is working a transition
from Christ to the Christian so that what Jesus is, will be
lived out in us. What Jesus is, presses ontologically for sub-
jectivization in men and brings to them not just knowledge of
Christ but also knowledge of themselves. The occurrence of
this event is by the miraculous power of the Resurrection and
the Holy Spirit. It cannot be based or maintained by any empirical proof, so it does not lead to introspection but to an
objective identification with the work of witnessing to the
world about Jesus Christ.

Here again there seems to me to be two unreconciled
strains in at least the language if not the thought of the *Dogmatics.* It behooves the reader not to identify himself too
easily with either one, or he will be preaching a partial and
a perverted gospel. The source of this particular lack of
coherence in the *Dogmatics* seems to me to be traceable to
Barth's basic indecision as to whether the communication
of the gospel to men by the resurrection and Holy Spirit
(the prophetic office of Christ, 4–3) is really part of and
the fulfillment of Christ's work of reconciliation or whether
the communication is of a past event completed on the cross
and now needs only to be told about. There is evidence for
both, although the latter view seems to dominate. I, myself,
would want to argue that the reconciling work of Christ
reaches its precise fulfillment in his prophetic encounter
with and conviction of men in the faith-event. I also think
this is the major issue between Barth and Bultmann and
that a harmonization can be worked out that guards ade-

quately against Barth's legitimate fears that existentialism
will make Christian faith into a repetition in me of what
happened in Jesus Christ. The importance and practical implications of this issue come out when we ask Barth about
the mission of the church, as to why Christ brought the
church into being, for what purpose has God allowed a
time between the time of reconciliation on the cross and
redemption at the end of time.

THE LIMITATION OF THE CHURCH'S MISSION

In the *Dogmatics* there is one theme concerning the
church that every reader should ponder with great seriousness. From its earliest volumes Barth has been working out
a revolutionary view of the church that is only now beginning to capture the imagination in some areas of the church's
life.[11] The church, he says, has only a provisional and
mediate role in God's whole plan and work for the salvation
of the world in Jesus Christ. It is not the continuation of the
incarnation. It is not the Kingdom of God, not an end in
itself. It does not convert the world to Christ or save souls.
It does not build the Kingdom on earth by Christianizing
the social order. It is not even responsible for the results of
its own mission. Reconciliation of all mankind *has been*
accomplished by and in Jesus Christ, and he will bring redemption at the end. So the mission of the church is not to
save the world but to proclaim to the world that it has been
saved in Jesus Christ, to tell the glad tidings. The church
consists simply of those who know this to be true and who
have been called into the service of Christ as he extends *in
fact* his victory over all that has already been won *in
principle.*

I personally applaud this limitation of the church's mission in most respects. But at one particular point I think it
is so weak that it threatens the very meaningfulness of the
church's existence. The same tendency to Christomonism

that threatens to relativize history, absorb humanity, and empty faith here tends to imply that everything has already been accomplished for the world in Jesus Christ. In some transcendent ontological sense, all humanity has been fundamentally transformed by a single stroke on the cross of Christ. One cannot help asking, then, why the resurrection and the final Parousia were not identical. Why the time between? Barth very occasionally tries to protect himself in this regard. He says the work of Christ is completed in content but not in "effective power," so a "genuine conflict" remains. (1–2, 677.) The relation of Christ's victory to the world must be interpreted as a "dynamic-teleological" movement that has not yet reached its goal. It must not be interpreted monistically, as if the opposition of the world's darkness has been so vanquished by Christ that it has been set aside and its limiting quality need no longer be considered. A historical dramatic battle is still to be waged. (4–3, 168.) This all sounds good but how seriously can this theme be taken in the total scope of Barth's Christology? He can relativize even the significance of Paul's mission to the world. (2–2, 256.) The historical battle for men's hearts and minds and lives seems to lose its importance when Barth locates the substantive event of reconciliation in the objective, ontological, isolated, hidden act of God in Jesus Christ in the incarnation and cross, and then makes the communication and subjective appropriation of this accomplished reality to be a separate, secondary, and hardly necessary transaction.

I have deliberately overstated Barth's view of the objectivity of reconciliation because this exaggerated statement can be found in the *Dogmatics*. If it is not balanced strongly by his occasional insistence that such a view is incomplete and that the subjective reception by man is an inseparable part of reconciliation (4–3, 3–11), then a very perverted understanding of the Christian experience and the church's mission results. I do not think that Barth has attained clarity and consistency on this problem, and this failure manifests itself in his shifting effort to answer his own question as to why God has allowed a time between Christ's resurrection and Parousia, in which the church has a mission to perform.[12]

THEN WHY KARL BARTH?

After reading this chapter there will probably be many who will wonder why I wrote this book. How can Barth's *Dogmatics* be recommended as a resource for preaching and teaching the gospel if it contains so many dangerous and threatening pitfalls? Of course it cannot be recommended to those who believe that the Bible provides us with a simple, final, and infallible set of doctrines, answering all our questions in a direct and clear fashion. Nor will the *Dogmatics* be congenial to those who believe that the Biblical message can be best grasped by forcing it into a single, preformed, human philosophy or *Weltanschauung*. Those who have received the impression that Barth has reduced Christian truth to a static and abstract system of dogmas must simply read for themselves and find in the *Dogmatics* a mind wide open to all truths and all viewpoints, a living spirit that struggles dynamically with ever-new material, a creative soul that is not afraid to follow wherever the light of truth leads. On the other hand, those who are afraid of what appears to be Barth's wild and radical Biblical interpretations and theological formulations must ask themselves whether Christian faith should expect to find anywhere the living truth of God in Christ caught in a simple creed or philosophy.

If you, the preacher and teacher, will enter into a reading of the *Dogmatics* as an adventure, as a questing, with a zeal for intellectual and spiritual wrestling, you will find here an unending stimulus for your thought and understanding. Of course, do not limit your reading to Barth. But the very critical questions that I have raised in this chapter should show you that the *Dogmatics* is no closed and final system but just the free-ranging experimental kind of theology that should arouse you to find your own way through to the truth for you and for your preaching.

How, then, does a preacher go about using the *Dogmatics* as a resource? In what follows in the rest of this book I am going to suggest a very direct, one might say, "practical" method. That is, by turning directly to Barth's interpretation of specific Biblical texts and passages. I am hoping that this book will give you enough rudimentary knowledge about the biographical background, the formal structure, the general theological contents, and the critical issues that you may dive into the *Dogmatics* where it directly impinges upon the Biblical text or theme on which you have chosen to preach. From Barth's discussions of the text, you may occasionally follow on out into the theological context and find further food for thought for the specific sermon you are preparing. But it should be very clear that you do not preach dogma or doctrine as such. You preach the forgiveness and the judgment, the claim and the command, the calling and the commission, the love and the holiness, the glory and the majesty—of God in Jesus Christ. Theology plays a role in the periphery of preaching, giving light and direction and correction from all the wealth of ways in which the Christian community has confessed and explained its faith to itself for two thousand years.

However, before I make some specific suggestions about the different ways to get at Barth's Biblical expositions, I do want to draw your attention to a couple of other rather obvious ways in which the *Dogmatics* may be helpful to you. On the one hand, if you are the "scholarly" type who sets aside some time for general background reading, you may occasionally pick one volume of the *Dogmatics* and read it through leisurely, stopping to argue with it, to make notes of ideas you can use in sermons and talks, following out leads to other literature, consulting and comparing the views of other theologians on the same topic, perhaps setting up a discussion group on the volume with a few fellow preachers. But *take your time* and enjoy it. Scope is not so important as depth in this use of the *Dogmatics*. On the other hand, you may be preparing a talk on a specific doctrine or teaching a class in which you are surveying a series of doctrines. From the complete Table of Contents and from the summary (Ch. IV) in this book, you should be able to find your way to one or two helpful discussions of the doctrines. Be sure to note that Barth gives introductory treatments to most of his major doctrines. These two ways of using the *Dogmatics* should enrich your own theological thinking and gradually enable you to give richer answers to the questions posed to you by inquiring believers and unbelievers.

Preaching, however, is quite a different business. For myself, I seem to come to a sermon from one of three starting points. A text grips me and I want to preach it. Or a deep need of man cries out to be met and I seek the answer from God in Jesus Christ. Or a luminous truth about life dawns in my mind, and I wish to proclaim it in a way that is rooted in God's Word and that is relevant for my fellowmen. If you have a specific text in mind, in any one of the three cases, it is easy to find Barth's commentary on it by consulting the index to Biblical passages in the back of each volume. To consult them all would be time-consuming but you never can know for sure where you will find the spark that will ignite your own imagination. Since I have started this book I have heard of a number of preachers who already regularly check their text with the *Dogmatics* in just this way. One of the brightest of the younger American theologians (by no means a Barthian) says he finds some of his most stimulating and creative ideas for preaching in this way. After a little familiarity with the *Dogmatics,* you may be able to guess in which volume and context Barth will give his most thorough treatment of a text. But often as not his most revealing remarks are incidental to what he is discussing.

Obviously, if you come to a sermon without a specific text, you must find the places where he treats the theme that concerns you and scour the pages for the Biblical grounds for his own thinking. Usually these will be found in the small print of the notes, which can be quickly scanned. To give some examples of how this may be done, I have set aside four brief chapters (VII-X) in which I will try to bring to light some of Barth's Biblical expositions on the main themes of his own theology.

Before we examine his specific Biblical expositions and their usefulness for preaching, we must be clear about one of the aspects of the *Dogmatics* that is most under attack by contemporary theologians, that is, his use of the Bible. This is such a major critical question, especially for the use of the *Dogmatics* in preaching, that I have assigned a whole chapter to its consideration.

Chapter VI

The Preacher and the Word

WHEN you stand up to preach why do you take your "text" from the Bible? Whatever else you quote in your sermon, why do the words of this one book remain the criterion for the judgment of all the others? Why not Shakespeare, Plato, the Koran, or the Bhagavad-Gita? What do you mean when you call the Bible the "Word of God"? Do you mean it at all? Is there no difference in reading from Deuteronomy, the Song of Solomon, The Gospel According to Mark, Paul's Letters, and The Revelation? What authority do these readings have for the life of the average person in the pew?

These questions go to the heart of the question not only of Biblical authority but of the authority and meaningfulness of the whole of Christianity for contemporary man. If you can answer these questions, you can answer the more fundamental question, Why be a Christian at all? The authority of preacher and priest, the right of council and synod, the force of church law and order, the power of sacrament and song—none of these can be established apart from answering the question of Biblical authority. And certainly before you open yourself to the impact of the Biblical and dogmatic theology of a man, you should have some general idea of his answers to these questions. This is an especially crucial question in regard to Barth, first, because of the central importance he himself gives to it, and, secondly, because it is just on this point that most Biblical theologians shrug Barth off as irresponsible.

THE FORMAL AUTHORITY OF THE BIBLE

There is no doubt that Barth places the Bible in a class by itself as the ground and judge of every aspect of Christian faith and life. "Christianity has always been and only then a living religion when it was not ashamed actually to be in all seriousness a book-religion." (1-2, 495.) He fully realizes that the Bible does not stand alone but in the midst of a long history and a rich community life. We recognize other authorities such as a creed, sacrament, tradition, liturgy, and polity. And we gladly give thanks to the church whose confession of faith we hear before we can make our own and who provides us with the canon of Scripture and with teachers. But for Barth, these other authorities, in spite of their necessary and interactive relation with the Bible, have only secondary and derived right and power. They all are indirect witnesses to the revelation of God. They can do nothing more than repeat and help re-create the original testimony of the prophetic and apostolic communities. The Bible, on the other hand, is the only direct source of that firsthand witness to the presence and activity of God in that community which centers and is fulfilled in Jesus Christ. So Barth warns that the church stands to lose its very faith unless it holds to the "Israelitish concern for the sentence, word, and letter."[1]

Because of statements like these in his early volumes, Barth was sometimes accused of being the proponent of a subtle variety of fundamentalist Biblical literalism. That this charge is absurd we will see in the next few sections of this chapter. But more serious critics have taken Barth to task for indulging in "a pneumatic, suprahistorical comprehension of Scripture," for using a "Christological exegesis of the Old

Testament," and "obscure conceptuality" and "arbitrary assertions" in his Biblical interpretation. We will analyze the basis and the justice of these criticisms later. But it should be noted that these harsh words have not deterred Barth in the least. In his latest volumes he still insists that the one true mark of the church is its apostolicity, and this means its subservience to Scripture (4–1, 721). "The Biblical Word," he says, "is the concrete *vinculum pacis* (bond of peace) of the church of all times and places." (4–3, 131.)

The real question, however, is concerning the basis for putting the Bible into such a position of eminence. Many who would criticize Barth's use of the Bible still admit it is the ground of the Christian faith and life. Even many Anglicans with their stress on liturgy and many Roman Catholics with their veneration of pope and tradition are coming to recognize that serious study of Scripture is perhaps the common bond that binds us all together. So the more serious problem is the one of approach to and use of the Bible.

The Material Authority of the Bible

Men may agree, then, to give formal authority to the Bible for different material reasons. Simply to say that the Bible is the most primitive record of the only direct witness to the original and decisive revelation of God in Jesus Christ does not solve the problem. Of what did that revelation consist? Of these statements in the Bible? How do we know this was and is revelation? By some theory that proves the Bible to be "inspired"? By "existential encounter" with the testimony of the Biblical authors concerning their own encounter with God? In what sense, then, is the Bible the "Word of God"? This series of questions will force us to ask what kind of trust we put in the Biblical documents and in the authors themselves. But first let us see what is Barth's general answer to the foregoing questions.

Revelation for Barth is nothing more nor less than the revelation of God himself. It is the event in which God makes his own self or person known by man. This means that revelation occurs only in an act. And this kind of *self*-revelation may occur because this act is the kind in which God and man are consciously present as persons (not as things), and present *to each other*. So the Biblical knowledge or revelation of God always has the character of the event of an encounter. And these encounters are always initiated by God, and in them he asserts his Lordship over man and demands acknowledgment and obedience from man (2–1, 23). But because man is compelled to be present himself as a person in this encounter—to respond to God's demand—something else happens besides man's knowing of God. Man is also enabled to know his own self. God reveals not only himself but us to ourselves. For the first time, we see by his light that we are truly sinners, but also we see the new man that we are meant to be (4–2, 300 ff.).

This immediate presence of God and man to each other, however, always occurs mediately, in and through some concrete medium, never in naked objectivity (1–2, 224 ff.; 2–1, 18, 24 f.). Or as Barth more lately prefers to say, God is present not so much *in* or *through* but rather *with* an actual event or person or thing. So God reveals himself always and only by hiding or veiling himself with some empirical reality. In this way God preserves his own freedom and holiness by never being identical with the empirical mode of his presence, never caught or bound in it. In this way he also honors and preserves man's identity and freedom, by not overwhelming him with the irresistible glory of his immediate divine presence. God has identified himself as such in perfect union with only one creature in the whole history of creation, the man Jesus. The heavens and the earth, male and female, the history of Israel, the church with its Book and its rituals—none of these *are* God.

He may encounter man *with* them, but he encounters us *in* and *as* only one creature, Jesus. Jesus *is* the revelation of God because he *is* God encountering us.

The Bible, therefore, can be said to be the Word of God only in an indirect sense, only because it is a creaturely object in conjunction *with* which God speaks to us. It has primacy over all other such creaturely modes of God's encounter with men only because of its unique connection with God's unique presence in Jesus Christ. We say the *Bible* is the Word of God because it witnesses to Jesus who *is* the Word of God. So the Bible has material substantive authority, not in itself, not in its own words on the page, not in the facts, events, ideas, images, or propositions recorded therein. The material authority of the Bible is identical with Jesus Christ, as the living Word of God who speaks here and now in "a divine act of majesty." So we give this Book primary formal authority in our religious life because it gives the *possibility* of hearing the Word of God. But it has no material authority of its own because the *actuality* of our hearing the living Word of God is something not even the Book can guarantee. Only the living Word himself can open this door and reach out to enclose us so that we come to know him. (1–2, 485, 530, 538; 2–2, 706; 4–2, 122, 160.)

This sounds clear enough, but can nothing more be said about how the poor, human, earthbound words of the Bible attain for us the majesty of the eternal, living, present Word of God? Barth clearly believes this event to be the miracle of Christian faith. It is not to be taken out of the hands of God to be arranged and guaranteed by some human mechanism or method. Yet it is not, for Barth, simply a brute fact, beyond all description and understanding. Within faith, we are led to "explain" this event by reference to Jesus' resurrection and the Holy Spirit. To hear the words of the Bible as the Word of God is identical with knowing

Jesus as the Son of God. This knowledge in turn is identical with "the knowledge of faith in his resurrection from the dead," which again "is itself nothing other than the self-witness of God by the Holy Spirit" (1-2, 485 f., 538). In traditional Reformed theology this kind of statement usually ends all discussion. After one has mentioned the Holy Spirit, nothing more can be said. "Holy Spirit" is invoked as a wholly undefinable, inaccessible act of God that is supposed to account for everything that cannot otherwise be explained.

Barth, however, will have nothing to do with the characterization of the Holy Spirit as a magical, mystical "indefinable whispering and compelling" in the depths of the human soul (4-2, 360). Holy Spirit is not a third separate "person" who works in his own obscure way independent of Father and Son. Rather, Holy Spirit is precisely the same One (God) who was incarnate as the man Jesus now effectively uniting himself with us in mutual self-disclosure (4-2, 331). This same union is describable as our sharing in the power and reality of Jesus' resurrection. And this sharing consists of "the power of the inconceivably sublime passage from what is real and true in Jesus Christ to what is true for us, or to put it more simply, from Christ to us as Christians" (4-2, 307). Therefore, the miracle and mystery of this event does not lie in any obscurity or in any tricky, under-the-table (subconscious) workings. This climactic event in God's saving work, this heart of the material authority of the Bible, occurs in inseparable connection with all the objectivity and light and concreteness of the life, death, and resurrection of the man Jesus and of his relationship with his disciples of all generations (4-2, 360-377). It occurs for us in the midst of our encounter with the all-too-human witness of the first disciples, as recorded in the Bible.

One very important point in Barth's presentation must be noted at this time, although we will discuss it at greater length in the last section of this chapter. It is this: for Barth,

the speaking of the Word, the seeing of Jesus as the Son of
God, the experience of the resurrection, the testimony of
the Holy Spirit, is not a purely objective event that may
occur in my awareness without really involving me subjectively in the depths of who and what I am. This single
event, which can be so variously described, does not occur
at all except insofar as there is a passage from what is true
in Jesus to what is true *for me* (*pro me*). The words of the
Bible do not become the Word of God, the man Jesus is not
revealed as Son of God, the resurrection has no power or
reality, there is no true communion with God at the level
of spirit, until *I see myself* grasped, challenged, judged, forgiven, and made new in Jesus Christ. In fact, Barth goes
even one step farther and insists that for all this to be real
I must not only see myself so transformed in Jesus Christ
but I must also begin to draw the implications of this fact.
It is in this latter act that I begin to become a Christian.
(4-2, 307.)

How Barth differs from Bultmann at this point (if at all)
we will discuss later, but let it here be underscored that Barth
does describe the revelation of God in a way that makes it
inseparable from man's own self-fulfillment and the revelation of himself to himself. Barth preserves the major concern of existentialism at the very heart of his system. He has
clearly stated that one cannot possibly hear and understand
the "speaking and acting Subject" of the Biblical records
unless the hearer himself "consciously participates in covenant history as partner of this covenant," unless the Spirit
himself who spoke to the Biblical people also speaks to their
readers and hearers (3-1, 92 f.). So these poor human words
of the Bible attain material authority as the Word of God
himself as they become the occasion for God himself, in all
the fullness of the creative power in his being as truth and
love, to break through the barriers of our sin, to convert us

to acceptance and obedience toward him, and to impart the power and the guidance of his own life to ours.

Now the question must be reversed: Does not this "subjectivism" run the risk of making our own faith, our human act of acceptance and obedience, to be that which gives authority to the Bible? To those at the theological right of Barth (the verbal dictationists and the historical positivists) it appears that he has completely sold out the objective authority of the Bible, and the radical degree to which he actually does contradict their position will become fully clear only in the next section of this chapter. From the foregoing material it is obvious that Barth does "spiritualize" the event of man's encounter by and with the Word of God. Granted, this encounter is never immediate but always mediate, essentially *in* and *through* the medium of the humanity of Jesus and so necessarily *with* the Biblical testimony to Jesus. Nevertheless, according to Barth, "the Bible *becomes* God's Word in this event, and, in the statement that the Bible *is* God's Word, the tiny word 'is' indicates the Bible's *being* in this *becoming*" (1–1, 124). Faith, therefore, as the responsible act of the human heart and mind and will in accepting God's judgment and forgiveness and new life of obedience, is an integral factor of that event in which the Bible becomes God's Word (4–2, 319).

This faith, however, is not initiated or maintained by man but is wholly the product of the power of the resurrection and of the Holy Spirit. Therefore, Barth sees the requirement of faith in the establishment of the authority of the Bible as the best possible means for safeguarding God's own freedom and sovereignty in his self-revelation (1–2, 534). God has not given himself over to man's control by being boxed up in a book of words and propositions. "As to when, where, and how the Bible establishes itself for us as the Word of God in such an event, we do not decide. Concerning that, the Word of God himself decides!" (1–2, 530.) Barth clearly realizes that the requirement of faith can be twisted to mean that the Bible is the Word of God only because and to the extent that I decide and condescend to believe it. "With this conclusion the divinity of the Word of God is done for." (1–1, 300.) But the alternative is not to try to prove by some objective means that the Bible is in itself the Word of God. Such a view denies the living sovereign nature of God's Word and actually subjects God the Creator to one of his creatures. "The Bible is the opportunity which the revelation of God has created for itself by the appointment of human witnesses. It is offered to us as the possibility which waits to be realized by revelation because it offers itself to be found there. Thus Holy Scripture is *the* source of revelation."[2]

THE AUTHORITY OF THE BIBLICAL DOCUMENTS

It might appear that the question of Biblical authority had been settled in the last section. Actually, we have just begun to approach the more difficult aspects of the problem. We have not yet talked about the Bible as such, the ordinary material book, composed literally of nothing but very human words placed on paper and bound together. What is the Bible's own "being" in the event of its "becoming" the Word of God? What part do these mere human words play in the event of revelation? Does God's own Word and Presence crash through these words with such power that man is delivered from the need of being concerned with their purely human form and meaning? Is one to prop up this book on a stump out in the woods (as did Billy Graham), kneel down before it, and cry out for God to change it from a fallible human book so that every single word in it is magically transubstantiated into God's own literal Word? Does Barth mean this kind of miracle when he says that the "door" of the Biblical words can be opened only from the inside? Certainly many preachers and theological students would whimsically welcome such a miracle in order to be relieved of the burden of learning Greek and Hebrew and of reading difficult books of exegesis.

By no means is such a view subscribed to by Barth. Even his more liberal critics know they go too far in asserting that he completely divests revelation of all human dimensions.[3] In the next section of this chapter we will analyze in detail the role played by human understanding in the establishment of Biblical authority. But first it must be made clear that when Barth says that the event of revelation can take place "only in an act of worship" (4-2, 341), and when he insists on a "Christological" interpretation of all Scriptures, he does not mean to relieve us from the necessity of a full scientific treatment of the Biblical texts. Barth rigorously and consistently derides the theory of verbal dictation. The fact that Christianity is a "book-religion" and preserves the Hebraic concern for the "sentence, word, and letter," the fact that Christian faith says that the Bible "is" the Word of God, "does not mean that the texts of this book are a revelation as such."[4]

Barth is well aware of the difference between, and the need of, both a kerygmatic encounter with the words of the Bible and also an exegetical theological interpretation of them. Faith itself demands a full scientific treatment of these words out of respect for them as God's self-chosen means of revelation.[5] Barth first of all presses with vigor the distinctions among scientific historiography (*Historie*), narrative of human events that points to something deeper than mere objective accuracy (*Geschichte*), and narrative of those human events in which God has been uniquely present in his work for salvation (*Heilsgeschichte*). He believes that the preacher has to wrestle with the fact that the apparently historical accounts in the Bible are not primarily or merely historical records in the scientific sense. Beyond this distinc-

tion he also insists that there are strictly nonhistorical materials in the Bible such as saga, legend, and myth, and that
the whole gamut of literary forms has been used by the authors. He further recognizes that these authors constantly
allied themselves with the current cosmologies and mythologies in their attempt to witness to the unique revelation of
God, just as the church and its thinkers have never hesitated
to use the prevailing language and concepts of their day
(3–2, 7). Barth does not hesitate even to assert that what the
Scriptures offer us is not "a consistently sustained outlook
on the world nor even a uniform theology." In fact, "not a
single verse of the Bible has come down to us with such
absolute certainty and clarity that alternative versions cannot
be suggested."[6]

These complex Biblical materials present complicated
problems of interpretation, and Barth agrees that they cannot
be ignored or circumvented in the name of "listening to
God's Word." Through the Bible, the Word of God comes
to us in conjunction with strictly human words, which because of their ambiguity always require interpretation. The
job of this interpretation is first to determine what meaning these words had for their original author, then to make
these words meaningful for today's reader, and to make
sure that these two meanings coincide. Therefore, all the
members of the church must share in the task of being the
interpreter between the men who speak in the Bible and all
other men, both in the church and in the world. Every
hearer of the Word depends directly or indirectly on this
work of interpretation. In the form of this interpretation
"the Word of God . . . is able to go its way as human word
on its own feet, so to speak," and on this basis "there can
be also a direct relationship and understanding between the
Biblical authors and their present readers" (1–2, 714).

As regards our attitude toward and our use of the Bible,
however, the crucial question is this: What is the relation

between the spiritual reality of revelation itself and this human "understanding" in the form of a human interpretation of some very human words? Does this understanding, made possible with the help of a "scientific" solution to all the complex problems of interpretation, (1) *replace* the revelation that comes in existential encounter, (2) *supplement* it, (3) *formulate* its contents, or (4) *prepare* man for existential encounter? Part of this question we will treat in the next section. But again it might be pertinent to note that here the distinction between Barth and Bultmann tends to be reduced to a matter of emphasis. Bultmann has often been wrongly represented as reducing Christianity to existentialist philosophy concerning man and as denying any knowledge of God. Actually, he clearly makes the distinction between encounter with God and interpretation of it. On the one hand, he notes a "paying simple heed to what the New Testament says—which is directed directly toward an existential understanding of the self"; on the other hand, lies "a scientific interpretation of Scripture" which "takes its orientation from the inquiry into the understanding of human existence which finds expression in the Scriptures."[7] And in discussing the analogical character of theological language, Bultmann makes it clear that in the existential event man is confronted with God in his love and judgment. "We are not only justified in speaking thus, but we must do so, since now we are not speaking of an idea about God, but of God himself. Thus God's love and care, etc., are not images or symbols; these conceptions mean real experiences of God as acting here and now."[8]

Bultmann does not, therefore, reduce or eliminate the reality of the revelatory event. But he wants to ask, How can one hear the Word in the words unless one *understands them*?[9] So he stresses the importance of the preparation that man brings to the Scripture and the self-understanding that he takes away from it. On the other hand Barth's concern

seems to be: how can one understand the Word in the
words unless one *hears Him?* He gives the priority to the
free sovereign act of God in making himself known. This
does not exclude the role of historical exegetical studies and
the play of human understanding, but they are in a sub-
servient position for Barth. "All exegesis," he says, "can lead
only to the threshold beyond which the Scripture as the
Word of God is clear in itself." (1–2, 712.) This clarity is
the power, intrinsic to the Word itself, to be seen and known
by men in a way that transcends all "historical understanding" and "interpretive skill" (1–1, 168; 1–2, 718). The Biblical texts have the authority to demand the service or
"subordination" of all our knowledge for the determination
of the original historical, literary, ideological contents and
context of Scripture (1–2, 715–719). But all this helps us to
grasp revelation only on the presupposition that we have
been grasped by the living Word of God himself.

What, now, does all this mean for the way the preacher
treats the actual documents and texts of the Bible? The consideration of the role played by the preacher's own spiritual
experience under the impact of Scripture, we again leave
aside till the next section. Here we are asking, What is it
that the exegete is looking for as he mounts his "scientific
interpretation of Scripture"? Barth answers this question by
recognizing the existence of a third term or reality between
our purely human presuppositions with which we come to
Scripture and the existential event of encounter with the
living God. Between these two there lies in Scripture a
theological content which claims to be knowledge and truth
about God, man, and their relationship. This content is the
real heart of the Scriptures as human documents and comprises the truly "historical" (*geschichtliche*) meaning that
exegesis and theological interpretation should be seeking.
Scientific studies of the Bible should seek to help in the
preparation of men for the hearing of the gospel, but they

should also be engaged in the search for this content of Scripture as a normative check on our preaching and teaching of the gospel. Let us give one of Barth's examples and then consider just what is the nature and authority of this theological content, or "kerygmatic sense" as he calls it, of Scriptural texts.

One of the best examples, in the whole of the *Dogmatics,* of Barth's exegetical, hermeneutical method and concern is his interpretation of the story of the spies sent out by Moses to scout the Promised Land. (Num., ch. 13; cf. 4–2, 478–483). Barth insists that an adequate interpretation requires us to recognize different elements in this story. There are the purely historical matters of time, places, and persons involved. But there is also "saga," by which Barth means a poetic expression of a vision of the transempirical origins and roots of some concrete historical event (3–1, 81 ff.). So the story is history but something more than history, as indicated by the presence of the giants, the two men carrying the bough of grapes. Finally, we must recognize what Barth calls the "synthetic" factor. That is, the story certainly did not receive its form, as we have it, contemporaneously with the event but perhaps as much later as the Babylonian exile.

These distinctions must be made but then must also be put aside, in order for the story to be read as a whole with the single intent that it has in the text. Reading the whole with such "tested and critical naïveté," one can ask why this story was preserved and given this form and incorporated into the Scriptures. In this way one may arrive at the theological content or "kerygmatic sense" that is the only reason for our interest in the story in the first place. And what is it in this case? Barth sees the heart of this story in its vision of the way in which man is held back, to a terrifying and threatening degree, from moving out of the "wilderness" of his life by himself into the "promised land" of life with God, for which God is working in the saving events of history. And what is it that holds man back? It is his "evil anxiety" before the threatening forces that stand in his way, and this is just the other side of man's basic sin of sloth or inertia (*Trägheit*), man's refusal to trust in the reality and power of God's grace.

Now there, preacher, is a text and a sermon! No preacher could read these pages of Barth's exposition without having at least one and maybe several sermons come to mind. But the point of interest here is that Barth claims to have broken through the fog of historical, textual, literary, and other problems that envelop this text and to have found the true kerygmatic meaning of it to be a statement about sin as sloth. He agrees that these technical problems must be faced and solved but insists that the more we allow them to become normative in the exposition of the text, the more we are in danger of never arriving at the spiritual meaning for which the story has been told and preserved. What, then, is the status of this kerygmatic sense of any text in the Bible? Clearly, Barth regards it as something *more* than an insight gained from the application of certain philosophical ideas and general principles of philology to some ancient Semitic manuscripts. And so does Bultmann. But Barth also regards this theological content of the Bible as something *less* than revelation itself, not identical with the event of encounter and the covenant relation of communion. And so does Bultmann. Barth will have nothing to do with "propositional revelation" or even with theological statement guaranteed by revelation. The fact that Barth calls this meaning of the texts "kerygmatic" indicates that he ties this meaning to the existential encounter with God on the part of both the original author and the most recent reader. After having used and left behind historical, literary, linguistic, philosophical, philological methods and having arrived at the story's inner meaning, one may have taken a step nearer the substantive, material authority of the living Word of God.

THE PREACHER AND THE WORD 183

But still it is a human step, dealing with human words that enclose not the Word of God himself but human formulations of images, stories, events, and ideas, all expressed in analogical language at best, by which these humans point to the occurrence of the speaking and acting of God himself in their lives.

After we have determined the kerygmatic sense, therefore, the question still remains, Why do we accept it as normative? On what grounds do we assume that we have arrived at the truth? We can no longer put off the problem we have been bordering on throughout this section. We must now try to determine more exactly the role played by human understanding itself in the establishment of the authority of the Biblical words as the Word of God, and the establishment of the Biblical meanings as the Truth of God.

The Authority of the Biblical Authors and Readers

We now approach the most difficult question concerning the Christian regard and use of the Bible. In its most radical form, it is this: Does not the authority of these documents in the end reside in the depth and force with which the *authors themselves* grasp the truth, and, in turn, in the depth and force with which the *readers* grasp their truth? Can any man, Biblical or contemporary Christian, actually tell about anything except his own world of humanly experienced and interpreted events, of concepts and images shaped and determined by the limits of peculiarly human existence? This question is the phantom (disease?) that dominates the modern mind. It was posed in inescapable form by Hume's radical empiricism; it was attacked but only intensified by Kant's analysis of the understanding; it was resolved in one way by Hegel's idealism; it was resolved in another way by Schleiermacher's religion; and it was pursued psychologically and theologically in endless refinement by Kierkegaard but with no clear-cut solution. At least it is still with us today and lies at the heart of the dispute between Barth and Bultmann. I personally believe that these two men are so close together on the issue that it is no longer helpful for Barth to accuse Bultmann of reducing all theology to "statements about the inner life of man," or for Bultmann to accuse Barth of using Scripture simply as "a compendium of dogmatic pronouncements" about God on the basis of which he makes "arbitrary assertions."[10]

Let us see what is at issue in this dispute by first of all asking how far Barth recognizes that, behind the admittedly human words of the Bible, the Word of God was first of all grasped and clothed in human *understanding,* in human concepts, ideas, images, feelings. And does he also admit that this understanding of the Word is inextricably interwoven with a new *self*-understanding? And does he see that both arose in the midst of historical (i.e., human) events within the conditions and limitations of human existence? There is no doubt that he does. A long list of relevant passages could be marshaled but just a few will do. "The Bible," he says, "was written by men in the language of men, at a definite time in human history and in a definite human situation. It follows that, in our search for an absolute, unconditional, supreme source of divine revelation we inevitably come up against the fact of the human relativity and limitations of the authors of the Bible. . . . They were human beings who lived and thought and spoke within the modes of thinking and feeling, the knowledge of nature and history and the intellectual tendencies of their age." Therefore, "the real question which the Bible presents and will always present is twofold: (1) How *do* these men speak with authority? and (2) Assuming they do speak with authority, how do we establish contact with them?"[11] Barth further notes that the record which the disciples of Jesus produced concerning him was completely impregnated with their faith-knowledge of him by the Holy Spirit. So "the

voice and the form of Jesus is in no way to be surely distinguished in the Gospels from the community founded by
him and participating in his life." (4–1, 320.)

Our questions are answered even more clearly when Barth
shows how the reader and interpreter of the Bible is subjectively involved in the act of "making contact" with the
authors of the Bible. For him, not only is God's living Word
veiled in the human words of the Bible, not even the Biblical *authors'* understanding of that Word lies on the surface
of the Bible, nor is it to be abstracted by some strictly scientific methods of critical interpretation. In addition to the
latter, there must be added the human act of "reflection,"
that is, a meditation upon what is said by which one enters
into the thoughts of another. By this meditation, while one
exegetes, there occurs that "moment of the passage of that
which is declared in Scripture into the thinking of the
reader or hearer of Scripture." No one can really see and
tell what is there in a purely objective manner. We are not
called on to make the *sacrificium intellectus* and accept the
Bible as brute fact of revelation. "How could we understand the text objectively without participating in it subjectively, that is, with our thinking?" (1–2, 727.)

And with what do we think and meditate? With some
supernatural gift of insight especially provided by God for
the occasion, devoid of human and historical viewpoints and
limitations? Certainly not! For Barth, every reader of the
Bible, from the most naïve beginner to the most sophis-
ticated scholar, thinks and interprets "with a specific espis-
temology, logic, and ethics, with specific ideas and ideals
concerning the relationship of God, world, and man. . . . We
could not read the Bible at all without such modes of explanation, without such spectacles" (1–2, 728). But Barth
does insist that we: (1) be conscious of what we are doing,
(2) use such systems only as hypotheses, (3) not allow the
system to be an end in itself and so let it control or become

identical with Scripture, (4) realize that one system is preferable only relative to the situation, and (5) allow the system finally to be controlled and corrected by the object within Scripture (1–2, 730–736). And this whole process calls into play the human capacities for "imagination" and "divination," and the results are best expressed in the perspective and speech of poetry (3–1, 80 ff.; 3–3, 373 ff.).

How far apart really are Barth and Bultmann at this point? In his essay "The Problem of Hermeneutics,"[12] Bultmann states his basic principle in this way: "The presupposition of every comprehending interpretation is *a previous living relationship to the subject,* which directly or indirectly finds expression in the text and which guides the direction of the inquiry. . . . Every interpretation is sustained by a certain *prior understanding* of the subject which lies under discussion" (p. 252). This prior understanding of the subject of the Bible (God) may be "in the form of the inquiry about happiness, salvation, the meaning of the world and of history, and in the inquiry into the real nature of each person's particular 'being' " (p. 257). But whatever its form, this prior understanding must somehow conform with "the intention of the answer in the New Testament" or otherwise the New Testament answer cannot be understood (p. 258). Thus a scientific interpretation of Scripture has to be aware of those concepts in which contemporary man understands his own existence and which are relevant to the Biblical message. The interpreter of the Bible must seek to speak in terms of these relevant concepts "if he wishes to make Scripture itself speak as a power which has something to say to the present, to present-day existence" (pp. 258 f.).

Barth clearly does not deny the operation of this "prior understanding" in the act of Biblical interpretation, but Bultmann accuses him of not using it seriously, sympathetically, and systematically. Bultmann agrees that "the inquiry directed at the New Testament must be prepared for a correction of the notion it brings with it in hearing what the New Testament has to say" (p. 258). But Barth accuses him not of allowing this correction to take place as radically as it must. "To wish to allow equal validity to both the witness of the Bible . . . and the autonomy of our intellectual life—that is an impossible hermeneutical program." (1–2, 721.) It seems to me, however, that Barth struggles with the problem of human interpretation and communication in his actual exegesis a lot more than his critics give him credit for. And it also seems to me that Bultmann takes the uniqueness and initiative of God's self-revelation in Jesus Christ a lot more seriously than Barth will allow. Before the real middle ground, on which both of these men stand, can be delineated, each side will have to listen to the other. A Barthian will have to be more explicit about the most relevant concepts with which to approach the Bible today and about the problems of imaginative and poetic interpretation. And a Bultmannian will have to lay to rest convincingly Barth's charge that Bultmann (*et al.*) sees Christian faith simply as the continuation and repetition in me of the same event as occurred in Jesus Christ (4–1, 767 f.; 4–2, 55 ff.). A Bultmannian will have to deliver on the master's assurance that existentialist theology can and must talk about "God himself" as well as about man.[13]

The supposed issue between Barth and Bultmann has important and practical implications for every person who undertakes to preach or teach the gospel. Let us try, therefore, to state the major problem without special reference to the accusations hurled by Barth and Bultmann at each other. Only if you have a clear vision of this problem can you safely use the Biblical interpretations, scattered throughout the *Dogmatics,* as a resource for preaching. For clarity of analysis let us first of all agree on certain terms by which to indicate certain factors. These definitions will in part be arbitrary but will help in simplifying the following discussion of the problem.

Encounter is the living, person-to-person relationship that God initiates with man by addressing man with such power and immediacy that man's whole existence is called into question and is made new as man now lives his life before God.

Within this event and relationship there is man's unformed, unconscious, direct *knowing,* the knowing that he is confronted by his Almighty Creator who has right and power over him, the knowing of this Creator's righteous judgment of him as sinner, the knowing of this Creator's acceptance of him into the communion of love, and also the knowing of man's own self-fulfillment and self-realization.

The man who "knows" in the immediacy of concrete event and relationship is also involved in *reflection,* which is that rather indefinable activity we call "thinking," as distinct from the immediate, intuitive knowing in the event. In knowing, man is grasped and transformed by the sheer power and reality of the other, and his response consists simply in his willingness and gladness to be so grasped and transformed. In reflection man makes his properly active response in his attempt to grasp the reality and the character of the event of encounter. Reflection is not something foreign or inimical to the encounter. Rather, the encounter seeks and demands to be "thought," because only so does the whole man respond and so fulfill the mutuality of love. Therefore, reflection is always called forth by encounter and operates so as to enrich the knowing in encounter because reflection increases man's willingness and gladness to be grasped and transformed and therefore leads to his being more deeply and more pervasively grasped and transformed. The modes of reflection are various but inseparable—sense image, symbolic picture, value judgment, generalized concept, metaphorical sign, analogical description, etc., with words being used but not exclusively.

For the task of reflection man uses a certain set of tools that we will call his *presuppositions*. He brings to his reflection about the encounter a set of images, symbols, values, concepts, analogies, and words that he already had before the encounter. There is not a single image, idea, or word in the Bible that was not previously in use in some pagan context. God's revelation does not provide man with a new language. Nor does encounter destroy the basic capacities of man as man, that distinguish him from other creatures. God's encounter with man claims and uses the language and capacities of man as God's own creation that he gave man in creation in order that man might be able to "grasp" and therefore respond to his being grasped by God in encounter. But the knowing of God and of one's self, that comes in the encounter, gives to man's images, ideas, and words a new and unique content, which man on his own can never discover or possess. Therefore man's true humanity, as his "covenant capacity" (Barth), can never attain its realization on its own apart from encounter.

The result of reflection by means of presuppositions is *awareness,* which is a form of understanding in which the knowing of encounter is brought to explicit consciousness. Herein, immediate unformed knowing has yielded itself to being formed in the shapes of man's presuppositions. Now man is consciously aware that he is judged, forgiven, loved, and loving in return. This awareness is one step removed from the living reality of the relationship of encounter with its immediate knowing. Yet it has not yet become something objectified and abstracted from that relationship but is still rooted in it and is a direct mirroring of it. This concrete formation of the reality of encounter, in the worldly presuppositions of man's reflection and awareness, gives to that encounter a definiteness and a duration that is very im-

portant for the life of faith. The warm glow and the self-
evident knowing of immediate encounter with God or
fellowman is a very fragile, fleeting, and intermittent thing
for most of us. The awareness of this knowing in the forms
of our reflection is something we can recall and hold onto,
even though we know that the living God is our only rock
and resource for life.

Man goes one step farther in giving definiteness and duration to the knowing of encounter. He engages in the
verbalization of his awareness. Here I mean the spoken and
written word. To reflect by means of words in silent inward
meditation is one thing. Words there are just one form of
thinking all mixed up with others without too much control. When we try to capture our knowing and reflective
awareness in the mesh of overt verbalization, all sorts of new
rules and restrictions come into play. At the same time
there is a gain in greater definiteness and clarity. How often
we have thought that we were clear in our own minds on a
subject until we have had to express it in words! On the
other hand, verbalization is fraught with fearful dangers.
We seek clarity at the cost of truth. We begin to equate
truth with an objectified statement or proposition, rather
than using verbalization for a means of enrichment of the
only living truth of the knowing in encounter.

Verbalization therefore gives rise to the problem of *meaning*. Words, phrases, sentences, and paragraphs are as such
only sounds or scratches on a piece of paper. They do not
actually contain the reality of a knowing event or relationship, nor even its secondary form of thinking awareness.
Words and sentences are only a special kind of sign or symbol whose meaning lies hidden behind them. The way in
which words are put together into phrases and sentences
arises out of the reality that gives them their meaning, and
the words point back to this reality as their meaning. To
say that certain patterns of words are "meaningful" is a

judgment as to their power and accuracy in representing
the reality they are meant to signify.

Usually meaningful verbalization is practiced with the
goal of communication. Therefore, there is the final problem of _understanding_ on the part of the hearer or the reader
of the words. To understand in this sense is to grasp the
meaning of somebody else's words. That is to say, to understand the meaning of the words of another is to share in
the awareness that the other sought to express in those
words. How does this event of understanding take place?
With this question we have not reached the far end of a
process, at a great remove from the event of revelational
encounter with God. Rather, we have come full circle right
back to the heart of that event. God effects the encounter
and the communion of love by "addressing" man, by "speaking" his Word to men. But his Word did not come to men
just in the form of words but in the form of events whose
meanings were verbalized by men. Finally, his Word came
in the form of a single specific human life, Jesus of Nazareth.
Now God addressed man directly, face to face, so to speak,
but through the form of common humanity, so the immediacy of encounter between God and men involved the
use of words, as is true in the encounter between man and
man. And as God addressed men through the life and words
of Jesus, some men understood, others did not. That is to
say, some men shared in Jesus' own _awareness._

At this point, Barth says, a crucial decision has to be
made. Is the awareness that dawns in us as a result of being
addressed with the life and words of Jesus identical with,
and a repetition of, the awareness that was Jesus'? The
denial of this identity and the assertion of the uniqueness
of Jesus' relation with God is, for Barth, the ground of all
true theology. We must see and say that Jesus _is_ the Son of
God, one of God's eternal modes of being now present in
human form. We men only _become_ the adopted sons of God

by our living in and through and with Jesus Christ. Bultmann, it seems to me, agrees on the uniqueness of God's act in Jesus and makes it the permanent ground of all salvation. But he insists that we have no grounds for talking about the inner life and awareness of Jesus, no grounds for defining *how* God was present in Jesus. Rather, what we have in the New Testament is a witness to what God-in-Jesus actually *did* to *men*. Of course, the New Testament authors are talking about God but always about God in his action on and to men. Therefore, our problem of understanding is that of sharing in the awareness of the first generations of Christians not in the awareness of Jesus himself.

We do not have time to argue further the case between Barth and Bultmann, but it does seem to me that there is no insurmountable conflict between them. Perhaps their varying emphases and interests could be put together as follows, as a contribution to our comprehension of the task of preaching.

The disciples of Jesus at least claimed to have come to an understanding of the meaning of Jesus' life, the meaning of the combination of his works and words. Whether or not we have any of the original words of Jesus, it is clear that he never acted to establish a living relationship with men without interpreting and aiding that act by means of words. Yet we must also note that the words attributed to him are not abstract theological propositions which claim to be in themselves the revealed truth. Jesus' language is represented as rooted in the creaturely things and conditions of the common life. Whatever he says about God is in the language of parables and analogies of man and nature, and makes constant reference to the historical events of Israel's past.

If the disciples came to an understanding of the meaning of Jesus' words and works, it seems an inevitable inference that they did share at least partially in Jesus' own awareness concerning his own relationship ("encounter") with

THE PREACHER AND THE WORD

God. But it also is very clear that Jesus' own awareness was not of a metaphysical or structural relationship but of an existential relationship. That is to say, Jesus was aware, with completeness and power, of the presence and impact of God's holiness and love upon the human condition. And insofar as his disciples understood Jesus and shared in his awareness, they too were aware that their lives and persons were in the grip of God in his holiness and love. The qualitative difference between Jesus' and their awareness they confessed by calling him Lord, Savior, Son of God, Word Incarnate. These are not metaphysical definitions but existential descriptions of the meaning of Jesus' life to them.

Much of the debate in the last seventy-five years has centered on whether Jesus understood himself in these terms. Many scholars have answered in the negative. Either this would mean that the Jesus of Christian faith is the creation and fiction of his disciples, which would be more incredible than the proposition that Jesus taught his own deity; or it would mean that the disciples in their awareness of Jesus pierced to aspects of Jesus' own unconscious knowing that never rose to Jesus' own awareness and that therefore were never verbalized by him. This would be an astonishing state of affairs, but it cannot be ruled out as a possibility. I am inclined to agree with a Bultmannian line of thinking here and to suggest that this is a moot issue. It cannot really be decided, and we have no need to decide it. What we have in the New Testament is the kerygma, that is, the confessed faith of the early Christians concerning the appearance of God in their midst in the life of Jesus of Nazareth. And we know this to be true, not on the basis of any amount of empirical evidence or rational argument. Rather, we join in their confession because we have come to an understanding of the meaning of their words and so share in their awareness of that knowing of God and themselves that was imparted to them in their encounter with God in Jesus Christ.

This is a technical long-winded way of saying that God has used their words as his Word in order to establish encounter and communion in love with us.

We can now face the decisive question for the preacher: How do twentieth-century men *come to an understanding* of the Biblical words so as to share in the first Christians' awareness of the knowing encounter with God in Jesus Christ? And what is the role of preaching in that event? We are agreed (1) that the Biblical authors verbalized their own awareness in the terms of the language, concepts, images, analogies, philosophies, religions, and mythologies current in their own times and inherited from their own cultures. We are agreed (2) that the verbalization in these forms is adequate to the subject to be expressed (revelation in encounter) because God's Word is correlative with man's God-given, indestructible covenant-capacity, which makes him restless till he finds his rest in God. On the other hand, (3) this verbalization is inadequate to the subject because human longing for God cannot supply its own fulfillment and in its sinfulness has attached itself to idols. We are agreed, therefore, (4) that contemporary man's encounter with the living God is not the guaranteed conclusion at the end of an unbroken process of careful, scientific explanation of the meaning of the Biblical authors' words, awareness, and basic knowing. Nor is it guaranteed by a kerygmatic preaching or an apologetic teaching of the Biblical words. A modern pagan may come with his own presuppositions and interpret the Bible in their terms and feel he understands the Bible. But in order for him to understand these words for what they meant to their authors, these words must become the unpredictable and uncontrollable occasion of his own existential encounter with the judgment and forgiveness of the living God. For the pagan, therefore, his understanding of the words of the Bible and his encounter with the Word of God are not two events, one preceding and producing the other, but are simultaneous or coincidental. Likewise, the Christian's perennial attempt to "understand" the meaning of some specific text is doomed to failure unless carried on in the conscious context of his faith-relation with God in Jesus Christ; that is to say, unless carried on in the light of his constant struggle to bring his own continuing paganism under the sovereignty of God's righteousness and love. Finally, we are agreed (5) that the encounter, God's Word using men's words, is not just sheer miracle that violates and overrules his own creation. Jesus was his own first preacher, interpreter, and apologist for the Word who he was. He struggled mightily with this task within the limitations of his immediate hearers.

This task and this struggle has been passed on to each generation of his disciples. And as the gospel has moved out of its original Jewish setting and across the centuries of change and into totally new cultures, the problems of preaching and interpreting have increased in complexity and difficulty. The twentieth-century preacher of the gospel is often hard put to uncover the existential meaning for himself of certain passages in the Biblical confession of the first Christians. It is so buried as to be almost lost in the obscurity of ancient language, customs, thought forms, images, and analogies. But it is a still more difficult thing when this well-trained preacher seeks to interpret some human word as the Word of God for the people in the pew who are often more pagan than Christian but who do not want their paganism disturbed by their Christianity.

Yet there will be no encounter with the living God by modern man without the full use of every critical, historical, literary, lexicographical, philological tool at our disposal. This means that the preacher and teacher of the gospel must be equally familiar with the "presuppositions" in terms of which the first Christians confessed their encounter with God in Christ, and with the "presuppositions" with which modern man comes to listen and to receive that changeless gospel of God's love. On this point I can see no conflict between Barth and Bultmann. Again it must be added that Christian exegesis and understanding of the Bible requires the operation of faith, that is, the operation of the existential problem and relation with God. For example, when Paul solves the enigma concerning the image of God in Gen. 1:26 f. by the daring direct equation of the man Jesus with the divine image (II Cor. 4:4; Col. 1:15), Barth asserts that the decision as to the validity of this connection "is not an exegetical question. It was then and it is for all times to be answered only in the form of faith or unbelief, only through proclamation or denial" (3–1, 202). Nevertheless, let the users of Barth's *Dogmatics* take warning: if you try simply to appropriate the theological fruits of his labors without checking them against both your own exegesis and our contemporary forms of Christian faith and understanding, those fruits will be reduced to a dead and sterile dogmatism, impotent to speak and to save. Even worse, if you attempt on your own to deduce further such theology from the Bible by some simple "faith-exegesis," then you will be breaking the basic rules and methods of Barth himself and will be led into all sorts of weird and fantastic notions that have nothing to do with the Word of God.

Barth himself has been accused of suggesting weird interpretations on the basis of inadequate exegesis. This has been especially true of his Christological interpretation of the Old Testament. Perhaps the most severe test case is his exposition of Lev. 14:1–7 and 16:1–22 as "prophecies of Jesus Christ, pictures and stories which have in him their meaning and fulfillment" (2–2, 364). Barth argues that the "meaning" of these passages can be "understood" only when we are "aware" that God is here speaking to us about the nature and purpose of his election. And since we Christians know God's election as fulfilled in Jesus Christ, we must read these passages as speaking of him and not just about the cleansing of a leper and a ritual for the Day of Atonement. Barth insists that this is not only proper but necessary because the mystery of election was the actual topic and meaning that the original authors had in mind. Otherwise, he argues, we would have to conclude that the subject of this Old Testament witness is an unknown quantity, or even worse, that there is no subject at all. He challenges others to find a better interpretation or to admit that they do not understand them at all (2–2, 363, 366).

The point here is this, that Barth's Christological interpretation is not at the expense of scientific exegesis. He does insist that we move behind it and ask what was the theological meaning of the authors, and ask how this meaning is enlightened and deepened by our own Christian revelation of the same God who was dealing with the Israelites. And neither of these questions can be answered without our own existential faith-involvement in the theological issue. Barth certainly allows for difference of opinion, but he would think it irresponsible for a commentator to see "religious continuity of idea and experience" between our Christian sacraments and the sacrifice of the birds in Lev., ch. 14, but then understand the scapegoat of Lev., ch. 16, as a concession to "crude and superstitious beliefs" (*The Interpreter's Bible*).

So we conclude our survey of some of the problems that face the preacher as he attempts to proclaim the Word of God. The point of this rather extended discussion is to surround your reading and use of Barth's Biblical interpretations with all kinds of questions and reservations. This is not in order to discourage you from being stimulated by them, but in order that you may not be hypnotized by them. As we have seen, Barth recognizes fully the human and therefore fallible character of the words, the presuppositions, and even the theology of the Bible. But one never finds him admitting a specific case of fallibility and so struggling with the problem of correcting one statement in the Bible by means of a normative theme of the Bible. Therefore, his expositions usually give the impression that he has infallibly discovered the infallible theological meaning of the text under consideration. And it might even appear that he identifies revelation with the Bible's theological meaning and, indirectly, with his exposition of it. As we have seen, nothing could be further from the truth of Barth's real views on these matters.

Barth wants and insists on full range for critical debate on both exegetical and theological problems in Biblical exposition. But even more he sees the crucial importance of going behind this debate to an existential encounter with the living Word, and a going beyond this debate to an obedient proclamation of the gospel that may serve as God's occasion for encountering other men. It is not his task as a dogmatic (systematic) theologian to give all the pros and cons of the debate on every passage. Nor is it his task to canvass all the questionable passages or themes or ideas in the Bible. Rather, he sees his task as the verbalization, in contemporary language, of the theological meanings of those themes of the Bible which will serve as the best check and stimulus for contemporary preaching and teaching of the gospel.

With this orientation, let us now look at a few of Barth's expositions on his leading theological themes in order to see how suggestive they may be for our own preaching of the gospel in America.

Chapter VII

Preaching: Jesus Christ

THIS and the following chapters have but one purpose:
to give you a few specific examples of Barth's Biblical
interpretation in the *Dogmatics*. The topics under which I
have arranged them are more or less arbitrary, being a few
of the major theological themes of the *Dogmatics*. Actually,
his exposition under one topic will often give you ideas for
a sermon on another. The examples also have been chosen
almost at random from a host of possibilities. I believe you
will find them quite typical. And of course each reader is
struck by different expositions as being particularly enlightening and relevant. So do not pay too much attention to the
types of examples I have chosen, or to the topics under
which I have put them. These are mainly a matter of con-
venience. But be alert as to how Barth's exposition of a
specific text would stimulate and affect your own preaching
on that text. As pointed out in an earlier chapter, I realize
that you do not always start the preparation of a sermon
from a text. Sometimes you start with a felt need or a serious
problem to which you wish to minister the gospel. Or you
start with some luminous truth that has been gained in
Christian experience, and you wish to have others share in
it. But sooner or later a Christian preacher will subject every
need and every truth to the criterion and enlightenment of
some Biblical theme or text. When you arrive at this point,

I suggest that you turn to Barth's exposition of the text to see what help he offers.

The content of all preaching for Barth must finally come to rest in Jesus Christ. Son of God who has become Son of Man embraces and fulfills every aspect of divine and human life that is proper subject matter for preaching. As we have seen, this is not a reductive or restrictive notion for Barth because "Jesus Christ" is equated with "the humanity of God," that is, with all of God's ways and works with men from eternity to eternity. He is God as God lives with man, for man, and in man. This means that you will find texts scattered throughout the *Dogmatics* from which Barth preaches Jesus Christ. Nevertheless, our central and normative knowledge of Jesus Christ comes from encounter with the one who lived and died and rose again as Jesus of Nazareth. It is therefore from Barth's volumes on reconciliation that we will take most of our examples for the preaching of Jesus Christ. It is only from the central event of God's reconciliation of the world to himself in Jesus Christ that we can also preach what we want to preach about the beginning and the end of God's way with man.

Reconciliation in Jesus Christ. How are you to preach this? One more comment introductory to Barth's treatment of this theme must be made for the English reader of the *Dogmatics*. The German word for "reconciliation" is *Versöhnung*. The dominant if not exclusive connotation of this word in German is that of the *reunion* of two alienated parties. It does not have at all the ring of the English word "atonement," especially as this latter word had become almost synonymous with the concept of penal satisfaction. When German theology wants to speak of satisfaction, it uses such words as *Sühne* or *Genugtuung*. At least this is true of Barth. Therefore, the translator of Vol. IV of the *Dogmatics* has done Barth a signal disservice and has hopelessly confused most English readers by regularly trans-

lating *Versöhnung* as "atonement." In the Preface (4–1, vii)
he says he has alternated the two English words according
to the demands of the context. This simply is not so. He has
regularly used "atonement" whenever possible, using "reconciliation" only when "atonement" makes no sense at all.

The point is that by using "atonement" he is changing
the sense that Barth himself intended. Barth clearly defines
Versöhnung as the restoration of *fellowship* (4–1, 22).
Therefore, if you are to read these three volumes with their
intended meaning, simply cross out "atonement" every time
you find it in the English translation, and substitute "reconciliation." "Jesus Christ is the reconciliation," not the "atonement" (4–1, 34). Reconciliation in Jesus Christ involves
suffering, but it is not correct to say that reconciliation *is*
the suffering. It is not valid even to say that it is the suffering *as such* that accomplishes reconciliation. A further in-
jection of this fundamentalist theory of atonement as penal
satisfaction into Barth's writings may be seen in the translation of the lead statement of Paragraph 59 (4–1, 157).
Here *"die vollbrachte Rechtstat"* is translated "a satisfaction." If Barth had meant "satisfaction," he would have used
Sühnung, or *Genugtuung,* or *Bezahlung.* He is speaking of
the completed justification of *man,* not the satisfaction of
God. Such twisting of Barth's meaning is inexcusable.
Barth's whole doctrine of reconciliation is clearly opposed
to that of penal satisfaction, and to use the English terminology, accepted in the description of the latter, is to misrepresent Barth in a drastic manner.

Let us first of all see how Barth handles this subject in
his exposition of the two "classic" passages of the New
Testament, John 3:16, and II Cor. 5:19 (4–1, 70–78). We
cannot repeat his whole treatment, but here are a few of
his major points.

On John 3:16

(1) "loved" points not to a static condition or attitude

of God but to a history, the story of an event, which
happened on earth, which men saw and heard and
touched.

(2) "the world" is man's world in its antagonism to
God, in its "darkness" not understanding God
(John 1:5), but which God still loves because it is
his creation and possession, even though it no
longer deserves to be loved.

(3) "so loved . . . that he gave": God loved this dark-
ened world of man *so much* that he *gave himself*
over to subjection to the forces of darkness, risking
his own existence, because he could not leave man
to continue in enmity toward himself.

(4) "that . . . shall not perish": the purpose and goal
of God's loving self-giving is not death and destruction, under which judgment man already
exists, but the conquest of this death, the refusal of
God to acquiesce to man's perishing.

(5) "whoever believes": believing is the act of man but
not of man on his own as sinful creature. The believing man is the man who is under the impact
of God's loving. Believing does not mean that this
man is any better in himself. Therefore he signalizes
what God has in store for the whole "world" that
he loves.

On II Cor. 5:19

(1) "God was . . . reconciling": the initiative for and
accomplishment of reconciliation is wholly from
the divine side. God reconciles, man is reconciled.
Reconciliation is God's act of "converting" man,
turning man away from himself and toward God.
It is man who actively turns but under the impact
of God's love "poured into our hearts through the
Holy Spirit" (Rom. 5:5).

(2) "in Christ": reconciliation is not accomplished at

long distance by legal fiat, with God remaining holy in heaven and man remaining sinful in the world. The heart of reconciliation is an "exchange," a "change of places," between God and man, accomplished in the unity of the life of Jesus Christ. God humbles himself to live with man in his sin so that man may be exalted to live with God in his righteousness (II Cor. 5:21). (Here again the translator radically misrepresents Barth by translating *Platzwechsel* with the theologically biased word "substitution," instead of using the only possible meaning of "change of places" [4-1, 75]. Barth's whole doctrine of reconciliation is built on this concept of an "exchange" [*Tausch*] or "change of places." Volume IV, Part 1, is the story of God's self-humiliation in assuming sinful flesh in Jesus Christ. Volume IV, Part 2, is the story of man's exaltation to righteousness in Jesus Christ. It is a two-way exchange, not a unilateral substitution.)

(3) "not counting their trespasses" is the negative way of saying "become the righteousness of God," which really means to become the covenant-partners of God (this rules out the ideas of penal satisfaction and forensic imputation).

(4) "entrusting to us the message of reconciliation": Paul, and therefore the church, do not themselves accomplish reconciliation. They are the ministers, or servants, or agents, of a reconciliation already accomplished in Jesus Christ and livingly present to men of all ages through the ministry of believers.

These, then, are some of the major points that Barth makes in a straightforward exposition of two Biblical texts. How do you, the preacher, use them? Let us remember that such exposition is an attempt to get behind the actual words of the text of Scripture to the *meaning* in the thinking awareness of the author. This meaning is something more than the literal words; it is something less than the knowing of immediate encounter. And preaching is both something more and something less than "telling the meaning" of a Scriptural text. Preaching is less because a meaning cannot be "told" in so many unequivocal words. This is true of all words, whether the words of Scripture, of Barth's exposition, or of your sermon. A meaning can only be *pointed* to by the externalized words of the speaker, and his meaning must be *caught* by the thinking, understanding, and awareness of the hearer. So Barth's exposition cannot *give* you the meaning of Scripture directly, any more than can the words of Scripture itself give you the meaning of their original author. So you must struggle with both the Bible's words and Barth's words and try to catch their meaning. And your understanding of their meaning is achieved by calling into play your own awareness of your own prior existential involvement in this world and its sin, and also your own existential encounter with God in Christ. Therefore, when you go to preach, you realize you can no more tell and give that meaning than could Barth or the Bible. Your preaching can only be a pointing to that meaning. And since it is *your* pointing to the meaning as caught by *your* understanding, your sermon must not be a simple repetition of what you read in Barth. Barth's exposition is to be used only when it is "meaningful," i.e., when it stimulates your own understanding to deeper insight into your own involvement with the world and encounter with God.

Your preaching is also something *more* than the attempt to tell a meaning by pointing to it. You preach with a promise and a hope that something more will happen than the communication of meanings that are the creations of human thinking. You preach with the promise and the hope that God himself will become a third party in this conversation between a speaker and his hearers. "For where two or three are gathered in my name, there am I in the midst of them." (Matt. 18:20.) The great promise is that words spoken in Christ's name may be taken up by him and used to instigate a conversation between the hearer and his God. The great burden of preaching is, therefore, to supply the greatest possible wealth and depth of meaning and relevance to the words of a Biblical text or theme, and yet not to so fix and harden that meaning as to pretend to be accomplishing the event of revelation itself. Preaching must make full use of every critical, exegetical, and theological tool, and yet must leave room and freedom for God himself to take over with the mystery of his own sovereign presence and power to encounter men with his own holy love.

Therefore, I cannot tell you, a specific individual preacher, how to use Barth's exposition of John 3:16 and II Cor. 5:19 to compose a sermon. But one more question remains. Points similar to those I listed can be found in this or that commentary. Why not read them? Certainly, read them. But reading these points in the *Dogmatics* has one distinct advantage. For example, Barth says reconciliation is the fulfillment of man's God-given capacity to become God's covenant-partner. But what does it mean to be God's covenant-partner? And what are the obstacles in the way that are removed by Jesus Christ? In the *Dogmatics* you find this interpretation of a certain text in the midst of a broad discussion of these very questions. And you find leads to even more detailed discussion in other volumes. For example, the new life that Christian faith has to offer man must not be proclaimed or explained apart from a realistic recognition of the man to whom it is offered, so-called "natural" man. The covenant fellowship offered in Christ is based on the nature of man as creature of God. So Barth gives a broad groundwork for the gospel in his treatment of such topics as "The Phenomena of the Human" and "Real Man" (3–2). Barth's Biblical expositions are not isolated comments dic-

tated by the primary interest of writing a scientific commentary, which often leaves the preacher with more questions than answers. Barth's interpretations are part of the
warp and woof of his entire theological system.

Another example: one of Barth's primary theological con-
tentions is that the real obstacles that prevent man from
achieving his destiny as child of God can be truly known
only by the man who encounters God in reconciliation in
Jesus Christ. So Barth's doctrine of sin is not to be found
under his doctrine of man in Vol. III but under reconciliation in Christ in Vol. IV. The preaching of sin, therefore, is
to be done only in the context of the preaching of God's
love and mercy in Jesus Christ. Let us see very briefly how
Barth lays the exegetical-theological grounds for this position, as another example of his provision of material for the
preaching of Christ.

Barth has a long theological section on this subject entitled "The Man of Sin in the Mirror of the Obedience of
the Son of God" (4–1, 358 ff.). In the middle of it he lists
a large number of Biblical passages that support his thesis,
especially those in The Gospel According to John which
specifically say that without Christ there is no sin, and the
rejection of Christ is death in sin (chs. 15:22, 24; 16:8–9;
3:18; 8:24; 12:48). Then Barth gives a lengthy exposition of
Rom. 1:18 to 3:20 (4–1, 392–396). Again we can give here
only a few of his many and diverse points. His basic thesis
is that in this whole passage Paul ties gospel and law in-
separably together. Gospel contains within it the judgment
that man is in the wrong. The law condemns and reveals
man's sin, as an act of God's love and mercy. So Barth
understands the revelation of God's wrath (Rom. 1:18) to
follow and to depend upon the revelation of God's righteousness by faith (ch. 1:17). So all human boasting is excluded
not by "the law of works" but by the "law of faith"
(ch. 3:27). And this law of faith has confronted all men

objectively in both nature and history (ch. 1:19–20). Therefore there is no abstract law that precedes the gospel and which condemns us so as to disclose our sin to us. Sin is not the breaking of rules or ideals. It is sin that sets up ideals in the place of God. So rules or ideals cannot breed a true sense of sin but only encounter with God in his mercy can do so. But mercy says that one needs mercy because he is in the wrong. So those whose inward heart and spirit are judged by Jesus Christ even now do the works of the law without possessing or using the Jewish law (ch. 2:14 f., 26 ff.).

Again, the real richness of these ideas and their relevance for contemporary preaching are brought out in the theological discussion in the whole section that serves as a context for this Biblical exposition. Here Barth explains that sin is something different from the antithesis of light and dark that runs throughout creation. He defines what he means by saying that sin is really an "impossibility." He shows how Jesus' own life of suffering and death "in our place" was necessary that sin in mankind might be judged and vanquished. Only in the light of God's love in Christ can we say that God hates the sin but (nevertheless!) loves the sinner. This is the miracle of grace. Perhaps this theme of Christian faith needs to be preached more than any other in the American situation. We have a long tradition of hellfire preaching that maintains that we must first convince men of their sin and damnation *before* we ever mention the grace and mercy of God. This is a form of legalism, which has its concomitant in the popular American conception of righteousness as the following of rules and the doing of good. The real tragedy of the American "self-made man" ideal will never be uncovered until we are made to see the real depth of our degradation as something against God, as lying in our very determination to follow the law *on our own* without God's mercy and gracious empowering.

And Barth gives us a profound analysis of the complex dimensions of man's failure and tragedy under the headings of pride and fall (4–1), sloth and misery (4–2), falsehood and damnation (4–3).

In concluding this chapter let me only briefly note a few of the other topics Barth treats that may serve as a foundation for preaching Jesus Christ.

2. When you preach the resurrection do you preach the Holy Spirit? Barth insists that you should. Holy Spirit is none other than Jesus Christ present in the power of his resurrection, and this in turn is his power of self-revelation. Before you preach or teach again on either of these dimensions of Christian faith and life, I suggest you read Barth's extended treatment of these themes in their relation to one another (4–2, 141–154, 302–319). While carefully maintaining and explicating the "historical" character of the resurrection event, his main emphasis falls on the fact that the "resurrection" takes its really meaningful form in the coming of a Christian to a new self-understanding (4–2, 307, 316 ff.). The reality of Jesus Christ's resurrection assumes for us the character of light, of liberation, of knowledge, of peace (4–2, 310–315). The presence and work of Holy Spirit means that our life is guided by the living Son of God. This guidance takes the form of setting us in a definite place with definite tasks, of placing us under warning and correction, or revealing a specific and concrete will of God (4–2, 363–377). I personally do not see how Barth could be more "existential" in his exposition. And in this connection you should also read his words on the "empty tomb" (3–2, 452 f.).

3. How do you preach the miracles? Or do you avoid them? I am willing to wager that if you read Barth's treatment of the whole phenomenon (4–2, 212–247), you will be eager to take up these Biblical accounts in your preaching and teaching. And this is important to do in this day of renewed and often morbid interest in so-called "faith healing." Barth

says quite bluntly that every account of a "miracle" by Jesus has a symbolic value and meaning, whatever might be its concrete substance. And it is in their symbolic or parabolic meaning that they are of importance in the life of the church (4–2, 218). Their real function was to set the "human situation" into a wholly new light, and it was this inexplicable new understanding that overpowered men and gave to these events their truly "miraculous" character (4–2, 220). What more could any Bultmannian want?

How do you answer the wonderings of people about the *4.* temptations of Jesus and his reputed sinlessness? And how does this help us to understand our own sinfulness? Barth gives a striking interpretation of the wilderness and Gethsemane experiences of Jesus and their relationship (4–1, 258–273). Have you thought of illuminating the story of the prodigal son by seeing it in parallel with the humiliation and exaltation of the Son of God in Jesus (4–2, 21–25)? If you want to preach graphically to the problem of the contemporary rush of man to fill the religious vacuum of our age with all kinds of fake gods, you will find an enlightening exposition concerning the golden calf of Aaron readymade for such a sermon (4–1, 423–432). But man in this depth of degradation is pitied by God, and he comes in mercy. Are all your sermons these days ones of condemnation and moral exhortation? How long has it been since you really preached the gospel, the good news, that God has come in compassion because the people are "harassed and helpless, like sheep without a shepherd" (Matt. 9:36) (4–2, 184–187)? Finally, let me urge you, when Vol. IV, Part 3, is translated, to explore the extended Christological exposition of The Book of Job, which is scattered throughout Barth's treatment of "The Falsehood and Damnation of Man" (¶ 70).

I am being perfectly honest with you when I say that these are but a handful of the numerous exegetical passages and treatments of Biblical themes that are scattered throughout the four big volumes (4–3 is in two parts) in which Barth develops the vast ramifications of God's coming in Jesus Christ to live with us, for us, and in us. You will not agree (I hope) with *all* of the theological positions adopted by Barth in these volumes. Some of them will strike you as abstruse and unnecessary. But I will guarantee that if you regularly check your texts with Barth's expositions of them in these volumes, your preaching of Jesus Christ as Savior will take on new richness and breadth.

Chapter VIII

Preaching: Man Between God and the Demonic

MAN'S bewilderment about man, and his conscious desire to understand himself, is probably more widespread today than at any time in his history. Our novels and plays are no longer crusading pieces on burning social issues but pictures of contemporary man turning inward and asking dumbly, Who and why am I? And unlike the ancient Greek and the Shakespearean dramas, our contemporary ones cannot even be filled with tragedy but only with pathos, because today's artists are aware of no certainties upon which man can be broken and remade. He simply drifts into an even thicker mire of meaninglessness.

In such a day the Christian preacher is faced not only by a frightening task but also by a wide-open door into the very hearts of his hearers. Can he proclaim the Christian faith in a way that gives a resounding answer to the ancient cry, What is man? and in a way that men can hear and understand? Or must men turn to the oracles of Freud and Jung in order to hear words that meet men where they really are? Preachers who are sensitive to the real need in this area, and who dare to face the risks and burdens of entering it, would not normally think of turning to Barth for guidance and help. Rather, they would look in the direction of Bultmann, Tillich, and the new existentialist psychotherapy. Again I suggest that you may discover unexpected stimulus in this regard from the *Dogmatics*. And what you will find will be existential enough to meet men where they are and yet point to the transhuman resource of help in God with such strength that they may be lifted out of their uncertainty and distress.

The first thing the preacher of the gospel must make clear to twentieth-century man is that Christian faith understands him, that is, understands man as he is in himself. Instead of always damning man for what he is and exhorting him to press on to some impossible moral ideal of what he ought to be, the preacher should be able first of all to help every man understand better what he is in himself as the creature made by God. Contrary to general opinion, Barth has a good deal to say about man "as such" throughout the volumes on the doctrine of creation. As we have already noted, he recognizes that there is a mystery or secret determination immanent in man's creaturely existence as such (3–2, 265). It consists of man's native capacity to live in "freedom of the heart for others." Furthermore, this built-in meaning of humanity can be seen, explored, and actualized by men on their own without any knowledge of, or help from, Christian revelation. In fact, sometimes "children of this world" seem to understand this basic humanity better than many Christians (3–2, 276 ff.).

The reality and common knowledge of this essential human capacity should impinge on preaching in several different ways. First, the preacher should resist the temptation to represent non-Christian man as a mere animal or a blackened devil with no good in him. The hearer instinctively knows this is wrong; he knows that men are capable of a kind of love quite apart from the gospel. So he concludes that the preacher is either a fool or a charlatan and so closes his ears to the gospel. Again, the preacher must remember that the clarification and strengthening of basic humanity

is not the unique concern and gift of Christian faith. The
gospel of Jesus Christ offers to men something new and
something more: love from God and love for God. Yet the
successful preaching of the gospel assumes, builds upon, and
corresponds with man's creaturely capacity to love his fellowman. Therefore, Christian faith in general and the preacher
in particular should be keenly interested in all phases of
man's self-knowledge and representation (scientific, philosophical, aesthetic). Being well informed in this field
should not be regarded as a hobby or luxury but as an indispensable part of theological preparation for preaching and
witnessing to the gospel. A knowledge of the picture of man
in contemporary social sciences and the arts is of immense
value. (3–2, 278 f., 200 ff.)

Finally, however, every informed Christian and especially
the preacher should realize that our faith provides us with
a criterion that should enable us to understand basic humanity more profoundly than does the non-Christian. Man's
natural inclination to live gladly with his fellowman is
neither self-explanatory nor self-supporting. It lies there in
the human mind and heart as a fond dream or potentiality.
It is explicated by the philosopher and extolled by the poet
but is actualized only in bits and patches by the human
race. It is so often involved in such failure and degradation
that an occasional voice (Nietzsche) will deride it as a
debilitating delusion. The love and truth of God present in
the manhood of Jesus has revealed the origin and the goal
of this essential human determination to live in love with
fellowman: God's creation of man with the destiny of becoming God's own covenant-partner, the children of his
own household, the sharers in his own eternal life. So, for
Barth, man's natural inclination toward love of fellowman
and the love of God that is the gift of grace in Jesus Christ
are bound together in direct correlation and interdependence
in God's overarching purpose. Therefore, Christian faith

that knows this has the task also of calling all men, inside and outside the church, to acknowledge their basic, given human determination as made to live with one another gladly.

How to preach this? If you look for Biblical expositions of this theme in Barth's volume on man (3–2), you will find very few. Rather, he limits himself pretty much to a detailed explication of one Biblical theme: the creation of man in the sexual differentiation of male and female. And you will find this exposition scattered throughout the volumes on the doctrine of creation. In his extended treatment of Gen., chs. 1 and 2 (3–1, 94–329), Barth comes to the crucial anthropological text of Gen. 1:26 f., "Let us make man in our image, after our likeness. . . . So God created man in his own image, in the image of God he created him; male and female he created them" (3–1, 181–206). Barth gives helpful expositions of the "let *us*" and of the distinction between "image" and "likeness." But his distinctive and stimulating treatment comes in his development of Bonhoeffer's suggestion that the likeness of man to God lies in man's being created for life with another, and that this nature of his being is posited and established in man's being created in the interrelatedness of male and female. Barth expands the point in his commentary on the story about the addition of female to the male in the second creation story (Gen. 2:18–25) (3–1, 288–306). He further elaborates the centrality of the sexual distinction in the Bible when he finds it used at the heart of the New Testament description of human fulfillment in Jesus and his community (3–2, 291–324). But his fullest statement of the implications of this definition of basic humanity comes in his ethics of creation. In his description of the good life as "Freedom and Fellowship," he opens up with a long section on "Man and Woman," in which he treats all the problems of sex and marriage (3–4, 116–240).

I will not try to summarize even the major points of
Barth's exposition and theology on this theme. But if you
will read through these various passages, you will find a
profound, practical, and moving analysis of man as he is
and as he finds himself as a creature among the other
creatures of this world. And you will find the exposition
grounded at every point in specifically Biblical theology and
on Biblical texts that you can preach. And you will find this
interpretation given in direct confrontation with contemporary scientific and secular thought (e.g., his commentary
on Simone de Beauvoir's *The Second Sex,* 3–4, 161 ff.).
Barth, of course, does not mean that to be sexual is to be
human. Animals and plants are also sexual. But sexuality
means something more for men because it is the basic and
inescapable drive that leads man to the discovery that he is
made to live gladly with others. If you can really understand
this structure of human existence in its depth and rich detail, and if you can preach it as the creation and will of the
Word of God, then you will indeed be encountering men
with the Word where they really live. Social sciences and
the arts are agreed that contemporary man is characterized
in two ways, by an overwhelming and pervasive sense of
estrangement and loneliness, and by a perverted absorption
with sex. Sex is by no means the only area in which men
are faced with the challenge to become truly human (as we
will see in the next chapter on ethics), but it is the basic
and most universal one. One does not become truly human
by trying to deny, or to ignore, or to transcend sex. The
pulpit has too long been prudishly silent on the basic issue
of human nature concerning which the Bible is quite frank
and voluble.

In pursuing this subject in the passages in the *Dogmatics*
mentioned above, you will find many related texts of the
Bible treated. You will also find other essential anthropological themes dealt with. How is man to understand his rela-

tion to the vegetable and animal kingdoms (3–1, 207–213)?
Also, Barth gives a very enlightening treatment of the difficult problem of human freedom in his interpretation of the
Garden of Eden and the meaning of its two trees (3–1, 249–
288). He also holds out for the meaning of love and marriage as something prior and more basic than the concern for
reproduction of the race, and here he appeals to the Song
of Songs and Hosea (3–1, 312–318). The question as to how
the Christian, with all his faith and revelation, can face up
to the problem of suffering as under God's providence is
directly attacked in connection with such texts as I Peter
1:6; Matt. 6:26 f.; Eph. 1:11; and Rom. 8:28 (3–3, 39 ff.).

Nevertheless, all of these aspects of human existence, and
many others, are regarded by Barth as no more than pointers
to or signs of an entirely different level of human capacity
and destiny. Man's natural inclination to seek a relationship
of love with another does not find its total satisfaction in
the fellowship of other men. And man's strange and enigmatic freedom does not find its fulfillment in his own self-
assertion or in his conquest of nature. Man's capacities for
freedom and love are gifts from God and find their ultimate
meaning in life with God. So in his sections on "Jesus, Man
for God," "Real Man," "Jesus, Man for Other Men" and
"Humanity as Likeness and Hope" (3–2), Barth pushes on
to the unqualified assertion that Christian preaching about
man must finally center in the preaching of Jesus Christ.
That is to say, you the preacher must help men find their
true selves in the humanity of Jesus. And this is true because
in him, for the first and only time in human history, do we
find human existence fully realized as a perfect living in
freedom and love "before God," and thereby also a perfect
living in freedom and love with fellowman. And, as the
whole previous chapter should have made clear, Christian
faith does not consist in a simple imitation and repetition
of what Jesus did but rather consists of the finding of a re-

flection of Jesus' true humanity in our own lives by means of our looking to the living resurrected Christ as our Lord who forgives, renews, and guides us on our way by his Spirit. In the sections referred to above you will find Barth laying his Scriptural foundation with expositions of John's Gospel and such Pauline passages as II Cor. 11:2 ff.; Rom. 7:1–6; I Cor. 6:12–20; 11:1–16; and Eph. 5:22–33. So, while the Christian preacher has today an unparalleled opening with modern man by helping him to understand his own creaturely existence and capacities, yet it is also clear that as preachers of the gospel we have fallen short of our calling until we have helped men finally to view themselves "before God" in Jesus Christ. With deep perception Barth has said that a man begins to be a Christian just at the point where he begins to draw the inferences and implications of the fact that he now sees his own true self there in the humanity of Jesus Christ (4–2, 307).

Is this the whole truth about man and so the whole content of Christian preaching about man? Would that it were! As we have seen, Barth contends that man's given creatureliness does not contain within itself the ultimate mystery that man is destined for life with God. This mystery is known and realized only when God speaks and reveals it to man. But Barth points out that there is a second mystery about man and his potentialities which also was not given and so is not explainable within his own creatureliness (3–2, 276). This is the mystery of man's sin and his corresponding fall, misery, and damnation. But just as man's destiny as God's partner does not have its ground and guarantee in man himself, so also man's sin is not to be understood, as to its possibility and its end, within the given structures and capacities of his creaturely being. The mystery of man's sin points beyond itself to the mystery of the demonic.

Just thirty years ago the demonic was little more than a subject of jokes and laughter in most of American Christian-

ity. But then we experienced the outbreak of all kinds of
irrationality during our ten years of world depression. These
were followed by the war in which man's brutal inhumanity
to man on all sides staggered the imagination. Then came
the revelations of the bottomless abyss of human horror out
of which arose the impulse to unutterable degradation in
the sadistic sacrifice of the Jews. Before such enormity the
human heart can only cower in an awesome terror, at an entirely different and deeper level than that of guilt and shame.
The result has been that the demonic has returned as a
serious concern in theology (even Tillich!) and hell has
become a commonplace topic in contemporary literature
(even Sartre!). If you are to preach to man about himself
in full realism, you cannot limit yourself to the life of man
with God. On the "other side" of man is another reality
quite distinct from both God and man. I have chosen to
call this reality the "demonic." This is a kind of middle
term between "devil," which overpersonalizes and over-
hypostatizes, and "nothingness," which is too static and abstract. Whatever the term chosen, we are dealing with a real
dimension of human existence. And if you are not clear as
to its character, and if your preaching does not always take
it into serious consideration, then your preaching will be incomplete and therefore irrelevant to a marked degree. This
does not mean that you proclaim and preach the devil as
such. You preach the gospel only, Christ crucified and risen.
But how can you preach that Christian faith "casts out
demons" unless you can make clear what the demonic is in
our lives?

Barth has constructed what is for me the most meaningful and helpful answer to this question to be found in contemporary theology. You will find it spelled out in one
comparatively brief section (¶ 50) at the close of his treatment of the doctrine of providence (3–3). But actually we
find the basic conception anticipated throughout his doc-

trine of God in Vol. II, and it is explicitly used throughout his development of the doctrine of Christ's reconciliation of man from sin in Vol. IV. The Biblical ground of his under-standing of the demonic, however, Barth develops most clearly in his exposition of Gen. 1:2, "and the earth was without form and void" (3–1, 101–110). In creation God asserts and establishes his purpose and will. This means that if men as his creatures are to share in God's life, they must accept the limits and determination that God has established for them. Apart from these conditions there is not another possibility for man, there is only impossibility. There is not something but nothing. When men therefore misuse the freedom God gave them in order to love him in return, men move out into that which God rejected or negated in his act of creation (Barth's term is *Das Nichtige*). It has no *being,* as do God and his creation. It is simply the shadow cast by God's positive will and purpose. Yet it hovers there as a seeming possibility to human freedom. Actually, it is an "impossibility," not in the sense that man cannot choose it, but that in choosing it man is not choosing another alternative life but is choosing death. In turning away from God and toward this impossible possibility, man gives this negated nonbeing a kind of limited reality. That which has been negated or accursed by God becomes operative in man, and the elements of "sickness unto death" (Kierkegaard) begin to manifest themselves in human existence.

In Barth's concept of *Nichtige* I believe we have one of those theological insights which is nowhere explicitly or comprehensively spelled out in Scripture, but which lies there below the surface of much of it and is arrived at by an intuition of the whole. Its validity and helpfulness, there-fore, is not determined by proof-texting but by its capacity to shed light on major Biblical themes. Observe, for ex-ample, the meaning it gives to the Bible's characterization of God's act of knowing. "I never knew you; depart from

me, you evildoers." (Matt. 7:23; 25:12.) To be known by
God is to live; to be unknown by God is to depart into
darkness and death (2–1, 567). In another direction we are
enabled to see by this concept that man's sinfulness is something more than his autonomous act of pride, sloth, and
deceit that might be reversed by his own act of humility,
resolution, and honesty. Rather, sin has given substance and
reality to a condition of human existence that has no ground
or origin in man as created by God, which is therefore
something alien to man and beyond his powers to cope with.
The "misery" and "death" that result from the "fall" are now
all too human, yet they are also something nonhuman (4).
In still another direction, therefore, Barth argues that the
doctrines of election (2–2) and reconciliation (4–1) center
around one all-important truth, that God alone can deal
with the problem of man's sinfulness and can deliver man
from it. The events of judgment, forgiveness, repentance,
and faith require the subjective play of human understanding and response. But below the level of man's guilt and
shame lie his subversion and subjection to the power of a basic
deceit, out of which have poured into human existence incredible forces of disintegration and destruction. This condition is subhuman and can be reached and vanquished only
by the immediate presence of God's own creative truth, love,
and righteousness. Yet this demonic power has its only occasion for activation in human sin and has its only place of
residence in fallen human existence. So God in Christ has
identified himself with man in his sin and has descended
into the depths of the hell of human degradation, there to
bear man's alienation and death in order to lead man into
the eternal fellowship and life of God.

I have taken time to give a brief summary of Barth's
analysis of the demonic because, although it is not something you should preach directly, it is a Biblical insight into
the human condition that should inform all your preaching

of man as creature and child of God. So I encourage you to read these sections of the *Dogmatics* and then test its power to enlighten the whole Biblical treatment of man. If men of today are to be helped to understand their need of a Savior, it will occur in conjunction with the ability to help them understand the abyss of chaos and annihilation that they see opening up all around them and within them.

Most Americans, however, are not inclined to contemplate the meaning of life and the despair of life in general philosophical terms. Many of our contemporary dramas and novels are doing so in a powerful way, and they may be used effectively for sermon illustration or in small study groups in the church. But for the average person in the pews, the questions of meaning and despair usually come to focus in the more concrete issues of what we call ethical problems. One of the notable features of Barth's *Dogmatics* is that these problems are not there set aside as secondary ones, to be treated elsewhere by someone else. For Barth, God's command and man's obedience occurs *within* the event of God's gracious forgiveness and man's repentance. Gospel encloses law within itself. So it may be that much of what we have seen in this chapter as content for preaching may very well be approached through a preaching to the specific ethical problems that every man faces.

Chapter IX

Preaching: God's Awesome Command

FOR Barth, man becomes truly man in that God addresses man, and man responds to God. If God were to cease to speak to man, the human would atrophy and die away. Even the No of God's judgment upon man's sin is a form of address that keeps man from drifting off into complete isolation and death. The ethical problem for man, therefore, is not the question of what is morally right or wrong and of man's relative achievement of the right. The ethical problem is the very question of human life: Does man hear God and respond? In his general introduction to this problem under his general doctrine of God, Barth deals exclusively with the fact that God's gracious election of man to life with him includes within it a *command* (2–2, 509 ff.). In his treatment of man's ethical response under the doctrine of creation, Barth explores all the aspects and problems of the *freedom* given to man in his creation by God (3–4). In his consideration of ethics in the context of the doctrine of reconciliation, Barth takes *fidelity* or faithfulness (*Treue*) as the key concept (4–4). But even these are not the only places where Barth develops his thesis that faith and ethics are inseparable. It naturally intrudes itself repeatedly throughout his *Dogmatics*. I draw your attention to only two notable examples. He concludes his doctrine of providence with a section on "The Christian Under the Universal

Lordship of God the Father" and develops the theme by a memorable exposition of faith, obedience, and prayer (3-3, 329 ff.). In the long volume on the prophetic dimension of Christ's reconciliation (4-3), Barth has a whole section entitled "The Calling of Man" in which he gives his clearest formulation of what it means to be called to and to live within the service of Jesus Christ (¶ 71).

Obviously, we dare not even begin a general analysis and evaluation of Barth's ethic. I would suggest that you refresh your memory of Barth's main points by rereading the summary of Chapters 8, 12, and 17 of the *Dogmatics* in the foregoing "Quick Tour" (Ch. IV). It should be clear that if you are going to use Barth as a guide for preaching, your job is not done until you come down to specific problems of Christian living. It is all too easy to preach about Jesus as our Savior and Lord, as Son of God incarnate, in whom God has already reconciled the world to himself. It is even easier to thunder at men for their sins and to exhort them to "walk in the Spirit." But preaching the gospel of Jesus Christ to man between God and the demonic really arrives at concretion and completion when the preacher can help the Christian draw the implications of his faith for his responsible decisions in daily life. Some preachers think they fulfill this duty by quoting a few general moral principles from Moses, Jesus, or Paul. Others are so concerned to avoid being "moralistic" that they shy completely away from the subject. Let me call your attention to a few examples of the way in which Barth draws these implications on the basis of Biblical texts. I believe that if you try to incorporate some of these materials in sermons, you will find your preaching more vital and relevant than it has been in a long time. Or if you already preach this way, you will find endless suggestions for new departures in this kind of preaching.

First of all, what does it mean to "follow" Jesus "in his

steps," to "imitate" his "example" (I Peter 2:21; John 12:26; Matt. 10:38; 16:24; 19:27; Eph. 5:1; I Cor. 11:1)? Barth discusses this question in a section entitled "The Content of the Divine Claim." He is attempting to define concretely what he means when he says that law is the *form* of grace. What is the "law" of Christian behavior? How can we speak of following or imitating Jesus without forming specific rules or principles of conduct? Barth interprets the above Scripture passages in a way that does not rob them of their concrete direction and yet also does not reduce the Christian ethic to a moralistic application of law (2–2, 569 ff., 576 f.). He does this by arguing that we are bidden to follow *Jesus himself*, not his teachings, that our "imitation" is but an extension in our lives of the power of God's gracious forgiveness toward us. And in the pages that follow these expositions Barth goes on to show that a disciple's conformity with Christ does not mean that he becomes a second Christ in himself. Rather, it means his whole life is open to spiritual determination by the living Christ.

One of the most troublesome and misunderstood problems of ethics is that of freedom. How can Christian faith be taken as a champion of free man when it speaks so much about God's law and command, about man's obedience, about the Christian as slave and servant of his Lord and Master, Jesus Christ? To properly define the nature of human freedom is one of the major concerns of Barth's theology. In his seminars he would never let go unchallenged a student's uncritical reference to human freedom. In a day when "free world" and "free man" have become unexamined clichés and political slogans, the preacher had best be clear about the Christian understanding of freedom.

Put very simply, Barth's main thesis is that man is truly free insofar as he lives gladly in communion with God. This is the "law" of his freedom. But as exemplified by the story of the two trees in the Garden of Eden, man seeks to be free of this law by claiming to be free to determine good and evil for himself (3-1, 249-288). The result is that man is subjected to another law, the law of sin and death. From this real slavery he cannot free himself. Now freedom comes only when men are restored to life under the true law of God in Jesus Christ, the law of love from and to God. Barth gives a full statement of this theme under "The Form of the Divine Claim" and in connection with an extended exposition of such passages as James 1:22 f.; John 8:31-36; Rom., chs. 7; 8 (2-2, 588-593). In the gospel we come to know that God's command does not come as a tyrannical compulsion (you must) but as a loving permitting (you may). The presence of God's Spirit in our hearts now allows us to be free to live with him in love. In this way we come to live gladly under and by God's command, because his command means freedom, freedom from anxiety (Matt. 6:25; 10:19; Phil. 4:6; I Cor. 7:32), freedom to stand and to abide (John 6:56; 15:4; I John 2:6; 3:24; 4:13; Acts 13:43; Rom. 11:22; etc.) (2-2, 597-602). Barth develops the theme again under the topic "Freedom Within Limitations." He shows how the Biblical conception of man's limited time is to be understood as "Unique Opportunity" (3-4, 580-585). He interprets the Biblical view of man's work as "the creaturely carrier and medium of God's own voice" in his consideration of the limiting factor of man's "Vocation" (3-4, 600-607). Finally, Barth concludes his ethics of creation with a section in which he explores the ultimately limiting factor on man's freedom, which is also the fulfillment of his freedom, namely, the fact that man's only and ultimate honor or glory lies in his being created and called to be the covenant-partner of God, the child of his household. This passage is replete with Biblical texts (3-4, ¶ 56:3).

One might think that the commands of God are arbitrary and unrelated if they cannot be reduced to some general principles, if the Christian must always seek the immediate

will of God anew in every situation. Barth's ethic has been
so charged. How do we maintain day-by-day obedience to
the living Christ without being overwhelmed by a sense of
relativity and uncertainty? We have summarized Barth's
general answer to this charge in an earlier chapter (IV).
But this is a serious question in the minds of many average
Christians as they face the moral chaos of our day and desire
something clear and firm to hang on to, and you should be
able to preach to this need. If we are to escape a simple,
legalistic moralism, then how are we to regard the Ten
Commandments and the Sermon on the Mount? Cannot we
take even these rules as eternal verities? Barth gives a clear
answer to this question in his exposition of the relevant
Biblical passages (2–2, 673 ff., 678 f., 683–700). And I believe he is able to give normative and serious place to the
Biblical ethical codes without at the same time leaving man
to apply a set of rules on his own inadequate moral initiative. Rather, he shows how these codes assume and are the
means for God's own living, personal direction and enabling
of man in his concrete daily decisions. Barth also gives a
telling exposition of Rom., chs. 12 and 13, in order to show
that there is an inner connection: (1) among all of God's
specific commands across the centuries and years, (2) among
all the men who hear and obey his commands, and (3)
among all the moments of hearing and obeying within the
life of each individual man (2–2, 713–732). This unifying
power of God's command is its goodness. It is good because
it is the power of love (*agapē*), and Paul makes clear that
the whole Christian ethic consists of conduct under the rule
and expressive of the reality of objective unsentimental
Christian love (2–2, 719, 724).

All the examples, however, that we have thus far given
of Barth's exposition of the Biblical ethic have been concerned with general problems of human behavior rather
than with specific concrete conditions. This is because the

examples have been taken almost wholly from his statement of a general Christian ethic within the context of his general doctrine of God. But when we turn to his special Christian ethic in the context of the doctrine of creation, we find Barth drawing the implications of our life in Christ for the most concrete and particular problems we face in living as God's creatures in God's world (3–4). That he is not constructing a natural ethic on the basis of a natural theology Barth makes quite clear in his opening paragraph on "Freedom Before God." In his discussion of the Holy Day, confession (of our faith to the world), and prayer, he gives a strong Biblically based argument for the position that love of God, as a conscious turning of man to stand before and for God, is something quite distinguishable from love of fellowman, even though the two cannot be separated.

In the rest of the volume Barth takes up one concrete ethical problem after another. And although the discussion is full of specifically exegetical notes, actually the whole text is an extended Biblical exposition. Again, instead of giving a lengthy summary of the contents of one or two of these expositions, I will briefly indicate the variety of problems dealt with.

In the long section on "Man and Woman" we find the following. "They two shall be one flesh" (I Cor. 6:16; Eph. 5:31) is interpreted in relation to modern psychological views on man's sexual needs (3–4, 134 ff.). Both marriage and celibacy are discussed as Christian possibilities in the light of numerous Biblical texts, including those which reflect Paul's ambivalent attitudes (3–4, 141 ff.). In commentary on the puzzling statement of Gal. 3:28 that in Christ there is "neither male nor female," Barth argues that this does not mean abandonment but fulfillment of sexual differentiation (3–4, 156, 164, 174). Barth explores the reciprocal contributions of man and woman in marriage in his treatment of Paul's peculiarly unmodern insistence that the husband is the "head" of the wife (I Cor. 11:3; Eph. 5:23) (3–4, 172 ff.). Barth also provides us with a commentary on Jesus' words concerning marriage (3–4, 185 ff.), on the contrast between the Old Testament and the New Testament concerning monogamy (3–4, 199 ff.), and concerning the permanence of marriage (3–4, 204 ff.), on the Biblical view of adultery (3–4, 232 ff.).

We will not try to be so explicit about the preaching resources in Barth's next section on "Parents and Children." It is a comparatively brief one (forty-five pages) and should be read in its entirety for suggestions when you are preaching on the family. This is surely an area that is of prime concern in the fields of sociology and psychology today, and the preacher should be aware of the Biblical materials on the matter. Recent studies have shown that neither the Bible nor the church is too clear as to the status and function of the family as a result of Christianity's separation of religion from the tribal and national life of the Jews. Certainly Barth does not give any final word on this complex problem. But he does attempt to draw the lines of connection between the relations of responsibility and dependence of parents and children, on the one hand, and the same relations of God and men, on the other hand. He sees in the establishment of the authority of God over men the ontological and existential grounds for the establishment of parental authority over children. But then Barth also insists that we must take seriously the possibility that man's new life in Christ may lead a specific person here and there completely beyond the family life (3–4, 259 ff.). This person's calling in Christ may demand a breaking off of his involvement with his parents and may lead to his denial of marriage and children for himself. Barth again discusses the Biblical case for celibacy. Then, in a very direct fashion, Barth defends the thesis that children are not absolutely required for the occurrence of true Biblical marriage (3–4, 265 ff.), and this is followed by a frank treatment of the use of birth control and its various methods. Many books are now available on these subjects with a supposedly Christian orientation. But very few of them will discuss them in such a solidly theological and Biblical context.

There then follows another brief section on "Near and Distant Neighbors." Here Barth seeks to clarify for the Christian conscience what it means to be a member of a particular nation or people, and at the same time a responsible member of the human race. Even though these two relationships are not given orders of creation, they are spheres that develop under God's providence. God meets men in these spheres also with his command. Therefore, these are areas in which Christians must act by decisions determined by their faith. Barth's major discussion is in the light of the perverted exaltation of the concept of "people" by the Nazis, and the section ends with a long consideration of the Biblical materials that undercuts such a perversion (3–4, 309 ff.). Again, in a day when there is increasing pressure to identify "Christian" with one certain narrowly conceived political and economic system, the preacher had better be sure of his Biblical and theological base on this crucial issue.

Perhaps the most striking theme in Barth's ethics of creation is the one that comes next, "Reverence for Life" (surely "Respect" in the British edition is a very weak and inadequate translation of *Ehrfurcht*). Here Barth deliberately takes up Schweitzer's famous phrase in order to give it what he considers to be its proper Biblical meaning. Barth argues that it is precisely the Biblical knowledge of God that instills a sense of wonder and humility before the mystery of the life of the individual person, because Biblical faith sees clearly that each individual life is a gift or rather a loan from Holy God himself. And therefore we must not only reverence life but we must also be concerned about "The Protection of Life."

These two sections on reverence for life and protection of life comprise a 145-page commentary and interpretation on one single Biblical command: "Thou shalt not kill" (3–4, 324–470). How many sermons could you get out of this one commandment? Under reverence for life Barth draws out six different positive meanings, and under protection of life he draws out six other negative ones. Of course he brings in many other Biblical passages to his assistance, but here is material for twelve sermons on just one of the Ten Commandments. Let me just list the topics he covers under these headings. The positive meaning of the commandment is simply to love life in all its forms. Under this theme Barth proceeds to discuss the Biblical way of understanding: (1) the impulse or will to live (344); (2) the proper use of animal and plant life by man (348); (3) the problem of health, with a critique of Christian Science (356); (4) the will to joy (374); (5) willing to be one's self (385); and (6) the will to power (390). Obviously, the literal meaning of "Thou shalt not kill" is a negative one, holding man back from committing murder. In this protective sense it is stated unconditionally. Yet, Barth points out, the life it applies to is conditional and finite. So he undertakes to explicate the Biblical meaning of this commandment for men as they face those borderline cases where exceptions seem to be justifiable or even inescapable. Barth proceeds to construct a Biblical view concerning suicide (400), abortion (415), euthanasia (423), self-defense (427), capital punishment (437), and, finally, war (450).

There is one final sphere of ethical concern that has not yet been mentioned, and Barth does not neglect it. Life is not only a gift and a loan from God; it is also a task. Preaching the Christian ethic must meet head on all the thorny problems in man's work. Barth takes up this aspect of Christian ethics in a section entitled "The Active Life" (3–4, 470 ff.). He recognizes that here is a dual problem for the Christian: how to understand the uniquely Christian calling as work in the service of Christ for the coming of God's Kingdom (474 ff.), but also, how to understand all forms of human work as under God's providence and therefore as a sphere in which man is under God's command whether he knows it or not (516 ff.) I leave you on your own to explore Barth's treatment of these ethical problems and its Biblical base.

I wish to close this chapter, however, by drawing your attention to the fact that the peculiarly Christian life of service to Christ and his Kingdom has its own unique problems of decision and obedience. Barth touches on them here as noted above. But in the general outline of the *Dogmatics* his full treatment of these problems that are unique to the Christian life can only come under the doctrine of reconciliation. And the ethical section has not yet been completed. But already you will find an extensive treatment of just what a man is called to do when he answers Christ's call to be his follower (¶ 71 on "Man's Calling"). Barth there explicates not only the event and the aim of that calling but also explores with true compassion and insight the "affliction" and the "deliverance" of the Christian in his service. May I suggest that your preaching of the command of God and the Christian life of obedience is not done until you have led the congregation to see and to accept the life of service which is the way of the cross.

Indeed, your task is not even done then. What Barth gives us in the yet unfinished ethics of reconciliation is not a definition of the task and work of the Christian but an explication of the *resource* for that work: life in Christ. As already noted, he does this by speaking of baptism, prayer, and the Lord's Supper. The heart of all preaching on Christian living must be preaching that leads men to an understanding and a practice of prayer. Perhaps you have already noticed how often this topic has cropped up throughout our references to the *Dogmatics*. This is no accident. For Barth, the Christian life is a life of prayer, because only so can it be a life before God. So, in conclusion, I suggest that you organize yourself to preach on prayer. And you will find few sources more helpful than the many passages in the *Dogmatics,* which you can find by simply looking in the index of each volume. You can begin with those already noted (3–3, 239–288; 3–4, 87–115). If you come to understand Barth's view of prayer, you will be prepared to understand the next and final chapter in which we will try to show that, for Barth, all preaching has really only one theme, God.

Chapter X

God's Joyful Partisan

FOR its main article in its issue of December 23, 1959, the popular German news magazine, *Der Spiegel* (*The Mirror*), put a large picture of Barth on the cover with this title underneath: "Gottes Fröhlicher Partisan." There could not be a more appropriate description of Barth in the basic intention and character of his person. Here is a man whose overruling aim in life is devotion to the cause of God, with joy and with humor. With joy because God is the only source of all true joy in living; with humor because man is so fallible and funny in his fumbling attempts to help the cause of his all-wise Father who is sovereign in his love and freedom.

Yet, God desires it so, because the community of life that is God's final aim with man demands the glad and willing response of man. In this sense the Christian life of glad obedience and joyful service to Christ's Kingdom is an image and anticipation of what God will eventually offer and ask of every man. "God's joyful partisan" could then well be the motto for the life of every Christian.

It should be made very clear, however, that for Barth the primacy of initiative and the finality of fulfillment is wholly with God. This is not because God is jealous of his rights out of weakness and of fear that men might rob him of his divine prerogatives. The decision and the power lie with

233

God simply because he is God, and he cannot give his own
being away to another even if he wanted to. Likewise, men
are not drawn to devotion to God by threats of doom and
infliction of suffering. Men finally come to God because they
see that he alone is truth and life, that his glory is their
only joy.

Barth therefore insists that the center of the Christian's
faith is God, not man or the world. The primary subject
matter of preaching and so of theology is God, not man's
knowledge of God or the world's reflection of its creator.
Of course not God alone by himself. Barth vigorously rejects the possibility of talking about the *logos asarkes*, the
Word without flesh. We know God only as God makes himself known, and God unveils himself to us only by veiling
himself with his creation, finally and perfectly in the creatureliness of Jesus of Nazareth. We who are creatures can talk
only about creaturely events and in creaturely language. But
since God actually does make *himself* known in creaturely
guise we can and must talk to *him* and about *him* in our
creaturely language. We do always talk about him in the
terms of his relationship with his creatures, specifically his
relationship with Jesus, with the first Christian community
that witnesses to Jesus, and so with us who receive that witness. There is no question but that, in the order of our
conscious experience, we move out of dimness and darkness
by feeling our way through the thick folds of creaturely
condition and event and language into the light of understanding and there profess to have come in touch with God.
Barth contends, however, that Christian faith must make
another confession. The understanding that comes from
being in touch with God in Jesus Christ brings to light
another path that has been trod. It comes to light that the
movement of man toward God is enabled by a corresponding movement of God toward man. And the knowledge of
God that we have in the knowledge of man in Jesus Christ

now makes it possible and requisite that we say something
of that primary movement of God toward man. The proclamation of this movement *is* the gospel. To speak of what
God has done for man, to man, in man is the good news.

For Barth, this means speaking essentially about God, even
if always about God with man. Christian confession and
proclamation is centered on God, for only so can man know
his true destiny. The Christian, therefore, is par excellence
"God's joyful partisan." And if this be true of every
Christian, it is true of the preacher in a very special form.
If you have learned anything about preaching and what it
means to be a preacher from reading this book about Karl
Barth, it should all center around this one image: the
preacher as the one who speaks up gladly for God. Of course,
while his heart is stayed on God, his eyes are on the people,
for he is filled with compassion as he sees them like sheep
without a shepherd. But in the end he knows that he is not
their shepherd, nor is even the church. God alone can suc-
cessfully shepherd them home. But the image breaks, because every Christian must learn from the preacher how to
be his own joyful partisan for God out in the workaday
world where he lives. The Christian people must be shepherd for the whole race of man and be able to point beyond
themselves to the God who is shepherd of all.

However down-to-earth and practical, therefore, the sermon may and must be in its treatment of man's ethical di-
lemmas, its primary task is to point man beyond himself to
God. According to Barth, you have not done this fully and
satisfyingly until you are able to preach meaningfully to
Christians about the movement of God *von oben nach
unten,* from above to below. This phrase, along with its
correlate, *von unten nach oben,* has become a favorite with
Barth over the last dozen years. I heard him using the combination in his opening lectures on the ethics of reconciliation (4-4), and he would almost sing it, fondly, as a kind

of mystic refrain or counterpoint to the whole line of his theology. To proclaim the gospel certainly means to offer to men acceptance, forgiveness and renewal, self-fulfillment in a life of freedom. But all this is from God and to be possessed only in the service of God. How, then, can we speak of God so that he and his glory remain the center of attention, even while we speak of his relation to men so as not to claim knowledge of an abstract God-in-himself? What does a speaking of the movement of God "from above to below" consist of? How do we preach God?

It is very appropriate to bring this book to a close with a brief exposition of Barth's answer to this question. As noted in an earlier chapter, Barth's whole *Dogmatics* is really an extended doctrine of God. While we must preach about man, his world, the devil, the church and its mission, we can unveil their true meaning only in terms of their relation to God. While all Christian preaching begins and ends with Jesus Christ, this is so only because he leads us into the mystery of God's life and action, only because he enables us to view and to understand all things *von oben nach unten,* from the point of view of God himself. If this results in a kind of Christian "gnosis" (Bouillard), Barth would say, so be it. What is the wisdom and mystery of God's eternal purpose that Paul says has been made known to us (I Cor. 2:6 ff.; Eph. 1:9 ff.; 3:1 ff., 7 ff.)? This is no gnosticism because this wisdom has come to us only by God's self-humiliation in his movement "from above to below." Furthermore, this wisdom is not imparted or grasped by the methods of human wisdom but by the exaltation of men "from below to above" into fellowship with God through forgiveness. Furthermore, this wisdom is not meant for a small elite circle but is to be shared with all men. And both the humiliation of God and the exaltation of man has occurred in the concrete life of Jesus of Nazareth.

On this basis, Barth insists that we are obliged to preach

about God in his acts of election and creation, as the visible circumference of his act of reconciliation. And even beyond this circumference he sees another that is the necessary ground or presupposition of all three: the eternal trinitarian being of God. This means that we must be able to ground our Christian faith and life not only in the existential realities of our personal forgiveness and renewal but also in the promise of God that this new life in Christ is his intended purpose for all mankind (election), and is the determining force in all the obscure movements of nature and history (creation). And there is no ultimate and wholly satisfying assurance for our faith and life until they find their rest in the eternal life of God himself as Father, Son, and Holy Spirit.

Bultmannian theology and preaching tends to believe in the total adequacy and self-sufficiency of the immediacy of the Word of God in the event of personal forgiveness and renewal. This point of view looks with suspicion on any talk about a "goal" for all mankind "at the end of history" if any temporal and spatial meanings are included in these terms. It sees no ground or need for the construction of a theory about a supposed relationship between the uniquely human event of faith and the infinitely explorable processes of subhuman nature. It regards as pure speculation and as the denial of faith itself any attempt to describe the Holy of Holies of God's own being, whether in trinitarian, dualistic, monistic, or any other terms.

At this point you, the preacher, face a crucial decision. Are you to preach only the existential kerygma that leads men to personal awareness of sin and forgiveness and of power to live a new life of freedom and love? Are you to leave this man of faith (as individual or church) with nothing to believe or to say about the relation of his God of faith to the long millennia of human striving for a better human society on earth? Are you to leave this man with the terrifying sense that the realm of his faith-relation to God faces an alien universe in which it has no roots and for which it has no concern? Are you as well as others to be left wondering if, behind the best Christian symbols and analogies for God, there still resides the ancient "unknown God"?

If that is really the most that Christian faith can do, it would indeed be folly to try to make it do more just because the human heart and mind desires more. Barth and Bultmann agree that Christian preaching and theology must not try to say more than the Christ-event warrants. But Barth insists that the Christ-event says a lot more. He would argue that its limitation to the impartation of meaning to the personal subject is being unfaithful to its own nature and leaves Christian faith hopelessly vulnerable to the attacks of inner doubt and external forces of opposition. Here we must be very clear, however, as to what Barth says about the limits of what Christian faith can say on these matters. He very clearly asserts that the Christian doctrine of providence must not be identified with any philosophy of history (3–3, 20 ff.). Likewise, the final Parousia and victory of Christ cannot be spelled out in the temporal and spatial detail of some particular apocalyptic but can be only the confession of hope born out of Christ's present Parousia in the Spirit (4–3, 289–296, 934–942). Barth also vigorously rejects any possibility of a "Christian cosmology" or an "ontology of the created whole" (3–2, 6). Finally, he readily admits that the doctrine of the Trinity is not identical with revelation itself but is a work of the church (1–1, 353 f.) and that we cannot speak of God except by the use of analogy (2–1, 225 f.).

Within these severe limitations, however, Barth insists that Christian faith not only can but must speak about these matters. First of all, how can we be truly met by God in the kerygma concerning Jesus Christ without being required to see in this God the same one who called Abraham, Isaac and Jacob, Moses, David and the prophets, Augustine, Hildebrand and Luther, as well as the Pharaoh, Nebuchadnezzar, Cyrus, Pilate, Constantine, Charlemagne, and perhaps even Hitler and Lenin, as the carriers, scourges, and comforters of his people? And how can we view all this from the vantage of the cross and resurrection without knowing that what we see in Christ is the secret original purpose from which sprang all of God's doings with men, as well as being the final goal for all men toward which God is still moving forward in history in his own mysterious way?

Barth provides not only vast theological defense and statement of this thesis in the *Dogmatics* but also innumerable Scriptural expositions as a basis for preaching it. He expounds John 1:1 f. to explain the eternity of Jesus Christ's election (2–2, 95 ff.). The election of Israel and the church is described on the basis of Rom., chs. 9 to 11 (2–2, 202 ff., 213 ff., 240 ff., 267 ff.). Barth faces up to the obvious counterpart of election in the rejection of men by God in the stories of the patriarchs, of Saul and David, of the two prophets in I Kings, ch. 13 (2–2, 354–410). He uses a series of New Testament passages to show that the calling to be a Christian is election not to privilege but to service of Christ's reconciling work (2–2, 419–449). Barth also gives a profound interpretation of the Biblical concept of God's reprobation by analyzing the relation of Judas and Jesus, and ends by suggesting that Paul really replaces Judas as apostle (2–2, 458–506). Relevant also is Barth's elaboration of the doctrine of providence (3–3). And in the third part of his doctrine of reconciliation (4–3), you will find in the section entitled "Jesus Is Victor" (¶ 69:3) Barth's latest formulation of his view of Jesus Christ as the one who battles in history to accomplish his goal, and this comes close to a Christian philosophy of history.

Secondly, Barth also insists that we cannot know the re-creating power of God in the Spirit of Christ without knowing that we have been met by the one who created us in the

first place. Since he created us from the dust of the earth
and as an animal among the animals—even though in his
likeness—we trust that the God of faith is the God of creation who numbers the stars, feeds the birds, clothes the lily,
and provides for our need of "all these things" even while
bidding us to put his righteousness and Kingdom first in
our lives. I will not list any special expositions of Scripture
on this theme because the first 330 pages of his volume on
creation (3–1) consist wholly of a running commentary on
Gen., chs. 1 and 2. But I would call your attention to another
section in his third part of the doctrine of reconciliation
(4–3). In a section entitled "The Light of Life" (¶ 69:2),
Barth gives a fully developed positive statement on the coordination between creation and reconciliation. He argues
that we must see the "order of reconciliation" in Jesus Christ
as the fulfillment of the "order of creation." Therefore, the
Christian must not look upon nature as a demonic sphere
but as the "external ground of the covenant" (3–1), the
stage on which Christ is enacting his drama of salvation.
The church must even listen for an authentic Word of God
that is received by the unbelieving world. And Barth concludes by arguing that scientific knowledge of the universe
is made possible by a God-given order and stability in creation and is for man's benefit even though not for his
salvation.

Thirdly, Barth contends with utmost seriousness that all
that we can say about reconciliation, creation, and redemption hangs in the air in uncertainty unless we can confess
with assurance that the One who meets us in reconciliation,
and claims to be our creator and redeemer, is truly God,
that there is no other who hides behind the veil as the "unknown" but "real" God. Barth maintains that the various
elements of the Biblical testimony, out of which the church
has formulated the doctrine of the Trinity, comprise the

answer to this final dilemma of faith. Such testimony amounts to this, that the God who reconciles us to himself in Jesus Christ, himself guarantees to us in this event that he *is* who he is in *this* event and no other. And the best and only adequate way the church has found of formulating this testimony is the doctrine of the Trinity. So Barth argues that he is not speculating about the transcendent nature of God in and by himself. He is simply describing the God who has made his *self* known in the relationship of reconciliation in Christ. Barth insists that knowing him, we finally know the wholly adequate ground and reason for the contexts of creation and history in which reconciliation occurs, and we know also the certainty of the hope of final redemption.

One never preaches doctrine as such. So you should not look for Biblical expositions in Barth that will allow you to preach the Trinity as such. But Barth would argue that all preaching of God must be Trinitarian. This means first that we must never preach about God as if he were a commonly and universally known phenomenon or idea, to which we add a few Christian attributes. We point to the One who is the sovereign giver of our life and arbiter of our destiny only by speaking of the Father of our Lord Jesus Christ. When we speak of the love and freedom, the grace and holiness of God, we are not using general concepts that everyone understands. We are referring to the actual being of God in his specific acts toward us in Jesus with the power of his living spiritual presence. That is why Barth's exposition of each of the "perfections" of God ends with a reference to Jesus Christ (2–1, Ch. 6), and in these sections you find a plenitude of very preachable expositions of Biblical texts concerning God. Secondly, Trinitarian preaching means that we never preach about the Spirit of God as if "it" were a magical energy naturally residing in every mountain, river, and human psyche, there to be tapped if we but have the magical formula. The Spirit of God is just God who has brought us into a communion of love with himself by speaking to us and reconciling us in Jesus Christ. Finally, Trinitarian preaching means that we cannot preach Jesus as the Word of God in the sense of his being the best example of the human attainment unto divine wisdom, whom we should therefore imitate and whose relation with God we should repeat in ourselves. Rather, we preach Jesus as the Word of God because in him the Creator and Judge and Savior, God, speaks decisively and uniquely and accomplishes the miracle of human belief and acceptance by the sovereign power of his own spiritual presence.

In a sense Barth's entire twenty-five-hundred-page elaboration of the doctrine of reconciliation is a continual repetition of this Trinitarian theme in an infinite variety of ways. If someday you were to attempt to preach the whole mystery and glory of God in one sermon, then, Barth insists, you would inevitably come to speak of God as Father, Son, and Holy Spirit. You would not use any of the traditional formulas of the creeds and the fathers. You might not even use the word "Trinity." But how could you avoid being Trinitarian? And once this is agreed upon, Barth is ready to take another step. He claims that the vision of the ultimate mystery and glory of God as Trinity in our faith-relation with God in Jesus Christ answers our ultimate theological questions. The fact that God himself lives in the dynamic diversity and unity of Trinity gives us the basis for understanding the possibility of creation, incarnation, reconciliation, and the assumption of mankind into an eternal sharing in the history of God's own life (cf. 2–1, 317; 3–2, 218 ff.; 4–1, 202–210; 4–2, 340–343). In the context of his statement of this thesis Barth gives us his Scriptural basis. Does this mean that you can and should preach God in this way? I myself am not yet convinced enough of the theological perspicuity and helpfulness, let alone necessity, of this principle of *analogia relationis* in order to answer in the affirmative.

The major question, however, is this: In order to be "God's joyful partisan" in your preaching, must you preach his Word in a way that lights a path for the Christian into the mysteries of God's relationship to the whole creation around us, and also into the enigmas of God's action in the hidden origin, the historical vagaries, and the ineffable consummation of the life of the human race? Must you preach the Biblical materials that have given rise to the doctrines of election, creation, providence, and eschatology (in the absolute sense)? Or may you, must you, limit yourself to preaching that Word which is directed toward personal existential judgment and renewal, with all else left to mystery and to God? I myself believe that the very Word that meets us in the kerygma of Jesus as the Christ demands that we follow him into these broader circumferences of our personal reconciliation, but never in a way that that relationship and reality of reconciliation is left behind. This is no mean trick, to be theologically inclusive and existentially relevant at the same time.

This book has been written to suggest that your preaching may gain immeasurably in depth and force if you try to be both. And it has tried to show how the use of Barth's *Dogmatics* can serve as a guide and resource for this kind of preaching. There are very real dangers in this program, but warnings and safeguards have been supplied. If you attempt it, and then discover that your preaching has become ponderously theological and dull, then you will surely have misused the *Dogmatics*. The man who takes God's part, Barth insists, must be joyful above all. We have been given *good* news from God to proclaim to all men. And let us close with Barth's reminder that if we witness to God with true joy in him, then we will also do so with humility. And if with humility, then surely also with rare good *humor!* (3–4, 664 f.)

Notes

CHAPTER I

1. Cf. Karl Barth, "The Need and Promise of Christian Preaching" in *Word of God and Word of Man* (Harper & Brothers, 1957), especially pp. 100 f.
2. *The Christian Century,* Vol. 77:3 (January 20, 1960), p. 74.

CHAPTER II

1. The sources for the following account are very diverse. There is no real biography of Barth as yet. I have not tried to give the source for every piece of information. Those who are interested may consult the following: Henri Bouillard, *Karl Barth, Vol. I, Genèse et Évolution de la Théologie Dialectique* (Aubier, Paris, 1957), especially pp. 79–262; Georges Casalis, *Portrait de Karl Barth* (Labor et Fides, Geneva, 1960); the three ten-year retrospects by Barth himself in *The Christian Century,* September 13 and 20, 1939; March 9 and 16, 1949, and January 20, 1960; a brief account of "Karl Barth's Theologie der Frühzeit" and some of Barth's letters presented by Eduard Thurneysen in *Antwort* (Evangelischer Verlag, Zollikon-Zürich, 1956), pp. 831–864; and more Barth-Thurneysen letters in *Gottesdienst-Menschendienst,* the Festschrift for Thurneysen's seventieth birthday (Evangelischer Verlag, Zollikon-Zürich, 1958), pp. 15–173. There are numerous biographical references scattered throughout

Barth's writings, some of which I have collected. There is also the cover picture and article in the popular German news magazine, *Der Spiegel,* December 23, 1959. I also have the lecture notes of Joseph Hromádka's course on "Crisis Theology" as given at Princeton Theological Seminary, 1940–1941. Finally, I checked a few items with Professor Barth personally.

2. *Word of God and Word of Man,* p. 100.
3. *Antwort,* p. 846.
4. *Karl Barth,* Vol. I, p. 85.
5. *Antwort,* p. 842.
6. Cf. Barth's own account of this in retrospect in his "The Need and Promise of Christian Preaching," *loc. cit.,* pp. 97–135.
7. *Antwort,* p. 843.
8. *Ibid.,* p. 841.
9. Both in *Word of God and Word of Man.*
10. For an excellent summary of this first edition, which is not available for most students, see Bouillard's full analysis, *Karl Barth,* Vol. I, pp. 90–95.
11. *The Epistle to the Romans,* translation of the 6th edition (Oxford University Press, London, 1933), p. 2.
12. *Antwort,* letters of May 21, June 3, 1919; also, cf. *Word of God and Word of Man,* pp. 287 f.
13. *Ibid.,* letters of June 7, 16, 1920. But for earlier references, cf. *Word of God and Word of Man,* p. 315.
14. For much of the following, cf. Bouillard, *Karl Barth,* Vol. I, pp. 98–118.
15. *Word of God and Word of Man,* pp. 272–327, and pp. 51–96.
16. *Antwort,* p. 856.
17. *Romans,* p. 10.
18. *Karl Barth,* Vol. I, p. 107.
19. *Antwort,* p. 843.

20. *Karl Barth,* Vol. I, p. 113.

21. Cf. his reminiscence on this point in *The Humanity of God* (John Knox Press, 1960), pp. 40 f.

22. *Word of God and Word of Man,* pp. 1 f.

23. *The Humanity of God,* p. 42.

24. See Thurneysen's last letter to Safenwil in *Gottesdienst-Menschendienst,* p. 15, and Barth's reply in *Antwort,* pp. 863 f.

25. *Word of God and Word of Man,* cf. especially pp. 98, 103.

26. *Antwort,* p. 857.

27. *The Christian Century,* September 13, 1939, p. 1098.

28. *Gottesdienst-Menschendienst,* pp. 88 f.

29. Heinrich Heppe, *Reformed Dogmatics* (George Allen & Unwin, Ltd., London, 1950), Foreword, p. v.

30. *Ibid.*

31. *Gottesdienst-Menschendienst,* p. 147.

32. *Karl Barth,* Vol. I, p. 133, and for the above, cf. pp. 130 ff.

33. These lectures were published in 1947 as *Die Protestantische Theologie im 19. Jahrhundert,* and some of them have been translated as *Protestant Thought from Rousseau to Ritschl* (Harper & Brothers, 1959).

34. *The Christian Century,* September 20, 1939, p. 1132.

35. *The Christian Century,* September 13, 1939, p. 1097.

36. Cf. Shubert Ogden's "Introduction" to *Existence and Faith* (Meridian Books, Inc., 1960), pp. 14 ff.

37. Cf. *Church Dogmatics* (T. & T. Clark, Edinburgh), 3–1, 81–90; 3–2, 442–447. Also *The Christian Century,* September 3, 1952, p. 993.

38. *The Christian Century,* September 20, 1939, p. 1133.

39. Cf. Bouillard, *Karl Barth,* Vol. I, pp. 232 ff.

40. *Church Dogmatics,* 1–2, 661–665.

41. For an account of Niemöller's activities, see Henry S.

Leiper's "From Pulpit to Prison," an epilogue to Niemöller's autobiography, *From U-Boat to Pulpit* (Willett, Clark & Company, 1937).

42. For an account of the development of the Confessing Church, see Wilhelm Niemöller's *Die evangelische Kirche im dritten Reich* (L. Beschauf, Bielefeld, 1956).

43. Most of the foregoing material in this section is drawn from Barth's own article in *The Christian Century,* March 9 and 16, 1949, pp. 298–300, 333–334.

44. *Ibid.,* p. 298.

45. For Barth's political writings 1946–1952, cf. *Against the Stream* (Philosophical Library, Inc., 1954).

46. Cf. Karl Barth, Johannes Hamel, and Robert McAfee Brown, *How to Serve God in a Marxist Land;* also, Charles West's *Communism and the Theologians* (The Westminster Press, 1958).

47. *The Christian Century,* January 20, 1960, pp. 72–76.

48. *Karl Barth,* Vol. III, pp. 293–299. Bouillard makes the following points in comparing and contrasting Barth and Hegel. Because the most recent fad in the speculation about Barth's "secret philosophy" is to dismiss him as one more Hegelian monist, I think it important to summarize briefly Bouillard's evaluation of this thesis. The Hegelian charge has been leveled most forcefully by the Roman Catholic scholar, Hans Urs von Balthazar. The latter sees a congeniality of Barth's thought with Hegel's in its form and style, in its use of the principle that posits and presupposes itself, in asserting the unity of the beginning and the end of things, in its tendency to rationalism. It must also be admitted that Barth's essay on Hegel (cf. English translation in *Protestant Thought from Rousseau to Kant*) is enthusiastic on many points, such as the recovery of the unity of the human and the divine, the definition of the object of theology as truth instead of historical and psychological phenomena, and the equation of truth as event. But Bouillard

points out that Barth also criticizes Hegel precisely on the same points for which he praises him. (The heart of Barth's critique is contained in a note in *Church Dogmatics* 4–1, 375 f.). Barth is radically opposed to Hegel's identification of the movement of absolute truth with that of human thought, and to the positing of sin as one of the necessary moments in that movement. Barth does not allow the freedom of God in revelation to be explained in the terms of the dialectical methods of logic. So Bouillard concludes that for Barth "the Logos, in which being is itself and thinks itself, is the Word of God incarnate in Jesus of Nazareth, not the logos of man as such. Instead of speaking *in* man and *by* man, God speaks *to* man. Man conceives being only in the measure to which it is spoken to him. A philosophical ontology is replaced by Christological dogmatic. So whenever Barthian thought appears in Hegelian dress, its content is wholly different."

49. *The Christian Century,* September 20, 1939, p. 1134.
50. *Karl Barth,* Vol. I, p. 117.
51. *Karl Barth,* Vol. III, p. 299.
52. Quoted in *Der Spiegel,* December 23, 1959, p. 81.

CHAPTER III

1. *The Christian Century,* September 13, 1939, p. 1097.

CHAPTER V

1. *Karl Barth,* Vol. III, p. 300.
2. *Die mündige Welt* (Chr. Kaiser, Munich, 1955), p. 122.
3. Hans Urs von Balthasar, *Karl Barth, Darstellung und Deutung seiner Theologie* (Jacob Hegner, Köln, 1951), p. 129.
4. For a penetrating but inconclusive discussion of this last question, cf. *ibid.,* pp. 124–131.
5. Karl Barth, "Philosophie und Theologie," in *Philoso-*

250 BARTH'S *DOGMATICS* FOR PREACHERS

phie und Christliche Existenz—Festschrift für Heinrich Barth (Helbing & Lichtenbahn, Basel, 1960), pp. 98 ff.

6. Rudolf Bultmann, *Jesus Christ and Mythology* (Charles Scribner's Sons, 1958), pp. 68 f.

7. Balthazar's book on Barth centers on the thesis that Barth's shift away from dialectical theology was a turning to a theology of analogy (pp. 93–181). Bouillard sees the concept of analogy as at the heart of Barth's discussions of both "The Limits of the Knowledge of God" (*Karl Barth,* Vol. III, pp. 178–217) and "Man in the Image of God" (Vol. II, pp. 197–206). There is a simple but in the end confusing review on the problem of "Analogy" by J. McIntyre in the *Scottish Journal of Theology,* Vol. 12:1, 1959. He draws upon the following sources: Ian Crombie's essay in *Faith and Logic,* edited by Basil Mitchell (George Allen & Unwin, Ltd., London, 1957); J. F. Anderson (a Roman Catholic), *The Bond of Being* (B. Herder Book Company, 1949); J. C. McLelland (Reformed), *The Visible Words of God* (Wm. B. Eerdmans Publishing Company, 1957); Susan Stebbing, *A Modern Introduction to Logic* (Humanities Press, Inc., 1950). For some brief definitions of "analogy" in its history, see also D. D. Runes, ed., *The Dictionary of Philosophy* (Philosophical Library, Inc., 1942), and Bernard Wuellner, *Dictionary of Scholastic Philosophy* (Bruce Publishing Company, 1956).

8. As quoted by Edwyn Bevan in his *Symbolism and Belief* (Beacon Press, Inc., 1957), p. 11.

9. I have done this in my book, *Human Spirit and Holy Spirit* (The Westminster Press, 1959), pp. 83–88, 147–151.

10. The following passages, as a few examples, lead us to the very heart of the practical impact of Barth's pervasive Christology: 2–1, 163, 252; 2–2, 177 f., 347 ff., 558; 3–2, 552; 4–1, 556, 770–774; 4–2, 822 f.

11. For a statement of the following theme, cf. 1–2, 421 ff.,

685 ff., 689, 744 f.; 2–1, 676; 2–2, 196, 209, 256, 317, 414–419, 428, 724.

12. Cf. 4–1, 353 f., 737 ff.; 4–2, 544 ff., 620 f.; 4–3, 304, 316 ff., 344 ff., 360 ff., 607, 657 ff.

CHAPTER VI

1. For this paragraph, see: 1–2, 538–541, 586, 589, 597–649; 2–1, 651–655; 2–2, 234; "The Christian Understanding of Revelation" in *Against the Stream,* pp. 218 f.

2. *Against the Stream,* p. 225.

3. Cf. Ernst Fuchs, *Zum hermeneutischen Problem in der Theologie* (J. C. B. Mohr, Tübingen, 1959), pp. 155 f.

4. *Against the Stream,* p. 217.

5. I have not bothered to document every sentence in the following paragraphs, but Barth's exposition may be found in: 1–1, 98–212; 1–2, 457–742; 3–1, 42–93; 3–3, 369–418.

6. *Against the Stream,* p. 221.

7. Rudolf Bultmann, *Essays Philosophical and Theological* (S. C. M. Press, Ltd., London, 1955), p. 258.

8. Bultmann, *Jesus Christ and Mythology,* pp. 68 f.

9. Cf. *Essays Philosophical and Theological,* p. 261.

10. For such an exchange, cf. *ibid.,* pp. 259 ff., and *Church Dogmatics* 3–2, 443–447.

11. *Against the Stream,* pp. 221, 223 f.; cf. also *Church Dogmatics* 1–2, 716–740; 4–2, 300–307.

12. Bultmann, *Essays Philosophical and Theological.*

13. *Jesus Christ and Mythology,* pp. 68 f.